GREEDY

GREEDY

Notes from a Bisexual Who Wants Too Much

Jen Winston

ATRIA PAPERBACK

New York   London   Toronto   Sydney   New Delhi

An Imprint of Simon & Schuster, Inc.
1230 Avenue of the Americas
New York, NY 10020

First Atria Paperback edition October 2021

ATRIA PAPERBACK and colophon are trademarks of
Simon & Schuster, Inc.

For information about special discounts for bulk purchases,
please contact Simon & Schuster Special Sales at 1-866-506-1949
or business@simonandschuster.com.

The Simon & Schuster Speakers Bureau can bring authors
to your live event. For more information or to book an event,
contact the Simon & Schuster Speakers Bureau at 1-866-248-3049
or visit our website at www.simonspeakers.com.

Interior design by Lexy Alemao

Manufactured in the United States of America

1   3   5   7   9   10   8   6   4   2

Library of Congress Control Number: 2021943024

ISBN 978-1-9821-7917-5
ISBN 978-1-9821-7918-2 (ebook)

To my parents,
who promised they wouldn't
read this

I have nothing to say
and I am saying it
and that is poetry
as I need it.

—JOHN CAGE

When you look at someone through
rose-colored glasses, all the red flags
just look like flags.

—*BOJACK HORSEMAN*
Season 2 Episode 10

CONTENT WARNING:

*This book contains subject matter
pertaining to sexual assault, mental health,
biphobia, homophobia, the gender binary, fatphobia,
ableism, and racism/white supremacy.*

*There are no closer shelves in the bookstore
than Dating and Horror.* ❤

CONTENTS

A Story to Ease the Author's Impostor Syndrome   xv

What I Talk about When I Talk about Bisexuality   xxiii

PART I: I WANT A WORD FOR THIS   I

Cuffed Jeans and Feeling Seen   3

Hot and Cool   17

Girl Crush: Clinical Observations   31

True Life: I Masturbate Wrong   39

Dating and Walking   53

A Girl Called Rhonda   75

**PART II: I WANT YOU TO LIKE ME
(EVEN THOUGH I DON'T LIKE YOU)**   91

Crush on a Couple   93

The Men Who Ghost Me   103

The Power Dynamic   109

The Neon Sweater   121

Knots   145

PART III: I WANT TO BE QUEER ENOUGH   **159**

Out of the Woods   161

Bisexuality in Men: A Retrospective   175

Do I Make Myself Queer?   187

Bad at Sex   205

Boundaries: A Fairy Tale   215

A Few Words on Platonic Love   225

PART IV: I WANT TOO MUCH AND THEN SOME   **235**

A Queer Love Story   237

Brinley James Ford   247

Gender Is a Drag: A Timeline   269

Acknowledgments   289

References   293

GREEDY

A STORY TO EASE THE AUTHOR'S IMPOSTOR SYNDROME

YOU'RE TOPLESS, PICKING a zit in the mirror, when a man on a dating app sends you the word "Hi."

You scoff. "Hi" barely warrants a notification; it hardly even counts as a text. Some people don't respond to openers like this, refusing to expend energy on someone who hasn't prioritized them. Those people have self-respect. They put themselves first. You desperately want to be one of those people.

You decide to ignore him. It's a good decision, one that gets you closer to your ideal version of yourself. You're a modern woman who knows her worth and acts accordingly—you'll only accept suitors if they shower you with attention (read: random CashApps) and gifts (read: memes about Ted Cruz). Besides, right now you've got better things to do than write back—that whitehead isn't going to pop itself.

But minutes later, your phone dings again.

Ghosting me? After I used my best pickup line?

An annoyingly strong follow-up. It might be his go-to—copy-pasted—but you can't bring yourself to care. Interest piqued, you look at his profile and immediately catch yourself vouching for his character. No shirtless pics? He must be a feminist. Holding a dog? It's probably a rescue. You click to his Instagram to search for a problem, but discover he has good taste in books and dresses like Harry Styles. Fuck—you're in love.

You type: Sorry for delay, was busy flirting with a guy who said "hello"

He responds: That dude again? Damn, he always wins

You: Five whole letters—tough competition

Him: Can I redeem myself by complimenting your nails in that first pic?

You: It's a start

He soon suggests dinner (one step above drinks because bitch, you're worth it). But your skepticism returns, this time for a different reason: You promised yourself you'd stop dating men.

You recently came out as bisexual to your friends, family, and Instagram followers, and the shiny new label still hangs over your head. You know you should be living your fabulous queer truth—not going on more mediocre dates with guys who will inevitably disappear. Sure, bisexuality means said queer truth can still encompass men, but let's be real: If you keep hooking up with dudes, no one will believe you're queer (least of all yourself).

You'd hoped announcing your sexuality on Instagram might help you stumble into a queer relationship—maybe prospective lovers would throw themselves at you, like some multigender version of *The Bachelorette*. A few people did slide into your DMs, but most were sleazy cis men masking their fetishization as support: Congrats!!! I love bi girls btw 😈 Though you cringed, part of you did admire their straightforwardness. Coming out as bi was intimidating, but coming out as lonely? Terrifying.

Recently you saw a post that said I LIKE ALL GENDERS BUT I'M ALL BI MYSELF and commented, "wish I could like this twice!" You put off coming out because you thought no one would care, but as it turns out, plenty of people do care, just not in the way you'd hoped. You notice that lesbians in particular tend to carry their bias quietly, losing interest especially fast. No matter how good the banter is, if you use the b-word, they'll drop the convo two texts down.

Interestingly, though, your bisexuality has barely influenced the app scene with men. There life is simple—if you tell a guy about it, he typically says "hot" or "sick" or nothing at all. These low-maintenance convos keep you coming back, an addictive combination of familiar and disappointing. You act unfazed, like they're all beneath you, but you know men are the romantic equivalent of shishito peppers—one out of every twelve will fuck you up.

You stare at your phone, weighing your options, trying to decide whether this guy is worth your time. Then you say fuck it—maybe men aren't so bad. After all, the devil you know.

✳

At dinner you're late and he's early, just the way you like it. You meet outside the restaurant while it's still light out—he's resting against a mailbox that comes up to his hips and you realize he's tall. You wish superficial things like height didn't affect you, but alas—your body registers him as Hot™ and a pang of longing inflates your chest. Before you can stop it you're imagining your future together, the two of you weekending in the Hudson Valley, navigating the bathroom acoustics of a tiny Airbnb.

Back in reality you're waiting in line—no New Yorker takes a brisk July night for granted, so the hostess warns the whole queue that the roof is already packed. But your date and his linen shirt have a plan: He steps to the front and leans onto the lectern, cracking jokes and touching the hostess's arm. This bothers you until it works—she leads you both upstairs, weaving through the crowd, dropping you off at the four-top she's managed to spare.

After you sit, your date reveals he doesn't drink, and you graciously respond that you'll limit yourself to three. Apparently he doesn't need alcohol to monologue—he talks first and goes on forever, using plenty of ten-dollar words like "loquacious" and "capitulate." An English instructor once scolded you for writing equally pretentious dialogue, saying, "No one actually talks like that." No one, meet Jen.

An hour later, you're at four glasses (and counting) when your date starts scrolling through his phone. Those same self-respecting people would be turned off by this, so naturally, you find yourself salivating. He's not interested? Perfect—challenge accepted. The blue light on his face ignites a fire in you, making you feel like you have something to prove.

In a desperate attempt to seem interesting, you tell him you want to write a book on the topic of bisexuality. It gets his attention—he puts down his phone, props an elbow on the table, and rests his chin in his hand.

"This book—would it be queer?"

"Er, how so?"

"Good art is always queer."

You scratch your chin, unsure how to respond.

Eventually you'll understand that his question wasn't a personal attack (although anyone who talks like a liberal arts student on the first date is at least a little out to get you). But in the moment, you're on edge. You feel like a fraud just for being here. Your brain short-circuits and you take his words literally: He must mean "queer" as in "gay." As in LGBTQ+. As in an identity you're not sure you can claim.

Is bisexuality queer? In your head you know it is—another few years and you'll realize you're just as entitled to *Chromatica* Oreos as twinks are. But in your heart, you can't deny that bisexuality has never felt queer *enough*. It's never felt queer enough to talk about. It's never felt queer enough to take up space. It's never felt queer enough to lead you to community, or to show you who you are.

"I—I'm not sure." You gulp, disappointed with your own lack of conviction.

"Whatever." He shrugs. "You want more wine?"

✳

Your gut insists that you should go home, so you go to his apartment. His building gives you another sign to turn back— it's a converted warehouse that smells like copper and gasoline. You breathe through your mouth and get in the elevator, refusing to take the hint.

When he opens his door, the first thing you see is a wall-to-wall bookshelf. It's stunning in scale, especially for New

York. The books lure you in and you can't help but touch them—you stroke their spines, fingering the embossed names of dead white men. Your date gawks at the scene, as if you, him, and his literature collection make up his dream ménage à trois. His gaze feels good, so you don't stop, but you do scold yourself for pandering to his intellectualism. This whole night you've been an enabler—one of the reasons shitty men have no problem getting laid.

Apparently the books were pretentious-art-boy foreplay, because you move to the bedroom next. There you strip, earrings and all, and sit on the foot of the bed. You wait naked and with good posture while he fumbles in a drawer until he pulls out a pair of handcuffs. They sparkle while he straddles you, dangling the chain like a hypnotist—*when I snap my fingers, you'll start having fun.*

"You down?" he asks. You study the bracelets, eyes tracing the outlines of their tiny teeth. You've only tried light bondage with soft things before (ropes, bedsheets, a college hookup's tie), but there's a first time for everything. You nod.

"Thought so." He smirks, and you try to figure out how he knew. If it's because you're bi you should be offended, but at the same time, you understand.

He pulls your hands behind your back and tightens the cuffs, the metal digging into your wrists. You were expecting to be locked to a bedpost, but his approach grows on you. *This is better*, you tell yourself, *precisely because it is worse.*

"Want me to call you a car?" he asks after he's done. You'd never planned on staying the night, but regardless, it stings to be hurried out. You decide that you hate him, but also hope he texts you soon—if only so you can leave him on read.

Five minutes later he does text you, but it's just to say you left your earrings in his room. Before you can suggest meeting up next week to get them back, he runs outside, gold hoops glinting in his palm. You thank him, but recognize that the urgency of his action wasn't intended as a favor. You're both adults. You both know why he returned them tonight: so he never has to see you again.

✳

A year later you're writing the book about bisexuality. You wring out your brain for moments that tormented you, and unfortunately this date comes up.

You remember being stunned by the man's rejection, but with distance it's hard to see why. His bookshelf was decent—beyond that, the night was average, disappointing, and straight as hell. Bad art by his standards, bad sex by yours.

Back then you thought of yourself as straight plus gay—an identity made of old ingredients rather than something all its own. The only thing you knew for sure was that you didn't know for sure—another bisexual who couldn't "pick a side."

But as much as you longed to transcend the stereotype, you're glad you never did. Because now you know that confusion isn't your detriment—it's your superpower. Your date might have introduced you to handcuffs, but you taught yourself that the only enemy is restraint.

Your mind keeps replaying that dinner conversation—specifically his question about your book. At the time, you'd been ashamed to admit you didn't know. But in hindsight, maybe your response said it all: Maybe confusion is as queer as it gets.

WHAT I TALK ABOUT WHEN I TALK ABOUT BISEXUALITY

NOW THAT THAT'S out of the way, I'd like to thank you for buying this book! Algorithms have clearly determined you're a bisexual, a social justice warrior, or a slut (if you're lucky, all three)!

If you're already considering picking up your phone, honestly—same. But let me reiterate: I'm so grateful you're here! You took a chance by reading this memoir, the personal history of a thirty-two-year-old white woman whose AIM handle was once jennibaby069. I can't promise I'll deliver anything meaningful, but to quote former *CSI* guest star Taylor Swift, "this is me trying."

This book is about my experience, which includes but is not limited to being bi. On the surface, bisexuality seems widely accepted: The hashtag #bisexual has more than ten billion views on TikTok alone. Representation is on the rise, thanks to cultural heroes like Carole Baskin, Obama's "ethereal bisexual" ex, and Woody in *Toy Story 4* (some of us are still clinging to those rumors, okay?). Even science has come a long way: In 2020, a Northwestern University research team who described themselves as "skeptical" ran some tests and FINALLY proved that male bisexuality exists (as if millions of bisexual men hadn't been proving this all along).

Okay—so even on the surface, bi acceptance isn't perfect. That's a problem, because for bi people the illusion of acceptance can do more harm than good. While normalization has many upsides, it can also have a silencing effect, perpetuating the assumption that being bi is "not a big deal." Bisexuality tends to feel ubiquitous and thus irrelevant, as if the subject isn't worth our time.

But I promise—however much anyone wants me to stop talking about bisexuality, I want to stop talking about it more. In the same sense that the mark of a dating app's success is being deleted (@hinge #ad), I hope that someday, this book becomes obsolete. I hope we progress past the need for these conversations. I hope we dismantle not just systems of oppression, but also binaries and binary thinking. I hope fluidity becomes so ingrained within culture that it becomes "edgy" and "subversive" to be straight. Consumers will praise brands like Expedia and Cheerios for commercials that bravely depict straight life. Straight people will host warehouse parties on the east side of every major urban area, doing lines in the bathrooms, projecting the walls with straight porn and *King of Queens.*

But this is the dream state—not the current reality. And that, my friends, is why I won't shut up just yet.

Since there are so many misconceptions about bisexuality, we'll need to agree on some terms before we begin. If you're already a scholar of bi politics, feel free to skip ahead (and to slide into my DMs). But if you're looking for a quick refresher, you're in luck:

- Bisexuality is a multisexual identity that includes all genders, and is often defined as being attracted to more than one gender.
- Bisexuality and pansexuality are not mutually exclusive.
- Bi people are oppressed by a binary system called "monosexism," which suggests that everyone should either be straight or gay.
- The reason people think bi women are "just experimenting" and bi men are "actually gay" is because patriarchy has manipulated us into thinking that everyone *must* be attracted to men.
- The notion of "bi privilege" overlooks the serious issues bisexual people face. To name a few of those: Nearly half of bi women are r-pe* survivors (compared to 17 percent of straight women and 13 percent of lesbians), and bi men earn an average of 15 percent less than straight men (gay men earn roughly 5 percent less).
- Bi erasure means we don't have much data about bisexual people—especially not intersectional data, due to a lack of studies on nonbinary bisexuals and/ or Black, Indigenous, Asian, and other bisexuals of color.

---

* Please note that later mentions of this word are spelled out in full. (Mentions are indicated at the beginning of chapters by Content Warnings.)

- People often accuse bisexuals of only talking about our sexuality because we "like to feel oppressed." So to be clear: I, the author, am not oppressed. I have many privileges—I'm white, nondisabled, cisgender,* and relatively thin. I speak English, hold U.S. citizenship, and was raised in an upper-middle-class environment. I don't incur oppression based on racism, transphobia, ableism, fatphobia, classism, or xenophobia. I don't have to deal with being misgendered on a daily basis. I don't fear violence from the police. I don't have trouble accessing buildings or climbing stairs. Doctors don't suggest I should "lose some weight" when I go see them for a broken arm. I'm not constantly engaged in exhausting mental labor such as translating to another language in my head. Bisexuality is not a privilege, but my other privileges certainly paved the way for me to write a book about it. My perspective will always be shaped by this experience, so if you're wondering whether you should be reading something by a Black, Latinx, Asian, trans, fat, and/or disabled author right now, the answer is yes.
- Saying "everyone is bisexual" is a microaggression because it implies bisexuality isn't worth talking about.
- Not all bi people are promiscuous—in fact, 89 percent of bi women are in long-term monogamous relationships.

---

* This means I identify with the gender I was assigned at birth. (Which I do—for the most part.)

- If you're worried that bi people will cheat on you, your issue is with monogamy—not bisexuality.
- I'm not here to tell you that bi people aren't greedy or confused.

On that last note, one of my favorite unlearning techniques is to look at any stereotype, assumption, or injustice, and simply ask: *Why?* If, like an incredulous three-year-old, we keep repeating that one-word question, each answer will bring us closer to our world's deepest truths. It's like peeling an onion—the more layers we remove, the more we'll confront ideas that are so entrenched within our realities that we wouldn't have dared to question them outright. Sometimes it's hard to see that there was an onion in the first place. And, to fully round out this metaphor, sometimes peeling that onion can make us cry.

It took me a while to apply this approach to bisexual stereotypes, and even after I did, I stopped short. I focused on "myth-busting," insisting that I wasn't confused, experimenting, or in a phase. But then I read writer Shiri Eisner, whose work questions the very existence of bi stereotypes and asks why we see them as problematic in the first place:

> If we're saying, 'No, we're not confused; no, we're not promiscuous; no, we're not greedy,' then we accept that it's wrong to be confused, it's wrong to be greedy, it's wrong to be promiscuous. And I want to ask, why do we have to work by their rules?

The problem isn't promiscuity—it's patriarchy, which vilifies sex and dismisses non-monogamy. The problem isn't confusion—it's binaries, which encourage us to make finite decisions (usually between two constructs that we never got to choose in the first place). The problem isn't being greedy—it's that systems function better when we don't demand what we deserve.

As it turns out, I'm not straight. I'm not gay. The only thing I am is a threat. Because now I understand that bisexuality isn't just an identity—it's a lens through which to re-imagine our world. This book is about desire—sexual desire, yes, but also the desire to exist beyond the strict boxes that social expectations try to put us in. *Greedy* is about a lifetime spent thinking that I wanted too much, and how that made me want even more.

These are personal essays about what bisexuality means to me. It's the book I wish I had growing up, and I wrote it on the off chance that you might need it too.

PART I

I WANT A WORD FOR THIS

CUFFED JEANS AND FEELING SEEN

SINCE THERE WASN'T much to do in 2020 besides fixate on the future, I've already played out an exchange I'll someday have with my kids. When these children inevitably climb onto my lap and ask how I spent quarantine, I'll respond: "Kids, it was a trying time. While health care and essential workers fought tirelessly, Mommy became a grand master playing the app version of Hasbro's Risk.* She got drunk exactly once when the United States elected a mediocre Democrat. And she had a mental health crisis trying to find purpose under capitalism, which drove her to domesticity and inspired her to have you."

There was one high point of my pandemic that I probably won't mention to my kids (mostly because it involved Twitter,

---

* I stopped playing after I realized Risk was basically "Colonization: The Game" (and after the seventh graders in the Community Tips forum insulted my strategy).

and I'm sure future parenting books will advise against bring-ing up the internet whatsoever). But between you and me, I did smile for a few hours that year after seeing a viral tweet by @thecherryghoul.

The tweet read, "Bisexuals will be 20 mins into a movie and type in 'cast of' on google," and it shook me to my core. That might seem dramatic until you hear the context: I saw this tweet while Netflix's *The Lovebirds* played in the background, moments after I'd googled the film's entire cast. In disbelief, I double-checked Chrome and sure enough found my browser still open to Kumail Nanjiani's IMDb. Then I glanced at the TV and noticed the film was exactly twenty minutes in.

Reader, I gasped.

Logically, I understood that looking up the cast of a movie was part of the modern human condition. Rationally, I knew that many people went down trivia rabbit holes, no matter who they liked to sleep with.

But emotionally, I was swept away. I felt seen, as if this tweet had been written just for me.

✳

This was not the first random trait ascribed to bisexuals, nor was it the first that we'd accepted with open arms.

Somewhere in the 2010s, an idea took off that bi people wore cuffed jeans. In 2019, on a particularly nasty winter day, @sianvconway tweeted a request to "pray for all bisex-uals' exposed ankles in this bitterly cold time." By the end of that year, the internet had so embraced cuffed jeans as a marker of bisexuality that many teens actually used their pants legs as a method of coming out. This usually came to life through TikToks that felt like low-budget dating shows (the formula: call your crush, cuff your jeans, make out, go viral).

Cuffed jeans are bi culture. But that's not all: Finger guns? Bi culture. Bob haircuts? Bi culture. Lemon bars? Bi culture. Sitting in chairs wrong? Some say it's gay culture, but according to Reddit (and my lower back), it's bi culture.

To understand how this bi culture phenomenon began, we have to look at theory—not queer theory (we'll get there) but the theory of memes. Richard Dawkins says the word "meme" derives from "memetic," a term that compares the spread of information to theories of Darwinian evolution.* This is probably best explained by him but unfortunately for you, it will be explained by me, in a reductive excerpt from my 2010 college newspaper column, "The Memeing of Life":

> A meme is generally defined as a cultural idea spread by imitation and repetition. . . . It is easy to look at [memes] and renounce them as stupid, beneath you, or devoid of cultural significance. And true, a banana singing "Peanut Butter Jelly Time" should probably not be compared to Faulkner. However, the fact is that millions of people are out there videotaping their reactions to "2 Girls 1 Cup." And if participation doesn't constitute culture, then what does?

---

* Richard Dawkins has previously explained that this term has been co-opted by the internet—when he coined it he was talking about genes, and digital content doesn't evolve exactly the same way. While I see the need for nuance, I'm offended anyone would try to distance themselves from memes—just say you hate fine art and go.

Every piece of bi culture was born out of the same concept: If you say something is bi culture, it automatically becomes bi culture. In this case, participation isn't just part of the meme—it's the entirety of it: For an object or behavior to constitute "bi culture," all you need is someone willing to proclaim it as such.

Bi culture is everything. Which means bi culture is nothing. As annoying as this logic loop might be, it reflects exactly what it's like to be bisexual: to be told simultaneously that you are asking for too much and that you don't exist.

The meme format has worked well thus far, given that there haven't been any real-world forms of bi culture to invalidate the internet's claims. Growing up in southern Indiana, I felt that lack firsthand—amid the cornfields, I found no queer community, no sexually fluid role models, and no context for the term "bisexual" (though I knew it had the word "sex" in it, which meant I couldn't ask an adult). In middle school, I swooned over a boy on my swim team but got butterflies around a girl who rode my bus. Yet even at twelve, I knew life would be easier if I squished down the gay stuff and pretended to be straight.

As a result, I became performatively "boy crazy," obsessing over cookie-cutter hunks like Josh Hartnett and Sean Faris.* I dove headfirst into straight culture, which basically meant I wore Hard Tail pants, pretended to like *South Park*, and only came from penetrative sex 10 percent of the time. I wasn't faking my interest in guys, but I did know I was hiding something. Whenever I heard that a female celebrity was gay, I felt a pang of envy—like when someone on TV starts eating

---

* You might not have heard of Sean Faris, but if you're curious what he looks like, just know that he recently shot a film called *A Veteran's Christmas*, and that tells you everything you need to know. (Also, I found this out by looking at his IMDb, because of course I did.)

and you realize your own mouth is watering. Any mention of queer women filled me with desperation to shout my truth—I longed to yell, "I want that too!"

But I didn't. The media told me there were only two viable options: gay or straight (preferably straight). I can still hear Phoebe Buffay singing in Central Perk: "Sometimes men love women / and sometimes men love men / and then there are bisexuals / though some just say they're kidding themselves! La-la-la-la-la!" When bi people were shown onscreen, they were always hot messes, emphasis on the "hot." Common tropes that persist to this day include cheating (Piper Chapman on *Orange Is the New Black*), being rebellious (Marissa on *The O.C.*), and generally ruining lives (Kalinda Sharma on *The Good Wife*—a personal fave).* Characters rarely identified themselves as bisexual out loud—instead they behaved their bisexuality, usually through an illicit queer hookup (followed by a breakdown because they're so "confused"). This taught me that bisexuality was something you do, rather than something you are. And since I hadn't "done it" yet, I figured I was straight.

I showed up at college with an overpacked suitcase (okay, four) and a sexual history that, save for a few drunken make-outs, only included men. Desperate to seem "normal," I mimicked the preppy girls in my dorm: I drank Smirnoff Ice, biked on a beach cruiser, and, after saving up, bought myself a Longchamp bag. Proximity to sororities† and their

---

* Interestingly, bi characters are often associated with murder—there's *Basic Instinct*'s Catherine Tramell, *House of Cards*'s Frank Underwood, *Oz*'s Chris Keller, and *American Horror Story: Hotel*'s Elizabeth (though I'll gladly take vampiric Lady Gaga as representation). The trend could be coincidental, but it still provokes a question: Is sexual fluidity so destructive that we have to associate it with death?

† I wasn't "in a house," but that wasn't for lack of trying—I rushed two years in a row and got rejected from them all. Shoutout to Lucía, the incredible RA who let me attend weekly meetings at Delta Co (Del Taco).

heteronormativity rubbed off on me, so instead of using my college years to experiment with queerness, I became laser-focused on getting a boyfriend. Junior year I finally fell in love (this relationship was generally boring because we were happy, which is why you'll find little about it in this book). We broke up due to wanting different things (rational decisions—also boring), and I thought, *Maybe I can finally date women!*

This, however, was easier said than done. I expanded my gender preferences on apps but struggled to gain momentum—every time I messaged a woman, I panicked and frantically switched back to guys. I felt comfortable dating men—they were my regular commute, my status quo. Flirting with other genders took effort, and so dealing with my queerness became just another item on my perpetual to-do list, sandwiched between other things I'd never accomplish: meditate, dust, fix printer, come out, pay that one bill that won't let you do it online.

When I did decide I wanted to come out, I literally couldn't find the words. Was "bisexual" the right one? How could I explain my identity without making people think of sex? Announcing myself as bi seemed like oversharing, and potentially an HR violation—unless I was already naked, stating my sexual preferences would feel out of place. My mirror affirmations turned into anxiety spirals:

> Okay, you beautiful bitch—let's think. What if you start dating someone? Guess that won't work since no singular romantic partner can convey that you're attracted to everyone. And how adorable that you would even consider this option since you can't hold down a relationship to save your life!

Guess you'll have to actually talk to people. But you can't do that at work! When anyone thinks of bi women, they think of threesomes—that means your colleagues who once respected you will now see you as a slut. Not that you're not a slut—just that you don't want your coworkers to know it. Unless . . . maybe that cool lesbian creative director? Pfft—even she's not worth it. If you tell people at work, they'll inevitably wonder how you figured it out, and your imagined sex scenes will live in their heads rent-free.

Don't even get me started on your parents. They love you. If you love them, why would you force them to think about your sex life? You'd call and say: 'Mom, Dad, remember my Barbies? FYI, I made them scissor.' Besides, you bought so much porn on the cable box that your parents probably already know—just leave them alone.

Though how can you even dream of talking to your parents when you can barely talk to your friends? They know you haven't had many (any) queer experiences, which must mean they think you're a fraud. On second thought, why are you considering any of this? You're obviously just straight."

Coming out never seemed worth it. I was attracted to men, so why ruffle feathers when I could just . . . not? It didn't help that hardly anyone seemed to relate—I knew a few people who'd toyed with the idea of bisexuality, but none had actually claimed the term (gee, I wonder why).[*] The sense of isolation made coming out feel even more high-stakes—if it didn't go well and I needed to find some new bi peers, I wouldn't even have known where to look.

✳

Coming out doesn't promise to heal everything, but it does promise community. After revealing your true self, you're supposed to be rewarded with a support system—fellow queers who can do your makeup, administer your stick-and-pokes, and hold you accountable for misquoting *Notes on Camp*. But that support system doesn't just magically appear—you have to seek it out. And if you're bi, it can be very hard to find.

Most LGBTQ+ people[†] go through a process of making queer friends, and the later in life you come out, the more intentional you have to be. But friend-dating can feel even more pathetic than dating-dating, which might explain queer people's tried-and-true strategy: hook up first, then regress into a platonic bond.[‡] It sounds fun, but the awkwardness is not for the faint of heart—if you're seeking a non-Grindr friendship origin story, it's probably easiest to grab a drink.

I'm far from the first person to suggest that gay bars play an important role in queer culture, but I recently learned that

---

[*] According to the *Los Angeles Times*, only 28 percent of bisexual people said they'd disclosed their sexual orientation to the majority of important people in their lives. That means the odds are that there's someone in your life who identifies as bi, and you have no idea.

[†] Throughout this book I'll be using the acronym LGBTQ+ to speak about Lesbian, Gay, Bisexual, Transgender, Queer, Intersex, Asexual, Two-Spirit, Pansexual, and other identities. All of these are important, no matter where their letter falls.

[‡] This strategy may also be explained by a lifetime of internalized homophobia weighing on our self-assuredness, making it ridiculously hard to discern between friend crushes and romantic ones, but TBD.

their significance goes deeper than I thought. Reading *Gay Bar: Why We Went Out* by Jeremy Atherton Lin, I was struck by a quote from San Francisco–based activist Harry Britt: "When gays are spatially scattered, they are not gay, because they are invisible." In this sense, gay and lesbian bars are responsible for the very existence of gays and lesbians. Queer bars give structure to queer communities, while literally putting those communities on the map.

Given this massive responsibility, it's no wonder LGBTQ+ people treat these bars like shelters—places where we can shed our comphet* tendencies and listen to Robyn in peace. But the queer community is just a microcosm of the larger, problematic world, and so these bars often wind up bringing only certain scattered gays back into view. Bar clientele is usually white and thin. Few establishments are fully accessible. Trans-inclusive practices (such as gender-neutral bathrooms, stating pronouns, and forbidding transphobia outright) remain the exception, not the norm.

And since many of these spaces reflect dominant social systems, monosexism shows up there too. That means for bi people, pan people, and anyone who isn't a perfect "gold star,"† gay and lesbian bars can feel like obstacle courses. Questions about your sexual history are lava—avoid them at all costs.

Unlike Oktoberfest or Fox News, biphobia is not exclusively a straight thing—plenty of it comes from gay and lesbian communities too. One study found that in queer online forums about bisexuality, bi people were more likely to

---

* Cute shorthand for "compulsive heteronormativity" (which is, of course, anything but cute).

† For cis gay men there's also "platinum star": a gold star who was born by cesarean section and thus has never penetrated a vagina.

encounter biphobic comments than messages of support. Another study said that only 8 percent of bi people reported feeling included within the LGBTQ+ community, despite the letter *B* being so prominently featured in the acronym.* According to a *them* article from 2020, even queer activism overlooks us—"sexually fluid people tend to get lost in the conversation; there are fewer [LGBTQ+] organizations that specifically exist to advocate for the needs of people who are attracted to more than one gender."

Biphobia has many forms, and one of the most common involves suggesting that bisexuality doesn't exist. Since many gay and lesbian people come out first as bi, it's common for gay and lesbian communities to assume that bisexuality is a gateway identity, or that bi people are "just passing through." Even if these communities do accept bisexuality as permanent, bi people will still be up against the usual assumptions (e.g., we're desperate for attention, we're seeking straight privilege, we're already planning to cheat on you).

Gay and lesbian bars, safe havens for some, are rarely safe havens for bi people. But where does that leave us to go? It's like the gay and straight communities are our parents and each thought the other would pick us up from school. We're left sitting on the curb, moping with our lunch box, until we decide to walk home.

At this point, the bi culture meme transcends the internet, serving as a reflection on bi erasure in the real world. We have to wonder: Why would a community accept lemon bars as

---

* If erasure happens to one of the letters used in the first four, imagine how much it happens to the identities we tend to relegate behind the plus sign—2S (Two-Spirit), A (Asexual), and I (Intersex) people, to name a few.

iconography unless they were desperate for symbols, representation, or acknowledgment of any kind? Arbitrary tropes like "bad at chairs" wouldn't stick to bi people if we weren't so eager to embrace them.

Sometimes I'm jealous of queer communities whose cultural archetypes seem derived from actual behaviors or ideas. To be reductive (as distilling the idea of "culture" requires us to be): Lesbians have U-Hauls, cottage core, and Tori Amos, reflective of emotional openness and matriarchal aspirations. Gay men have Janet Jackson, voguing, and a tendency to walk fast, reflective of a generations-long dialogue with femininity and a tendency to have places to be. These may be massive generalizations, but at least they're relatively neutral ones. Clichés can be harmful, yes, but they can also help our brains process information—they give our gaydar (or in my case, "BiFi") something to search for. Growing up, if I'd known anything other than negative bi representation, it would've been much easier to figure out where I belonged.

But ironically, I'm now glad that bi culture exists only in meme form—at least an abstract idea can remain an expansive one. For lesbian and gay communities, even the stereotypes tend to align with that microcosm of society thing, influenced by patriarchy and white supremacy. Many tropes associated with "lesbian culture" (including those mentioned above) primarily represent *white* lesbian culture, which is notoriously also thin, rich, and cis. "Gay culture" has a similar history of racism and body dysmorphia, and today, bars and Scruff profiles alike still disenfranchise "fats, femmes, and Asians."

As individuals, bi people are not perfect—many of us contribute to the same systemic issues and perpetuate the same harmful ideas. But we don't really exist as a collective, and while that's generally infuriating, I'm relieved it makes our spaces almost too invisible to be exclusionary. Picture the meme with the guy tapping his head: Your community can't be problematic if your community doesn't exist.*

But this does bring up another question: If bi culture consists entirely of random nouns, does it have any significance? Without community to enact it, what's the point? In my eyes, bi culture's meaning depends on one thing: whether bisexual people can make it meaningful to us.

The bi culture meme reminds me of shitty horoscopes, the kind you might find hung in a coffee shop, torn out of an old *USA Today*.† These one-liners rely on vague aphorisms ("Virgo: Be wary of love this week" or "Taurus: You deserve to relax today"), and they make actual astrology‡ look bad. But the watered-down genre's success does tell us something about human nature: We're all seeking information about how to act, how to be, or how we already are. It doesn't matter if it's wrong. It doesn't matter if it could apply to anyone. If it speaks to us by name, just like that: We feel seen.

I read @thecherryghoul's tweet during the closest thing to an apocalypse that's happened in my lifetime, and it gave me a glimmer of hope. Not the kind of hope the masses could've used in 2020 (e.g., hope that the murder hornets would die

---

* I can only speak for NYC here, but it also makes sense that the queer nightlife scenes most affirming of fluidity (events like Papi Juice or Bubble_T) intentionally center Black, brown, Asian, and Indigenous people. This is a helpful reminder that binaries are another construct of colonization that queerness must work to undo—but we'll talk more about that soon.

† Before Astrology Twitter cancels me, let me clarify: I'm not referring to legitimate, need-to-know-your-birth-time astrology, but to pop-psychology's sun sign–only appropriation that makes the real thing look bad.

‡ And to the haters: Yes, I believe in actual astrology. It's the only interest I have that actually makes me feel queer—please don't take that away.

out, or that white people would do more to fight systemic racism than posting black squares on Instagram). Just hope in the form of reassurance that my bisexuality does, in fact, exist. I took a screenshot and felt better knowing I had the tweet on my camera roll. It could serve as a North Star—a tool to help me find my way, just in case I got lost.

HOT AND COOL

THERE ARE MANY things the Midwest thinks they understand, but autumn is one that they actually do. Nowhere else in America can September cloak the streets in such color (except Vermont, but few of us have the money or leftist parents to pull that off).* Every year, deep reds and burnt yellows paint the parks, skies, and sidewalks, and the majority of residents take this for granted, showing their appreciation the old-fashioned way: by denying that climate change is real. People often mock Indiana for having a flat landscape (that is, when they talk about it at all), but growing up there, these views never struck me as dull—they were the best I could get.

In 2004, the first night of fall brought with it two other milestones: It was the night before my first day of high school

---

* The rest of the Northeast? Don't @ me.

and the night I first smoked weed. The daytime still clung to summer: The humid air felt thick and the temperature hovered above eighty degrees. Even my family's dogs were lethargic, strewn around the kitchen like discarded fur coats. They barely stirred when the phone rang—I skipped over them to pick it up.

"Hello?" My voice lifted, as if there were any question as to who it might be.

"Laney's on the line," Sloane said, "but she's calling Erin." I knew what that meant—it was my job to three-way-call Becca; to not slow anything down with questions.

I dialed. Becca answered after half a ring. I clicked the flash button to join the group again—and then there were five.

"As you might have noticed, it's hot." Sloane's voice always commanded my attention—it was deep, especially for a fourteen-year-old girl, and made me want to do whatever she said. "This is an emergency call to talk dress code for tonight."

Two minutes of discussion led to a unanimous vote: We would stick with the plan to wear cute loungewear, but instead of doing sweatshirts with jeans, we would pivot to Soffe shorts, rolled at the waist a maximum of twice. Ideally this would help us seem spontaneous—high school started the next morning, and we wanted to look like serious students who'd snuck out on a whim.

"Can I sleep at Laney's?" I asked my parents. "Tomorrow's a big day—I'll feel better if I show up with friends."

My dad jumped at the idea. As a mathematician he hadn't grown up with a robust social life,* so he reacted to each of

---

* My dad's favorite college story to tell involves the one (1) time he blacked out while drinking beer. His friend dragged him home from a party on the MIT campus while he drunkenly shouted, "Give me any matrix and I'll invert it!"

my sleepover invitations like they were guest-list spots at the Met Gala (as if he even knew what that was). He taught decision sciences at the local university, and whenever we ran into one of his students around town, they would inevitably kneel to my eye level and ask me if I knew that my dad was "a genius." I said I did but felt confused by this, as to me, Wayne Winston seemed quite obtuse: He pronounced Nissan as "niss-ahn" no matter how many times I corrected him; he often left his backpack wide open or tucked one sweatpant leg into a sock. Quirks of this magnitude require a sense of humor, and thankfully he's always had one—loves telling jokes but loves being the butt of them even more. I admired him, but knew I didn't want to follow in his footsteps. I wasn't strong enough to make my way through life as a punch line—I longed to fit in, to even be cool if I could. My genes made it clear that I'd only achieve social success by way of a calculated pursuit, though getting caught trying too hard would be a dire fate. My safest bet was to go all in on conformity, so that night I put on my best Hollister sweatshirt and begged my dad to give me a ride. Thrilled for me, he agreed, then dropped me off at the end of my childhood, pulling away with a wave and a smile.

I was last to arrive. My four best friends were upstairs, doing their makeup and waiting for the adults to go to sleep. Laney's room was an early-aughts dreamland, complete with an inflatable chair, Backstreet Boys posters, and several white grommet belts from PacSun (for all your styling needs). I sat on her tie-dye comforter and picked at my cuticles, trying not to seem as anxious as I was.

"Who all's gonna be there?" Sloane stood in front of the mirror, applying the coffee-colored Bonne Bell lip gloss we all

swore by. Her brown curls grazed her shoulders and she kept
her neck long, which reminded me to sit up straight. I did.

"I'm not sure," I admitted. "But I do think he has people
over a lot."

"His parents don't care?" Erin chewed her lip. She was
the most nervous, but in her defense, she was also the only
one on an Ivy League track—that meant she had the most
to lose. Today the notion that a joint could ruin a white girl's
life seems laughable (I'm high as I write this), but back then
the fear was real. We believed our parents when they insisted
that getting caught with "reefer" would tarnish our college
applications, and we certainly didn't want to go to jail. Conversations about legalization stayed confined to coastal cities,
so as far as we knew, smoking pot was illegal and dangerous
enough to stay that way. We didn't realize that our whiteness
had already lessened our risk of consequences—that we were
one-third as likely to be arrested for this type of crime than
Black people were, and that we'd done absolutely nothing
to secure those odds. We were barely cognizant of our skin
color, let alone the privileges it gave us. We just knew weed
was "bad," and if we tried it, we could be bad too.

"He lives with his grandma." I shrugged. "I don't think she
knows."

When the hallways at Laney's house were quiet, we gathered the items AskJeeves told us to bring—eye drops, gum,
hand lotion, perfume—and tiptoed downstairs, slipping past
the screen door into the backyard.

"We'll cut through the woods," I whispered, and the group
nodded in unison. I was the leader now, a position I'd earned the
noble way: by having dated the drug dealer in seventh grade.
"Dated" was a liberal term—Wolf had been my boyfriend for

an impressive six days, though back then I knew him as "Walter," the notorious spikey-haired kid who'd stolen a roll of Subway Sub Club stamps and now ate every meal for free. We met at the Fun Frolic, an objectively disgusting carnival that came through our hometown once a year, and though Wolf didn't win me any goldfish, he did give me my first kiss. It happened as we said goodnight, standing awkwardly near the Gravitron—without warning Wolf's face zoomed into mine, his hat brim tripping on my forehead and tumbling to the gravel below. Our relationship ended a few days later, when Wolf sent a breakup IM explaining that he wsnt felin it [*sic*] but hoped we could stay friends. I cried for more days than the total time we'd dated, and though in a flicker of dignity I'd considered blocking him, I was glad I hadn't. Tonight we needed him.

The five of us considered ourselves independent thinkers (as middle schoolers who dress identically are wont to do), but it was hard to tell whether we'd sought to smoke because we actually wanted to try it or because weed was a boy activity that girls could do to become "cool." I craved cool as a title—as a way to rebel against my dad, but mostly because I needed a persona to own. I wasn't the cutest or smartest girl in my group (those were Sloane and Erin, respectively), and while I couldn't change my face shape or my IQ, I could listen to Radiohead and do drugs. I didn't realize yet that I was seeking a cool girl ideal created by patriarchy, the media, and underwear-clad men posting on 4chan—built by everyone except for women themselves. Even then, my vision of womanhood was hardly mine at all.

To this day, it can be hard to tell where I end and the male gaze begins. I still hate being caught off guard when a guy mentions an album or movie I don't know, but back then it was my worst fear—like being caught naked in public, my girlish ignorance revealed for all to see. As a preventative measure, I spent high school consuming traditionally masculine media, striving to connect with *Saving Private Ryan* or find meaning in the curb-stomp scene of *American History X*. I wanted to become an encyclopedia of cultural references, as if these could camouflage my femininity and let me tiptoe through patriarchy unnoticed. My college prep consisted of reading *Rolling Stone* cover to cover and downloading every song it mentioned—I needed the full Pink Floyd discography on my laptop in case a guy in my dorm happened to see. I didn't realize that the canon I'd studied to impress men had been designed primarily by—and for—those men. No wonder they liked it so much.

Every time I visit my childhood room, I'm confronted with evidence of this blue period: Led Zeppelin CDs, a poster from the movie *Blow*, and a purely decorative Sega Genesis. A Blink-182 poster still hangs on my door, raising the question: Which boyfriend was I trying to impress? (Answer: Grant, who loved the *Enema of the State* nurse more than he'd ever love me.)

In accordance with those cool-girl aspirations, I'd been the one to suggest that the five of us smoke weed. I hadn't expected the vote to be a unanimous, enthusiastic yes, but apparently none of us wanted to show up at high school without this experience under our (PacSun) belts. I could tell Sloane and I had similar motivations—we both longed for success milestones beyond standardized test scores, and knew that to get there we'd need to unearth a new set of social tools. I wanted to avoid my fate as an outcast, but for Sloane, the search was higher stakes—she wanted to escape her home life, where her divorced parents fought and money was tight. She'd grown up too fast but had gained street smarts as a result, and now had an ability to read people that made her (and me) certain she could get away with anything. Both of us thought weed might be the first step toward a deluxe version of ourselves, that it would grant us the keys to more rebellious and independent futures. Maybe that was why they called it "the gateway drug."

The streetlights were out so the five of us walked through the darkness together, softly singing what few lines we remembered of "Soco Amaretto Lime." Even then it felt like a pivotal moment that everything hinges upon—the kind that makes you see the rest of life as simply Before and After.

We stayed the course toward the woods, and if we were scared, we didn't show it. Led by the fluorescence of flipped-open Motorolas, we followed the sidewalk until it abruptly stopped, as sidewalks in Indiana suburbs often did. I'd always imagined the construction crews had picked up and left, tired of building Stepford neighborhoods with sunny street names.

"You said it was light blue, right, Jen?" Laney pointed at a flat rectangular house with pink curtains. She stood at the front, clearly wanting to be the first inside. Though you couldn't see her red hair in the dark, you could feel her fire—her desperation to evolve from an unsullied teen into a savvy adult. From the outside, most people assumed Laney ran our group—she was the one who'd publicly referred to us as the "best best friends," turning us into a "group" in the first place. But inside, it was clear that Sloane was the boss—because of her street smarts, yes, but also because boys thought she was the prettiest one. She had the power—no one would walk forward until she said the word.

"Hear that? Back there." Sloane gestured to the fence at the top of the driveway. What looked like a shed faced the backyard, the laughs of high school boys echoing out into the night.

Sloane stepped forward, passing all of us, wiping a trace amount of sweat off her brow. She lifted the fence gate and walked inside. We each took a deep breath and, like lemmings, followed suit.

Inside were three boys, each with different hair—together they looked like a pubescent stoner remake of *The Three Stooges*. In hindsight, their outfits had been curated to look uncurated—cargo shorts paired with T-shirts from intramural sports and local restaurants, each topped with the pièce de résistance: a hemp necklace. It took me years to understand that my cool girl persona had been a performance, but it took even longer to recognize that these boys had been acting too. They chased a version of masculinity defined by the ability to keep emotions hidden; to never show pain, weakness, or—god forbid—tears. A practiced insouciance had become their behavioral gold standard—sure, it stunted their emotional growth, but at least it upped the odds that other high schoolers might describe them as "chill."

The shed was long and narrow, two couches against opposite walls facing each other, and though I wasn't yet familiar with the concept of feng shui, I knew this aesthetic didn't work. But on the plus side, I also didn't understand weed clichés yet, so the Bob Marley poster seemed intriguing instead of basic. I realized I'd never heard his music before.

Maybe you haven't been ready yet, I thought.

Wolf brushed some greenish crumbs off his thighs, then stood up and walked toward me. His JNCOs sagged low, riding his thin waist like a Hula-Hoop.

"Jenny Jen-Jen! Glad you guys came!" He actually seemed sincere.

"Us too—we're stoked," I said, fully monotone. "We wanna get high."

One guy on the couch exhaled, and smoke filled the room.

"Your first time?" The guy coughed, regaining his vocal cords as he spoke. I glanced at Sloane, hoping for a look that would give me permission to lie, but she was busy thumbing through trinkets on a nearby shelf.

I turned back and nodded. "First time."

"You won't get high, then," he explained. I acted surprised but already knew this (again, thanks to AskJeeves)—it was rare to feel the effects the first time you smoked. The website said that even the first five times might not get you there, but there was one thing that might help: Knowing what to expect. That's why we'd spent the past week searching for "marijuana high symptoms"—we were prepping to beat weed at its own game.

I squeezed onto the couch between Wolf and the coughing guy, crossing my arms to avoid touching even a sleeve. I studied the room, noticing a blue glass vase that had fallen over on a low table.

Drug-induced carelessness, I thought. *Guess that's the life I should expect from now on.*

I looked around the room, noticing each of my friends, their faces instantly making me calm. These were my favorite people, the girls I called BF4E (AEAEAEAEAEAE, ad infinitum) and who called me the same. I loved them like family, or something stronger, because not even for family would I have put Vertical Horizon lyrics in my AIM profile. (We each included a different line from "Best I've Ever Had"—again, this was Laney's idea.)

Our group had formed two years prior, when all five of us were cut from our middle school's dance squad. The taped-up list of names seemed to confirm that we'd forever be pigeon-holed as nerds—we were smart girls who no longer had the option to redeem ourselves by looking cute in a uniform. We solidified our friendship a week later at a twenty-person birthday party for someone who'd made the team, disguising our hurt as a distaste for the host's childish sleepover activities like makeovers and prank calls. We wanted to do drugs, kiss boys, and rebel, and since we were misfits who didn't align with an existing clique, we created our own. We ached to be grown up, and now, hanging out with sophomores to smoke weed on a school night, we were proving we could handle the maturity we craved. These boys looked at us like freshly delivered pizza, as if something they'd been waiting for had finally arrived. Their attention didn't feel creepy yet; it was too new. All we knew then was that we liked it.

Wolf grabbed the blue vase and placed it in my lap. I stared for a moment before realizing: It wasn't a vase. It was a pipe.

"Go for it," he whispered. Sensing his eyes on me again felt good, but I caught myself waiting for Sloane to look too—I wanted to impress her as much, if not more than, the boys. Eventually she did, only to see me fumble with the piece, and I felt my cheeks heat up. I spun the pipe around a few times before figuring out which side to suck, then lifted it to my mouth with pride.

"Wow." Wolf chuckled. "You gonna do that without a flame? Impressive."

I tensed up, frozen in embarrassment. But Wolf's smirk revealed he'd been teasing—he handed me a lighter, then placed my thumb over a hole.

I sucked in, clenching every muscle in my body, hoping this might help me not cough. It did, and after I exhaled, I stared at the smoke in awe, shocked that so much air had come from me.

"Niiiiice," Wolf assessed. I grinned, honored to be the teacher's pet. I passed the pipe to my left and once we'd all taken a hit, the boys made small talk while us girls waited for something to change. Nothing did, except for the time— somehow we'd been there over an hour, and it was suddenly ten p.m.

"We should go," I said to no one in particular, but my friends were more than ready—they jumped to their feet like students at a lunchtime bell. Wolf gave each a goodbye hug, and when he got to me, he paused.

Ah yes—the money.

"How much?" I asked, my voice shaking.

He shrugged. "First time's free."

"Thanks for being so chill," I said. Apparently this was the magic word. He beamed.

We filed out the door, moving up Wolf's street, around the corner, and back toward the woods. I didn't feel high, but I was relieved to be out of that shed, my friends and I alone together again. There were no headlights in either direction, and we took that as permission to walk in the middle of the street.

Once we were out of the shed's earshot, we exchanged uncertainties.

"I don't feel anything." Erin gulped.

"That's normal," Laney replied, positioning herself as the

expert. Becca and I sighed, annoyed at the thought that we'd have to go through all that again.

Right then, without saying a word, Sloane took off running, her Vans thumping against the asphalt.

"Where the hell are you going?" I yelled. She took a few more strides, then turned back toward us. Sloane rarely smiled—both because she was a cynic and because she had slightly crooked teeth that she preferred to hide (lest they impact her position as the hot one). But there she was: mouth agape, like she couldn't help herself.

"You guys," she shouted. "Try RUNNING."

We raced toward her, zigging and zagging on the pavement, sweat condensing on our skin. I wasn't sure if I felt high, but I felt something—a bodily haze, one that brought brighter colors and blurry eyes. Now there was no Wolf, no Bob Marley poster, no need to perform. We ran for six blocks until, out of breath and laughing, we reached the woods.

Laney's screen door was slightly ajar, just as we'd left it—we quieted down and tiptoed upstairs. After making it inside her bedroom undetected, we hugged each other close. None of us could believe it: We'd actually pulled this off.

"Whew." Sloane sighed, her eyes still glittery. The other girls might have thought she was reacting to the weed, but I knew she was thinking bigger, processing our futures. The exhilaration wasn't because we'd snuck out and done a "bad thing," but because of how many doors we'd suddenly opened—doors to more drugs, yes, but also to maturity, which included the possibility of sex. We felt a rush of empowerment that seemed endless, a sense of agency that, in hindsight, stemmed from ignorance about the way the world works. We didn't yet understand that gender had already stacked the decks against us—or that white supremacy was cheating on our behalf. We felt lust or something like it: a drive to consume the entire world and to have it consume us back.

We switched into ratty T-shirts, assuming bedtime positions around Laney's room. As the one who'd arrived last at the start of the night, I got the floor.

"Can I open this?" I gestured to the window, wanting to feel like we were outside again. Laney nodded, then clicked off the string lights above her bed. Fumbling through the dark, I got up and lifted the glass. The breeze poured in—just cold enough to help us fall asleep.

GIRL CRUSH: CLINICAL OBSERVATIONS

BACKGROUND

Femme-affective homoinfatuation disorder typically falls into one of two classifications:

1. **Benign Girl Crush (BGC):** Common—occurs in >95 percent of patients. Frequently caused by platonic jealousy. No significant long-term effects.

2. **Malignant Girl Crush (MGC):** Earth-shattering. Life-altering. Will devastate you—as in "cry in the bathroom during third period because you hate her boyfriend and what the fuck is wrong with you, you're not supposed to think about girls like this you fucking CREEP." Occurs in roughly 5 percent of patients (as far as we know). Most prevalent in bisexuals and lesbians, though may also occur in other multisexuals or individuals who "don't like labels." In severe cases, MGC may simply be referred to as "a crush."

Diagnosis can be challenging, considering both classifications have similar symptoms (memorizing her outfits, starting a Tumblr together, thinking about her every time Broken
Social Scene comes on). But distinction is critical: Stubborn
MGCs may persist for decades, while BGCs tend to abate
after changing friend groups or unfollowing—a phenomenon
known as "out of sight, out of mind."

CLINICAL STUDY

This study follows an edge case—a Patient (henceforth referred to as "Jen") who believes she's experiencing MGC as
a result of contact with Stimuli ("Sloane"). Objective is to
determine if Jen's self-diagnosis is correct, or if this is classic
BGC—nothing to see here.

Predisposition (seventh grade): Given Sloane's attractiveness
(*see*: freckles, button-nose), Observation Team considers Jen
high risk for confusion: She will never be sure whether she
wants to be Sloane, kiss Sloane, or both. As a result, Jen primarily communicates using objective facts, such as "Sloane,
your features are so symmetrical" or "Sloane, your eyelashes are
so long." The format allows Jen to talk openly about Sloane's
attractiveness while keeping her own attraction a secret—even
from herself.

Onset (eighth grade): Jen reports that she and Sloane hang
out every weekday, going to Jen's house after school to sit on
the dusty brown sofa and sneakily watch Gwen Stefani on
MTV. Cherry Coke cans, gum wrappers, and beads from a
jewelry-making kit cover the floor—the living room is a mess,
and Jen's heartbeat increases upon realizing her parents will

be home soon. Despite her sympathetic nervous system, Jen seems certain the harshest punishment she'd get would be an exaggerated sigh—while some parents show their love with discipline, Jen's never scold her (not even when she deserves it). As a result, Jen demonstrates low recognition of her privilege, along with exceptionally low awareness that anyone else's home life could be different from her own. (Meanwhile, Observation Team notes that Sloane's descriptions of her own mom include outbursts, temper, and mentions of manic behavior. We wish we could give her a hug.)

Jen does not recall how escalation begins—just knows that she and Sloane are suddenly play-wrestling in the middle of the room. (Observation Team recognizes this feels extremely on-the-nose. Participants look like repressed teens on a CW show: *Spotted: Jen and Sloane in a brawl. But is it more love than war? XOXO.* But despite the cliché, Jen demonstrates physiologic signs of "having fun." Observation Team hypothesizes that "queer teen wrestling" may be a TV trope for a reason.)

Acute event begins: Sloane tackles Jen to the floor, pins her arms down, and kisses her, emitting a cartoonish *Mmmmwah!* Sloane keeps her mouth on Jen's for roughly five seconds before pulling away, erupting into hysterics. Then Sloane stands and says she's, uh, going to the kitchen to, uh, get water. Jen remains on the floor, dazed.

Latent Phase (sophomore year): Jen reports that she and Sloane have not spoken about their wrestling match, and it seems understood that they never will. Instead they spend high school in close proximity to Alternative Stimuli ("Guys"), doodling each one's name in their notebooks alongside Something Corporate lyrics (a common behavioral pattern circa 2004).

Jen reports excessive flirting during fifth period, as well as dry-humping in several grocery store parking lots. (Observation Team notes that Jen enjoys encounters with Guys, which, according to classification guidelines, decreases likelihood of MGC.)

Interestingly, Jen's serotonin levels peak after the hookups, when she drives loops around town with Sloane in the passenger seat. Both Participants exhibit mild logorrhea, swapping advice for hours: "Guys like when girls ignore them," "Girls should do everything except for sex," "Guys think it's hot when girls hook up with other girls . . . but only if they get to watch." (Observation Team vehemently opposes these ideas but has included them in this report to acknowledge how formative they were. Like it or not, this conversation constitutes one of Jen's earliest exposures to bisexuality, suggesting that a woman's queer behavior matters only if it has an audience.) Through high-risk body language (*see*: watching Sloane instead of the road), Jen indicates that she would realistically take any excuse to kiss Sloane again, regardless of whether or not it would "count."

Guys remain background noise until junior year when Sloane loses herself in one: a charismatic asshole that Observation Team refers to as "Threatening Alternative Disruptor" (aka "ThAD"). ThAD intimidates Jen—he towers over Sloane's small frame. His R-naught contagion score is extremely high (Observation Team notes that he even describes himself as "a player"). Sloane knows this, but pretends she doesn't care.

Neither Participant expects ThAD to ask Sloane to prom, but he does. When Sloane says yes, Jen demonstrates mild aphasia (*see*: loss for words, confusion), yet still agrees to go with one of his friends. The night ends at ThAD's house with Jen straddling her date in the hallway—when angles allow, she peers into ThAD's bedroom through a crack in the door. There, Jen witnesses Sloane on top of ThAD. She finds herself transfixed even as her heart sinks. Sloane's eyes are closed but ThAD catches Jen watching. He glares back, as if to say, "She's mine."

Aggressive Phase (junior year): After realizing Sloane might be having trouble at home, Jen's Observation Supervisor ("Mom") proposes Sloane sleep over more often. This idea may be thoughtful, but it causes Jen's jealousy to metastasize: One day she sees Mom and Sloane laughing together; the next they're sharing morning tea. Jen assumes Mom must prefer Sloane for the same reasons other students do: because she is prettier, skinnier, and better than Jen will ever be. Jen begins binge eating and sneaking to the bathroom to throw up, relieved to have something she can control. One afternoon, when Jen takes the blame for finishing the Cool Whip, Mom stares at her and blinks twice. (Based on several studies with Polite Midwestern Participants, Observation Team interprets this as "not mad—just disappointed.")

Jen demonstrates frustration with Mom, but not with Sloane. On the contrary—Sloane and Jen grow closer than ever. Mom has set up Sloane in the guest room, so every night Jen sneaks down the hall, climbs into the bed, and listens to Sloane talk. Some nights she talks about wanting to raise a family. Some nights she talks about ThAD. But if Sloane has recently spoken to her mom, she doesn't talk—instead she puts on twisted indie movies like *Hard Candy* or *Brick* that shift her focus to fictional pain instead. The DVDs always skip and Sloane always dozes off before the credits. Eventually Jen tiptoes back to her room, watches *Aqua Teen Hunger Force*, and goes to sleep.

Complication (senior year): Sloane falls in love, but not with Jen.

Incident occurs during a Senior Spring Break trip to Panama City Beach, Florida (Supervisor allowed Participants to attend, despite Observation Team's recommendation against it). Jen and Sloane find themselves immersed in a phantasm of a week—hookahs, Keystone Light, and Mardi Gras beads, a Harmony Korine film come to life. One day at the beach, a Guy approaches and gets Sloane's number, then proceeds to spam her with texts. After hanging out with him and his friends at a house party, Jen is shocked to discover he fulfills Sloane's "Full Package" criteria: cute but not too cute, great at board games, certain that he wants kids.

It turns out Spring Break Man lives in Ohio, three hours away from Participants' hometown, so he and Sloane keep hanging out when they get back. Each weekend, Jen waves goodbye as Sloane leaves to go visit him. (Jen reports feeling supportive, but Observation Team notes a dramatic rise in her cortisol levels, indicating otherwise.)

End-Stage Disease (senior year): Both Jen and Sloane have a history of crying when they're angry (at the time of this report, Jen's car seats are damp with tears). Jen sits in the driver's seat, elbows on the steering wheel, head in her hands, unsure how their fight has come to this.

Possible cause: Jen revealed that she wanted to go out of state to college, leading to harsh insults from both sides.

Sloane shouted: "You're spoiled" (Observation Team confirms), Jen snapped: "You're not brave enough to leave Indiana" (Observation Team confirms again). Now thirty minutes later, Jen's car remains parked on the quiet suburban street, engine on and the Killers' *Hot Fuss* playing at low volume. Both Jen and Sloane indicate strong unironic attachment to this album, though its queer undertones go over their heads. (Observation Team would like to point out the gender-fluid themes in "Somebody Told Me" and the bisexual rage in "Andy, You're a Star.")

Jen seems to process the evening like a breakup; says her chest feels like it might cave in. Yet it is not a breakup. She and Sloane are just friends. (Observation Team notes background noise: "It was only a kiss.")

Long-Term Follow-Up (post-college): In weeks following End-Stage, neither participant speaks to each other. Jen indicates reluctance to amend things, and since she has historically been the one to offer olive branches, Jen assumes GC has run its course. (Observation Team agrees—we're sad about it too.)

Jen does not know how to mourn, so she simply avoids Sloane until after college, when Sloane moves in with their Mutual Friend ("Erin"). Even then, Jen and Sloane barely talk. It takes years for the raw emotions to fade, but the friend group insists on staying in touch—it's a foundation so solid that neither Participant can escape.

Eventually Sloane decides to get married. When she asks the high school group to be her bridesmaids, Jen knows she can't say no. Besides, for once she's a fan of Sloane's Guy—a man whose earnestness and ambition put ThAD and Spring Break Man to shame. Jen shows up to the event in the requested Reformation dress, then smiles for the cameras and abuses the open bar. She reports boredom, lethargy, and general malaise. Sloane, however, says it's the best day of her life.

When Sloane and her Guy have a baby ("Sloane Jr."), Jen joins a Google Hangout to *ooh* and *ahh*. The infant's face looks like a pixelated candy apple resting soundly on Sloane's chest, and Jen's heart rate lowers (this either indicates a depressive mood swing or the opposite: some long-awaited tranquility). Sloane seems happy, and this appears to make Jen happy. Over the laggy connection, she tells Sloane congratulations and insists that she'll make a great mom.

FINAL DIAGNOSIS

While MGC remains plausible (*see*: underlying risk, mental preoccupation, internal torment), results still favor BGC. Common things are common—with only one kiss on record, it's hard to argue anything else. Observation Team understands that emotions roiled throughout the course of study, but stands by the recommendation to bury these feelings deep down. It's in everyone's best interest for Jen to write this off as benign, get a boyfriend, and move on.

TRUE LIFE: I MASTURBATE WRONG

I FIRST REALIZED I masturbated wrong the same way I discovered most of my other flaws: from a stranger on the internet.

It began in middle school, an era of spaghetti straps and gel pens, when no adrenaline rush quite compared to logging on to AIM. My first handle was glitz766, a reference to Mariah Carey's magnum opus that illuminated how innocent my digital habits once were. glitz766 felt like the username of a picture-perfect middle schooler: a girl who played sports, had sleepovers, and definitely didn't touch herself at night.

I'm not sure which came first, my handle change or my sex drive. But after I made the shift to jennibaby069, nothing was the same. I'd included the 69 after watching a popular eighth-grade boy doodle it on his notebook (in hindsight: gross). I didn't know what the number meant, but guys seemed to like it, and my buddy list continued to grow.

In high school, my family graduated to multiple phone lines, and I became an AIM regular. The high that had once felt special gradually turned into an addiction, and before I knew it, I rushed home to get my fix. Every afternoon I waited for the deadbeat junior I wanted to marry to log on (so I could say "hey" and he could say "sup" and the conversation could end there), but one day, when my parents weren't home and my future husband wasn't online, I decided to take a risk. I opened the tab that let you browse chat rooms and, feeling brave, I joined one.

The messages appeared fast: "oh yeah," "love it," "send more." Without thinking too hard, I typed "hi." Within seconds, three gray windows popped up—IMs from users I wasn't "buddies" with yet. A lump formed in my throat as I hovered the cursor over one of the messages—the only thing I remember about the username is that it sounded adult, probably because it had the word "Daddy" in it. I swallowed hard and clicked "accept."

a/s/l?, Daddy asked. I typed the letters into the AOL search bar—"age, sex, location."*

18/female/Boston, I lied.

nice, Daddy wrote. *send me your tits!!*

I'd never heard the word "tits," so I once again looked it up. Learning the definition made me feel hot all over, seared by shame and longing at the same time. I glanced down at my boobs, trying to see them as worthy of this new erotic name. I felt a warm glow throughout my body, the initial flutter of getting turned on.

---

* I could spend sixteen pages analyzing the use of "sex" over "gender" in the a/s/l context, but I'll spare you.

I don't have a webcam, I replied. There was a beat of silence, so I panicked myself into following up: But I'm touching my tits right now!

oh yeah??? send a pic baby.

I can't, I just told u. I scoffed. Daddy wasn't a great listener.

bummer!! how do they feel tho?

They feel good, I guess?

rad!! now touch yourself!

One sec.

do it now!!

I just need a sec.

what's the hold up??

I need to lie on my stomach. And use both hands.

weird. and no pics?

Before I could say no again, Daddy logged off.

Though today I have hundreds of nudes floating in the ether (brag), I've still never sent a photo where I'm masturbating. Sure, I've sent ones where I'm *touching* myself—my fingers elegantly opening my labia, a nearby thigh pimple left un-Facetuned in an effort to seem "real." If these photos convince anyone that I'm actually getting off, that's merely a testament to production value. (I'm far more talented with a selfie stick than a Hitachi.)

Composing these shots, I copied what little I'd seen about female masturbation in the media. Recent years brought a surge in realistic portrayals (some visionary performances that come to mind: *Pen15*'s Maya Erskine straddling her mirror, *You*'s Elizabeth Lail giving us cylindrical pillow representation,

Big Mouth's Maya Rudolph referring to orgasms as "pussy screams"), but in the early 2000s, accurate depictions were few and far between. Most representation featured a woman on her back, effortlessly and sexily bringing herself to completion (despite not even taking off her jeans). These scenes filled me with gay panic, but also masturbation panic. Pouting, I wondered, *Why don't I jerk off like that?*

Maybe early aughts fictional characters could get results while being delicate, but not me. My clit requires significant pressure, thus my masturbation style involves trading aesthetics for thrash—it's the bedroom equivalent of a monster truck rally. Though I own plenty of sex toys (another brag?), I have little patience for charging them, so a typical mastur-date with my hand goes like this:

Step One: Flip onto stomach.
Step Two: Tuck arms under body.
Step Three: Smoosh face into pillow.
Step Four: Attack.

If that doesn't paint the picture, search "Undulating Monk Seal" on YouTube—you'll get the idea.

✳

It's okay if you're ashamed, right, Jen? Your style can be your little secret, right, Jen? Wrong.

Because, as the world has finally started to understand, self-pleasure is beautiful—and it's even more beautiful when shared. Touching ourselves can be a magical component of intimate relationships. It can help us learn what feels good so we can share that knowledge with others. And in the event that our partners can't get us off (or vice versa), never fear: mutual masturbation is here! It's the sexual equivalent of participation trophies—everyone wins as long as you're having fun!

Female pleasure now also holds a prominent role in the self-care spotlight, where it's positioned as a lightweight act of feminist resistance. The assumption is that, if women and femmes openly share stories of our orgasms (along with our vibrator affiliate links), we're actively smashing the patriarchy and challenging sexist norms.

These outcomes—better sex and equal rights—are objectively positive things. But for those of us who get off by way of belly flopping onto our palms, masturbating in front of other people poses a unique challenge. Like so many aspects of modern empowerment, the self-love movement often filters through the male gaze. As a result, it comes with a subtext: If you're gonna get yourself off, you'd better look hot while you do it.

To be clear: I'd love to look hot while I do it. And trust me—I've tried. I've tried a lighter touch, but it tickles. I've tried lying faceup, but my mind wanders, and I inevitably pull a Beth Harmon and start running chess drills on the ceiling. I've even tried not giving a fuck, logging on to Chatroulette in search of a faceless partner that I don't feel obligated to perform for, but each time, I chicken out. Anxious at the thought of putting myself first, I usually wind up pushing my boobs (ahem: tits) together and saying "you like that?" until the stranger comes.

None of my attempts worked. Well, they *sort of* worked, but the orgasms were never the same. According to r/sexover30 (the best gynecologist I've ever had), my technique represents the vaginal equivalent of a penis-owner's "death grip," meaning that it gets one hooked on a high level of intensity, making it nearly impossible to feel sensations any other way. You'd think these consequences would deter me, but instead they've convinced me I've found the most potent drug on the market—a high I couldn't dare give up.

I'm immensely supportive of masturbation's good press—three cheers for the self-love revolution!—but I do miss pretending my onanistic insecurities were just another side effect of being a woman. Now that female masturbation is chic and mainstream (to reiterate: yay!), I have to acknowledge that it's my own personal shame, and it's my specific method that's strange. For context on exactly how strange, know that my friend Joey* has walked in on me before (we were roommates for three years—it happens). Afterward he described my splayed position as "either vaguely *Exorcist* or extremely *Exorcist*" (both of those being euphemisms). This happened one morning while I was peacefully obliterating my clit—Joey came into my room and lingered in the doorway. He later explained that, because my style seemed so visually removed from the realm of sex, he didn't realize he needed to leave.

My technique has never been a huge burden—just an oft-annoying, socially awkward quirk. Alone, I was usually desperate enough to push through the embarrassment. But with someone else, whether via screen or IRL, the shame consumed me. Before logging onto a digital sex session, I went through the glamorous pre-sex rituals of setting up a ring light, contouring my boobs, and googling "how to add filters to video chat." But once the session began, that work fell by

---

* More on him later.

the wayside and I faced a Sophie's Choice: Did I want to get off or look cute?

As a seasoned video-chat vet (I can proudly say I had Ye Olde Skype Sex back in 2011, long before the seamless user experience of Zoom), you'd think I would've learned how to choose the former. For the last decade, the angel on my shoulder has done her best to guide me: "Make it a teaching moment! Tell them what you like!" But the devil—presumably the one Joey thought I'd been trying to exorcise—always came up with a simpler plan: "Fulfill your obligation to get this guy off, then fake it, baby! The sooner you end the call, the sooner you can rub one out before bed."

✳

We do get our happy ending (pun intended), because eventually, I did gain confidence in my masturbation technique. Surprisingly, the thing that got me there wasn't a Savage X Fenty membership, a pole dancing class, or Gwyneth Paltrow's $75 vagina-scented candle—it was sociology 101. (This essay will now do a dramatic shift in tone—go ahead and call it a switch.)

In 2016, shortly after a white guy with a fake tan was elected president of the United States (what was his name again?), I read the blogger Erin McKean's quote: "You don't owe prettiness to anyone . . . pretty is not a rent you pay for occupying a space marked 'female.'" As a budding feminist (*listens to *BEYONCÉ (self-titled)* once*), I understood this, at least intellectually: Women and femmes were not obligated to look attractive to please men. Yes, adhering to specific beauty ideals would probably make our lives easier, but no one could force us to comply.

Since I'd skipped most of my Gender Studies elective in college, my unlearning process started late, but began picking up speed. I found myself developing a healthier relationship with my looks, accepting that my appearance changed daily and that my worth wasn't tied to my weight. One mind-blowing revelation feels embarrassingly obvious to me today: The fact that beauty itself was a social construct, originating from Western beauty ideals. This meant that attractiveness as I knew it was rooted in systems like racism, ableism, and patriarchy (to name a few)—this made sense, considering that the idea of "hot" essentially referred to Emily Ratajkowski and Emily Ratajkowski alone.* But before it shattered my entire reality, I'd simply never thought about it—a sign that I benefited from those oppressive systems more than I knew.

So I did what white women tend to do when we show up late to a movement: I took up space, eager to relay the recent revelations that had changed my life. Online, I evangelized my new knowledge through the noble pursuit of posting progressive memes. Yet behind the screen I hadn't made nearly enough progress—I still spent exorbitant chunks of my salary on skincare products, felt naked without my lash extensions, and scooped out my bagels while pretending that wasn't fatphobic as hell. For as much as I'd learned about the emptiness of beauty's ideals, I still felt terrified that I'd fall short of its expectations.

I wasn't afraid of being "unattractive" per se. Unattractiveness

---

* That's not to say Emily Ratajkowski doesn't deal with her share of shit—I refer you to her powerful essay in *The Cut*, "Buying Myself Back," wherein she recounts a sexual assault, revenge porn, and the myriad ways her image has been stolen from her in the name of "art." (Emily's battle did inspire me to send a cease and desist to the creators of "Where's Waldo," who have unapologetically profited off my likeness and poor sense of direction for several years.)

had basically become *attractive*—the word implied long armpit hair and a Riot Grrrl defiance of social norms. I was afraid of the extremes, and of slipping as far away from beauty as possible. Specifically, I was afraid of four letters: U-G-L-Y.

Ugly, I thought, was the worst thing a person could possibly be—and that wasn't referring to the emotional type of ugly that actually *is* the worst thing a person can be. No, I was scared of the superficial kind vilified in playground chants: "fell from a tree and got beaten by an ugly stick on the way down." Ugliness seemed like a scarlet letter—if just one person described you as such, you'd wear the *U* for eternity, doomed to a life of insults, ostracization, and friendships with donkeys (Source: *Shrek*). But if you'd asked me what made someone ugly, I couldn't have told you—unpacking the adjective seemed too scary, especially since I already knew it was a designation I didn't want to receive. Since I couldn't define ugliness in specific terms, it was easiest just to live in fear. I stayed vigilant about which photos my friends could post on social media. I never picked up a FaceTime before ten a.m. And, aside from my unlucky roommate, I kept my masturbation style to myself.

But fortunately, part of my unlearning journey brought me to disability theory—specifically, the work of Mia Mingus and, more specifically, her 2011 speech "Moving Toward the Ugly: A Politic Beyond Desirability." Almost a decade before I found my way to the transcript (late again, Jen), Mingus spoke these words to a room of self-described femmes:

> If we are ever unsure about what femme should be or how to be femme, we must move toward the ugly. Not just the ugly in ourselves, but the

people and communities that are ugly, undesir-
able, unwanted, disposable, hidden, displaced.
This is the only way that we will ever create a
femme-ness that can hold physically disabled
folks, dark-skinned people, trans and gender
non-conforming folks, poor and working-
class folks, HIV-positive folks, people living in
the global south and so many more of us who
are the freaks, monsters, criminals, villains of
our fairy tales, movies, news stories, neighborhoods and world.

At first I found this tough to wrap my head around—
wasn't ugliness something we wanted to avoid? But sitting
with Mingus's work helped me understand that ugliness was
also a socially constructed idea, which meant my fear of it had
been socially constructed too. Inherently, "ugly" wasn't good or
bad. It was simply a word—a word that was often employed to
degrade disabled people, trans people, fat people, non-white
people, and others who didn't fit into a narrow, colonial vision
of "perfection."

Recognizing that ugliness was also a construct made it
clear that the entire system was a scam. Beauty, a false ideal,
had required the creation of ugly, a false opposite, in order to
uphold its reign. There couldn't be a top tier without a bottom one, and so to keep the structure in place, beauty relied
on scarcity, ensuring only a few paragons could ever fulfill its
demands. The system was rigged, yet we were all encouraged
to chase the same aspirations and strive for a singular vision of
success. Years later, I'd be able to see the similarities between
beauty's false promises and the ones made by capitalism. (Note

to my past self: if you're surprised that ugliness is made up, just WAIT until you hear about money.)

Despite being a construct, ugliness had been persecuted in a very real way for quite some time. In 1867, San Francisco had an "Ugly Law" that banned "any person, who is diseased, maimed, mutilated or deformed in any way" from being seen in public. The further someone was from the Barbie-and-Ken standards, the more their looks were held against them. It continues today: For example, a Pennsylvania study showed that over 50 percent of doctors described their fat patients as "ugly and noncompliant" (this impacts treatment too—other studies say doctors spend less time with fat patients and offer less emotional care). "Ugly" might be fake, but increased risk of incarceration, state violence, and discrimination is still very real.

In a 2018 interview with *them*, Mingus pointed out that marginalizing people based on their appearance was ultimately "a way to create and reinforce normative identities." I realized I'd been duped into a state of hypocrisy—by running away from ugliness, I was upholding the exact systems that had made me self-conscious in the first place. My fear of ugly inflated the value of beauty, thus reinforcing them as opposite poles in a hierarchy. I'd been doing the exact thing I thought I was fighting against.

Today the internet is full of blog posts, think pieces, and Instagram captions from disabled, fat, and trans people reflecting on the ways their appearances are perceived. I've learned from Aubrey Gordon (@YrFatFriend), who writes about the world's hesitancy to speak the word "fat" out loud: "The fat people I know don't mind being called fat, in large part because we are—what's the use in denying that?" I've learned from Imani Barbarin (@crutches_and_spice), who writes about the social response to having a disabled Black body in a gym: "Exercise brings me the most anxiety because it is inevitable that a complete stranger will comment on my body, how it moves, how it doesn't, how brave I am to display it in public." I've learned from Jacob Tobia (@jacobtobia), who writes about gender non-conforming representation and its potential for radical change: "We have the power to glorify our own sacred understanding of beauty and to do so in public. We have the power to redefine what we've been told about the desirability of our bodies." And as I've learned about all these layers of oppression, I haven't experienced any of it directly.

Regardless of how I saw myself, I carried significant unearned "pretty privilege" according to Western ideals, and that remained true no matter what I did in bed. My ugly moments were just that: moments. Like a bad Christmas sweater, I could take them off.

For a while, I thought rebelling against desirability politics was enough, but Mingus's work reminded me that we have to go beyond that—we have to embrace "ugly" and celebrate it, both within our communities and within ourselves. Mingus's work focuses on those who are most significantly impacted by systems of oppression, and while I would never compare my experience to theirs, I was still surprised to learn how relevant their experiences were to my own. I'd heard that all liberation was bound together, but now I could see it for myself: As long as ableism, fatphobia, transphobia, and white supremacy (et al) remained in place, none of us could feel comfortable in our own skin.

In my case, the fear of ugliness had taken a deep internal toll: I'd ignored my own needs even at the moment of orgasm—the time I should've been focusing on myself the most. I finally realized what it meant to masturbate wrong: to masturbate with something other than my own pleasure in mind. If I spent those sacred moments trying to conform to narrow beauty ideals, I wasn't practicing self-love—I was playing into harmful systems, undermining others, my sex drive, and myself.

The internet still tends to position female masturbation as an empowering act (I'm part of the problem, since I'll readily do #sponcon for a butt plug to make a buck). But it's worth remembering that empowerment isn't the end game, because for anyone to feel free in the bedroom, everyone must feel free outside of it. And getting there means seeking a whole different type of release.

DATING AND WALKING

I WENT TO college at the University of Southern California, a school that had all the clichés: a sprawling campus, a good football team, and a Greek system that threw parties with themes like "Naughty Teachers and Mythical Creatures" or "ABC: Anything But Clothes." (It also had the cliché of several faculty sexual predators responsible for hundreds of assaults, but that news didn't break until years after my graduation.)

Hooking up in college (or "dating," as I optimistically called it) was as easy as the Los Angeles weather—you could meet people anywhere, from the dining hall to the library to a frat party's endless bathroom line. In stark contrast to high school, the campus felt too big for anyone to monitor my behavior, so free of impending "slut" accusations, I slept with anyone who would have me. All those people were men, but at the time that didn't seem too off base: I loved MGMT and played cornhole—how could I not be straight?

I carried this ignorance into my twenties, where it collided with two important cultural touchstones of the 2010s: (1) the proliferation of swipe-based dating apps, and (2) my coastal migration from LA to NYC.

I arrived in New York as so many do: imbuing the skyline with promise, hoping every day might lead to a book deal, a boyfriend, or both. But the city's realities came at me faster than a delivery guy on a bike. Careerwise I struggled to find freelance work and was too focused on making ends meet to write anything personal or worthwhile. Romance felt even more dismal—instead of meeting men at bookstores or on the train, I met them in my phone, where conversations lacked verbal cues or body language. The idea of "being myself" became relatively moot since I made my first impressions through curated profile pictures. Dating evolved into something passive, low-priority—an activity I could do while commuting, walking from the train station to my office door. Did it count as a meet-cute if you got hit by oncoming traffic while swiping right? Only if it caused you to accidentally super-like someone (that is, assuming they don't think super-likes are a red flag). It took only a few months for New York to turn me into a cynic, and before I knew it I'd become a study on self-sabotage: I fantasized about meeting someone on the subway but also refused to make eye contact on the train.

Despite being lonely, I was never alone. I lived with three roommates, the four of us college friends who had somehow managed to shlep across the country after school. We rented a tiny Williamsburg apartment with no character—glossy wood cabinets, a perpetually dirty bathroom, and lower ceilings than was probably legal. One living room wall featured a small window into a bedroom*—the landlords had allegedly done this to allow for more (any) natural light, but it felt like a child had built a dollhouse wrong and their parents had been too polite to correct them. When sunbeams did peek in, they refracted off the eggshell walls, manifesting in a putrid yellow tint. Our lives were just as together as this setting suggests.

The first roommate was Jamie—a dirty blonde who worked in merchandising, but dressed like she wanted you to know she majored in art history. Today, Jamie is the rare breed of white leftist I actually respect†—she divested from Bank of America, organizes for reproductive rights, and composts without bragging about it (you can only tell from the smell). Back then, though, I knew her as my friend who liked politics but loved to party. On nights out, Jamie always indulged me in conversations about fashion, makeup, and other "girl stuff"‡—when we moved in together, she'd recently gotten out of a toxic relationship with a celebrity hairstylist who taught her about the benefits of Moroccan oil, which she, in turn, taught me.

Next was Ben, best described as a cross between Seth Rogen (for his looks), a dachshund (for his loyalty), and *Pitchfork* (for his obnoxious music taste and the self-loathing we felt when we agreed with it). Ben was shamelessly up-front

---

* Mine, of course.
† In case this wasn't clear by now: I'm a white leftist and absolutely do not respect myself. I'm far too much of a hypocrite—in the words of a Bratz-themed meme I once saw, "I'm a communist with a shopping addiction." Avoid trusting me at all costs.
‡ Could someone please tell my younger self that fashion, makeup, and literally everything that exists is gender-neutral? Smh.

about his needs, to the point that we once joked his entire personality was just asking for favors (real example: "Can you feel my cat's nipples to see if she's pregnant?"*). But we never let this get to us—when the day came that we needed a favor of our own, we knew he'd have our backs.

Like me, Ben identifies as bi. I learned this through several drunk conversations when we each confessed that we wanted to have a threesome someday (in our early twenties, threesomes still felt like a bold, original kink). But before either of us came out, Ben presented as your average lovestruck straight dude—a Jewish Ted Mosby, always searching for the right girl. Friends warned me about living with him—they said he was "in love with me" and "in love with Jamie" and "in love with both of you, watch out." While these rumors might have been true, that was meaningless, as Ben was "in love" with everyone—both Jamie and I knew that if we let his interest deter us from this apartment, we'd miss out on a friendship (and very cheap rent). Sure, Ben and I did have a trace of chemistry, but we had a tacit understanding that we'd keep this to ourselves. Hooking up would disrupt the fundamental order of our friend group. I felt content sitting by his side, helping him find someone else to date. (At least for now.)

Joey didn't technically live with us then†—as a freshly out gay man, he'd insisted on a West Village shoebox he could call his own—but he stayed over almost every night, our Craigslist black leather sectional becoming his throne, our living room the cramped backdrop to many a tryst with

---

* She wasn't.
† It would be years before he'd walk in on me "making Rosemary's Baby" (which is what I now call masturbation).

some of Brooklyn's finest men. Joey was a tall blond who, while closeted, had been known for desexualizing himself with a wardrobe of Old Navy slides and oversize Life is Good tees; his style had since done a complete 180 and now consisted entirely of mesh and athleisure. Though we went to college together, we met while interning at an ad agency the summer before our senior year, and after some small talk in our cubicles, discovered we were embedded in the same group of USC friends. We had our first internship lunch at the finest Panera Bread in Irvine, CA ("Order anything you want!" said our generous boss), and after our leadership team deserted us, we realized neither of us was full. Joey asked whether I'd judge him if he finished the untouched sandwich that a high schooler had left on an adjacent table—I said I wouldn't, and from then on, we were inseparable, bonded by low disgust levels and a mutual adoration of each other's brain. The next few years, our friendship leveled up—Joey cleaned my puke when I got food poisoning from a kale salad, accompanied me to the Hustler store when I bought my first vibrator, and consoled me after I made out with a guy I later realized was a Juggalo. In hindsight, meeting Joey felt like meeting a soul mate, though neither of us had enough emotional intelligence to make a statement that heavy about a best friend. All we knew was that we couldn't handle living on opposite coasts—right after I moved east, he followed suit.

The apartment made all four of us codependent before we'd had enough therapy to know the term. As proof of our attachment issues, our favorite activity was to online-date as a unit: On any given weeknight, we'd gather in the yellow living room and hold court, collaborating on replies to one another's matches. We debated when to use exclamation points and how much emoji was too much emoji. We overanalyzed, overthought, and overhyped complete strangers based on tiny clues within their profiles:

- If they had photos with an ex, they were desperate.
- If they had professional headshots, they were fake.
- If they had pics in other countries, they were cool (but if their bio said "Love to travel!" they were not).

We spent hours working together, crafting witty comebacks and effortless opening lines. Perhaps it was a function of the windowless living room, but slowly our phones, banter, and dates began to merge. When one person's match replied, we all celebrated the victory. When one of us got laid, we collectively climaxed (well, metaphorically). And when the inevitable happened and one of us got left on read, we all felt the sting (though the subsequent trashing of that suitor was almost thrilling enough to offset it). We always speculated about why we'd been rejected but we never considered that it might have been our own fault—that maybe we were already spoken for by one another, our needs for connection more than satisfied by our chosen, albeit dysfunctional, family. We didn't consider that each overthought text might make it obvious that there was a team of writers on the other side of the screen, nor did it occur to us that we weren't writing for anyone but ourselves. No matter how much we *wanted* to fall in love, we didn't *need* to fall in love. Dating was only a game.

At that time I exclusively used OkCupid, mostly because it had a gamified element, asking users to answer several questions on their profiles. These felt like mini personality tests, with prompts like "In a certain light, wouldn't nuclear war be exciting?" (no) and "Would you ever eat something out of the trash?" (um, would you not?!). Because this platform encouraged introspection and also happened to be free, I had faith that it would help me attract smart people who wouldn't judge me for being broke.

But, like a wild night that ruins your relationship with tequila, there's always one bad date that makes you switch to a different app. For me and OkCupid, that date was with Stephen, a twenty-eight-year-old with a sparsely filled-in profile. By contrast, my own About Me was a novella, a heavily embellished piece deserving of a PEN/Faulkner award. It mentioned crosswords (I'm clever!), spicy food (I'm adventurous!), and *Channel Orange* (there's a good chance I'm gay!). Jamie, Ben, and Joey served as editors, ensuring my profile toed the sexist line of how much personality women could get away with. Somehow the final product felt confident yet inoffensive, funny yet soft, smart yet not-smarter-than-you. In reality, I was extremely self-conscious, left my contacts on the floor, and used my plunger more than my oven. But on OkCupid, I was the perfect girl.

Stephen's page, however, was an exercise in brevity—it simply said: "Comedian. Not funny." I was intrigued. I hearted him, and boom—we were a match.

"Look." I stretched out my arm to show his profile to Joey, who'd sprawled out on the couch's opposite end. He grabbed the phone without a word, then evaluated, drafted something, and put the device back in my hand. I looked at the screen: You're lucky I'm a sucker for mediocre men.

"It's perfect." I hit send.

Twenty minutes later, Stephen replied: I sure am

What's your number

I suck at this app

He'd responded in under an hour, so the last line was clearly a lie, but I gave him my number anyway. Exactly twenty minutes later, my phone buzzed again:

Hi

It's Stephen

We met on Christian Mingle

No punctuation in sight.

"Can I respond with 'lol'?" I asked, showing Joey the phone again.

"Of course not," he replied without looking.

"Yeah, no." Ben turned to face us, taking a break from his Crockpot.

"Right, right." I scrunched my forehead. "Wait—why not?"

"Jen." Joey sighed. "You know 'lol' practically means admitting defeat."

"Also didn't he *just* send that?" Ben asked.

"Wait like twenty minutes!" Jamie shouted from the shower.

"Fine." I clenched my jaw. "Then we have twenty minutes to write our response."

The four of us donned our figurative monastic habits and dug into our limited pool of religious references, crafting a reply as if my hymen depended on it. After wrestling with jokes about Jdate, altar boys, and Jesus himself, we settled on a two-text combo:

Thought it was FarmersOnly?

Guess Stephen's a common name

FarmersOnly jokes still had clout back then, so Stephen replied fast:

Yeehaw

I showed it to Joey. He seemed impressed.

✳

My bisexuality stayed on the back burner—dating guys (or trying to) was hard enough. Men controlled my emotions, the world's color brightening or draining entirely based on their attentiveness, and this was true regardless of whether or not I'd met them yet. Every exchange felt high stakes; each text had the potential to make me sulk for a week.

A few days later, I hadn't heard from Stephen, so I jumped back in to escalate (though I did this in secret since my roommates would've advised against it). I covertly texted: Wanna get a drink sometime? and patiently waited for his reply. It didn't come immediately, so I forced myself into the distraction of "running errands"—a euphemism for "checking my phone in a few different bodegas, then coming home with detergent."

EXT. 5th AVENUE & 19TH STREET—DAY

JEN walks out of a Duane Reade onto the sidewalk. She's carrying a shopping bag filled with makeup remover, dandruff shampoo, and a drugstore string cheese that she bought against her best judgment.

JEN approaches a street corner where a WOMAN and her TWO KIDS wait to cross the street. Something vibrates in JEN's purse, and she pulls out her PHONE. (Similar to a city in a romcom, PHONE is now a character in the story.) JEN's face lights up, implying she's received an important text. The walk signal appears. Staring down at PHONE, JEN steps off the curb onto the crosswalk.

> WOMAN
> (to her kids)
> See that millennial? Promise you'll *never* use your phone in an intersection like her.

JEN scoffs, then returns her eyes to the screen. We cut into PHONE and see a text from an unsaved number.

> SMS FROM 1(696)555-5569
> Hows Thursday

> JEN'S INNER THOUGHTS (v.o.)
> It's him! Time to do what I do best, aka spiral and overthink! Let's unpack that missing apostrophe: Is he lazy? Disinterested? Bad with the punctuation keyboard? Oh! Maybe it was autocorrect— let's go with that.

Cut wide. JEN clutches PHONE to her chest and smiles, then immediately frowns.

                    JEN'S INNER THOUGHTS (v.o.)
Shit. I think I have a dinner thing on
Thursday.

Cut to PHONE where we locate Thursday's
calendar event, which indeed says: "Dinner
Thing." JEN taps back to STEPHEN's text
and the cursor blinks.

                    JEN'S INNER THOUGHTS (v.o.)
Should I say, "Sunday?" Or maybe, "What
about Sunday?" Is that punctuation too
much? What if he associates question
marks with a childhood trauma? What if
his grandpa capitalized proper nouns in
the last letter he wrote before he died?

JEN realizes she can't do this alone.
She takes a screenshot of the exchange,
then sends to BEN, JAMIE, and JOEY on a
thread.

We hear a HONK. The traffic light has turned
red, but JEN remains in the intersection,
a few feet from the sidewalk. A taxi
speeds past and narrowly avoids her, and
as she yells, pretending this isn't her
own fault, she stumbles into a mailbox.
We hear a THUD, then an "OW!"

Lights fade to black.

Clutching my bruised elbow, I walked home. I could hear my roommates talking even before opening our apartment door—the walls were so thin that our conversations often floated down the hallway, giving you a preview of what to expect. As you got closer, you could feel your heart rate quicken, body filling with FOMO, hungry to get up to speed.

I turned my key, not sure who or what I'd find inside. Jamie wasn't home, but Joey had taken over the long side of the couch while Ben cooked chili and waxed poetic about his latest Ok-Cupid dream girl. Moving slowly to avoid further injuries, I set down my purse, then settled into the sectional's corner seat.

"She's from Pittsburgh!" Ben exclaimed, scooting past Joey's seat to show me his phone. Ben was also from Pittsburgh and had a tendency to overstate the city's cultural relevance, singing high praises of its art and tech scenes. He acted as if the almost-Midwestern metropolis was the modern incarnation of Florence during the Italian Renaissance, the Terrible Towel our generation's version of the David. He flipped through his match's pictures, shaking the phone in excitement.

"And she listens to Darkside!" He practically skipped back toward the stove. "I'm going for it."

"What are you gonna say?" I asked.

Ben leaned against the counter, eyes on his phone. *Clack-clack.*

"Ahem?" I cracked my knuckles, eager to wrap this up so we could discuss my stuff instead.

"And why do you have your keyboard noises turned on? So selfish." Joey rolled his eyes.

Ben kept typing—*clack-clack, whoosh.*

"Did you just . . . send something?" Joey stared in horror while Ben, excruciatingly proud of himself, lifted his chin.

"Yep. I said 'hey.'" He smirked.

"Ben, we're on your team here." I slowed down my words, remembering a YouTube video about how hostage negotiators communicate under pressure. "Tell us—what *exactly* did you say?"

Why hadn't Ben consulted the room? Maybe he wanted to prove something—that he didn't need to over-strategize; that he'd be fine showing up purely as himself. Sure, being "authentic" on apps might prove effective in the long term— you weed out people who didn't like you for you, ultimately serving as a shortcut to finding the right person. But where was the fun in that?

Whatever Ben's goal, he was far from achieving it—he turned the phone around, revealing the text he'd sent. The screen read: Hey!!!

"Ugh, no." Joey winced, each exclamation point like a dagger to his heart.

"Come on, guys." Ben stuffed his phone in his pocket, his smug smirk fading from his face. "It's fine."

"Oh my god, I wish it were fine." Devastated, I put my face in my hands. "Such desperation. So much thirst."

"I've been saying, you need to lean into other punctuation," Joey replied. "Semicolons have big dick energy; start there."

"How do you use those again?" Ben asked.

We groaned.

Our conversations were always this dramatic—in a way, the absurdity had always been the point. Deep down, we must have known that none of our matches would evolve into an actual relationship. We hoped they would—because we felt compelled to move toward the goalposts of love and marriage, but also because we could barely afford New York as it was, and romance seemed like an express ticket to a better life. But as much as we wanted to stop eating dollar pizza, we weren't ready to part ways just yet. We were a family, and this cumin-scented, one-bathroom apartment was our home.

❋

Stephen and I cemented plans for Sunday, and he picked a bar on the Lower East Side. I promised myself I'd get a good night's sleep, but when Saturday rolled around, Joey dragged me to a Ladyfag party where we danced under an inflatable penis until dawn. Eventually he went home with a first-grade teacher and I remained on the dance floor, surrounded by throbbing house music and men who wanted nothing to do with me.

Sunday, I woke up late and hungover, a victim of weekend jet lag. I attempted to heal myself with a bagel and *Project Runway*, but even after five hours of Tim Gunn, the last thing I wanted to do was make small talk over a ten-dollar beer.

Stephen and I had stopped the back-and-forth texting after locking in a date, and somehow I found it difficult to summon my interest again—wild how you could have a near-death experience for someone one day, then feel too dehydrated to see them the next. But my Midwest roots told me not to flake, so I put on some clothes and dragged myself to the train.

By 9:03, I'd somehow made it to the bar. Stephen had selected a nameless dive in Alphabet City, described only as "to the right of the banh mi place" (a destination that already sounded more appealing). The bar was so far from the subway that I started resenting him before I even reached the door.

INT. DIVE BAR TO THE RIGHT OF THE BANH MI PLACE—NIGHT

JEN enters the bar, encountering several men: BARTENDER, BAD AT BILLIARDS GUY, TOO INTO PINBALL GUY, and PERFORMATIVELY STRAIGHT BEST FRIENDS. She considers that female representation in dive bars still has a long way to go.

JEN spots a bearded guy sitting at the bar who indeed happens to be STEPHEN, though his hair seems much longer than in his photos. He reminds her of a troll who asks three riddles before letting you cross the bridge, and sits hunched over the counter, nursing his beer.

JEN approaches. Though STEPHEN is the one who's borderline catfishing, she still manages to undermine herself, yelling to him from halfway across the bar:

> JEN
> (gesturing at forehead)
> Sorry, I have bangs now!

JEN walks toward STEPHEN and discovers that he's chosen two stools with armrests. She tugs at one, realizing it doesn't spin.

Struggling onto the seat, JEN maneuvers
her body between the armrest and the bar.
It takes her a comically long time (a
'90s sitcom would've put Final *Jeopardy!*
music over the edit), and STEPHEN doesn't
acknowledge her struggle, which obviously
makes it worse.

When JEN finally sits down, she realizes
that the chair structure forces both her
and STEPHEN to stare straight ahead.
JEN's line of sight leads directly to the
pool table, where BAD AT BILLIARDS GUY
misses a shot.

                    BAD AT BILLIARDS GUY
Aw, man!

Ignoring this, JEN asks STEPHEN the one
question she already knows the answer to.

                    JEN
So. What do you do?

                    STEPHEN
I'm a comedian.

                    JEN
Oh yeah! I forgot, ha-ha. What do you,
er, *comede* about?

                    STEPHEN
               (sipping his beer)
Damn, a couple more zingers like that and
you'll put me out of a job.

                      JEN
I *have* taken two improv classes, so you
could say I'm due for a Netflix special.

STEPHEN coughs.

                      JEN
               (backpedaling furiously)
Um . . . do you wanna workshop any material?
We could see if the bartender has a mic?

                    STEPHEN
That's not really how it works.

                      JEN
Okay! Got it.

Thanks to the silence between them, the
bar background noise seems to get louder.
JEN coughs and it echoes. "Little Wing" by
Jimi Hendrix comes on, and PERFORMATIVELY
STRAIGHT BEST FRIENDS put their arms around
each other, singing along to the sounds of the
guitar. TOO INTO PINBALL GUY does something
good, apparently, because he cheers.

```
                    STEPHEN
        (shouting over Jimi Hendrix, BEST
     FRIENDS, and whooping pinball machine)
        So, what do you do?



                      JEN
         (mouth falling open in shock)
     You didn't read my profile?



                    STEPHEN
                  (shrugging)
        It was long.
```

"Little Wing" trailed off, and Stephen checked his phone. I leaned away in disgust—using a device in front of a date was off-limits, no exceptions. (If there were exceptions, I'd find a way to be one.)

I watched Stephen's fingers formulate a tweet, wondering why he couldn't at least pretend it was an urgent email. The whole night felt informal and underthought—the equivalent of not using punctuation in real life.

"Tell me your . . . personal history," I blurted. I'd read this first-date question prompt somewhere—it was cheesy, but at least it would get him to ramble so I could zone out again. He started talking, and I prayed that the angle of our chairs would hide my face, allowing me to take a nap.

"I was born in Missouri, and . . ."

After three minutes of not sleeping I pieced together that Stephen was thirty-five and his parents still bankrolled his lifestyle while he pursued a seemingly fruitless career in comedy. I started to roll my eyes but remembered that, in some small way, I'd asked for this, asked for him. I'd claimed to be a sucker for mediocre men—all Stephen had done was deliver.

As I considered why someone whose parents gave them money would ever pick this bar, Stephen oriented his face toward mine. When I noticed, I almost jumped. For one, he was slightly more attractive head-on. But . . . were his lips pouting? Was he going for . . . ? No way.

After three long seconds, I realized that Stephen did, in fact, expect me to kiss him, and it seemed like my one way out was, unfortunately, through. I considered that maybe I deserved this—though I wanted to believe I was out of this hirsute man's league, maybe we were on equal playing fields just for being here in the first place.

The pool balls clacked. Pinball guy cheered. Stephen blinked. I exhaled. Then with sympathy, misery, or some string of both, I leaned toward him, the armrest jutting into my ribs. He tasted surprisingly sweet, like a nostalgic candy that made me both wistful and sad. Fun Dip? Necco Wafers? Whatever it was, it bummed me out—but still felt better than nothing.

After we pulled apart, I decided it was time to go. At that point in my life, most men could've still convinced me to go home with them, but Stephen's lack of effort was actually impressive. I realized his laziness had probably been responsible for the casual nature of his profile, then heard Maya Angelou's voice in my head: "When people show you who they are, believe them."

We were taking the same train in opposite directions, so we walked the too-long walk to Essex Street together. As we neared the station, he pressed me against a McDonald's for another embrace.

"This was fun," I said for some reason.

"It was," he said. I hoped he was lying.

"Let's do it again," I said for some reason.

"Yeah," he said. I hoped he was lying.

✳

The next week Jamie, Joey, and I took Ben to his favorite Mexican place to mourn the loss of Pittsburgh Girl—despite his aggressive Hey!!!, she'd actually replied to his first message, and they'd managed to get so far as coordinating a date. But after a few days she'd stopped responding, and now it was our job to console him.

"Maybe she lost her phone," Jamie offered.

"Or died." I shrugged.

"Or reread the 'hey' text," Joey said sweetly as he patted Ben on the back.

My pocket buzzed as we left the restaurant, announcing a text from Stephen: a question mark–free Jen what's up.

Ugh. I hated the phrase "what's up"—I was always inclined to answer "the sky," and that just made us both look bad. His text felt hurried—I'd literally had dentists who put more effort into communication.* But there was still an appeal to Stephen's casual style. I liked his no-punctuation. I liked that he'd written my name. I could almost taste the Necco Wafers again, and considered how to respond.

But before I could do much brainstorming, Ben shoved his

---

* Gramercy Smiles, while I do appreciate feeling wanted, I'd like to take this opportunity to say: PLEASE CHILL. If I respond to your text, you don't need to call AND email me—I'm not canceling my appointment, I swear. You have an anxious attachment style. May I suggest therapy? I promise, it's just because I care.

phone in my face. On the screen was a twenty-four-year-old with natural curls, sunbathing on a speed boat—her About Me said, "Sundays are for pancakes and D'Angelo." I glanced up at Ben, who was already beaming.

"She's cute, right? What should we say?"

A GIRL
CALLED RHONDA

*(Content Warning: Contains mentions of
homophobic and queerphobic violence)*

IF I'D BEEN hiding from my queerness, it managed to find me at church. Not church in the sense of priests or Catholic schoolgirls, but church in the sense of a nightclub: cyan and purple bulbs that flashed like cameras; accessories whose appeal was mostly tactile—sequined bras glittering like disco balls, feather boas begging to be touched. Perfume mixed with the smells of bodies, smoke, and sex. Looping disco synths became the soundtrack to my life—or at least the life of someone I could become.

I understand the inclination to assume that nightclubs suck. In fact, I agree—plenty of them do. Before I experienced good ones for myself, the only nightclubs I encountered in real life were establishments of the "models and bottles" variety— glitzy bars where thin women flirted with slimy men, where overpriced vodka granted access to a table, waitstaff, and the ability to sit down. Bravo shows had fed me this image as the gold standard of a social life, and for a long time I believed it—even craved it, in a way. After I moved from middle-of-nowhere Indiana to Los Angeles, I felt obligated to experience Hollywood's nightlife, though it never occurred to me that Hollywood might not welcome me with open arms. One Wednesday night during the original heyday of *The Hills*, I paid a promoter $150 to get into Les Deux and immediately regretted it—I'd had a hunch I wasn't "hot" enough for this scene, but the hardest way to learn that for sure was to be ignored at the bar while wearing my tightest dress. With this rejection came some semblance of clarity, and I could finally see these clubs for what they were: long lines, drunk people crying, and $25 vodka sodas (not including tip).

My first positive nightclub experience occurred during my study abroad in Amsterdam, though technically it was less of a nightclub and more of a warehouse party (my now pretentious self would consider this a critical distinction). The party was in Rotterdam, two and a half hours away from me by bus, and it began at midnight. A girl on my dorm floor had invited me: Heidi, a quiet Bostonian who wore thick glasses with a cloudy pink rim. She didn't talk much but she dressed loud, like a twee extra in a Wes Anderson film. We'd been abroad for two months, and she'd already learned to speak fluent Dutch— thanks to this and her ability to look so natural on a bike, Nederlanders often mistook her for one of their own. We had a class together wherein we'd developed a casual friendship, and I could never decide if I was attracted to her or if I just wanted to be indie chic like she was. Still, I knew she didn't like to hang out with other Americans, so when she asked me to join her, I felt proud.

I spent hours planning my outfit, ultimately deciding on a burnt-orange bowling shirt, a black skirt, tights, and stilettos, though when Heidi appeared at my door in Doc Martens, I promptly changed my shoes. Cheeks flushed, I threw on a pair of beat-up Air Force 1s, slipping my nylon-covered feet inside. On the bus, we drank whiskey from a small bottle inside a paper bag—Heidi talked about books and art while I nodded along, pretending to have read and seen everything she referenced. Though it was pitch-black outside, she wore sunglasses on her head—when she explained that they were for the morning light, I pretended I'd forgotten mine, rather than let on my shock that we'd be out that late. I felt smug, convinced I'd successfully maintained the illusion that I belonged. Then I asked her if this club had bottle service, and she laughed so hard she almost spit out her drink.

We arrived at the venue: a brutalist building surrounded by gravel, the muffled music growing louder as we approached the door. I soon realized sensible footwear wasn't just preferred but essential—our night would include hours of dancing in place and trudging across the dirty ground. I felt like smiling but knew it was more European not to, so I widened my eyes instead. The hallway lockers and maple wood floor suggested the space was an abandoned high school gym, filled with ghosts of teenagers laughing and memories of another era's youth.

The music pounded around us, hypnotic thuds that helped my brain shut off. I would've described it as meditative if the rest of the surroundings hadn't been so unhinged: People tossing pills into their mouths. Chain-smoking cigarettes indoors. Fingering each other by the sound booth. Piling into

bathroom stalls to do lines, fuck, or both. After a few minutes of dancing, Heidi mouthed the words "find you later"
and vanished. (Years later, Heidi told me she'd taken Molly
that ended up making her nauseous. She also told me that
in her memory of the night, she'd been the uncertain one—
apparently I'd seemed in control, as if I'd done this kind of
thing before. Consider this your reminder: Memoir consists
of recounted experiences, but by its nature, memory is unreli-
able. That means maybe—in someone else's story—you actually know what you're doing.)

I was jealous, yet I understood the desire to be alone
while doing these things; I could rationalize the benefits of
shedding me as a witness. I danced by myself for an hour
before sitting against the wall on the sticky floor, popping a
piece of gum into my mouth and gazing out at the hedonism.
I longed to participate and wondered if I would ever be brave
enough to actually do it—I longed to be sexual in public, to
kiss a girl, to sleep with one. But the only courage I could
muster was enough to eventually stand up and dance alone
again. I let the music wash over me, and after a few whiskey
gingers, my loneliness disappeared.

In the following years, during my early twenties in Los
Angeles, I got better at losing myself. I justified my club habit
by intellectualizing the music, studying the names of DJs,
learning too-specific genre names. I spent weekdays working
at an ad agency, keeping one browser tab open to a Flash website called Ishkur's Guide to Electronic Music, studying every
chance I got. I spent weekends out until five a.m., forgetting
everything I'd learned.

Before long, my nightlife had one unifying characteristic,

and I didn't have a better word to describe it than "gay." I assumed I'd found myself in so many queer spaces not necessarily because I wanted to be there, but because my friend group consisted almost entirely of gay men. Their presence somehow allowed me to subtract my own motivations from the equation, to pretend that I was just along for the ride. In a sense, I felt different from the other straight girls and "f*g hags" who frequented the scene—more legitimate, in a way—but I wouldn't have dared express that out loud. I never considered that the queer aspect of these spaces could have applied to me directly, that there might have been a deeper reason I felt so connected to them. All I knew was that gay bars made me feel understood, and that it was socially acceptable for straight women to love them too.

Eventually my friends and I got bored with WeHo and its circuit scene, citing the lack of diversity, the prevalence of bachelorette parties, and the incessant EDM. We became nightlife snobs (far and away the worst kind of snob—self-righteousness and ketamine make for a lethal combination), spending most of our time at warehouse parties so we could stay out after the bars closed. There was only one bar that could rally us: Los Globos, a Silverlake staple known for bringing together an international queer crowd. Our favorite event was "A Club Called Rhonda," a monthly happening that described itself as "a pansexual dance party where everyone's invited." Today I know that pansexuality falls under the broader multisexual (or Bi+) umbrella, and that it means to many people the same thing that bisexuality means to me. But back then, I had no idea—my friends and I often speculated about definitions, and the conversations wouldn't age well.

"I think it means you're attracted to the third gender?" I remember someone saying.

"What's the third gender?" someone else asked.

No one could answer that.*

I don't know much about what Rhonda's like today—I just hope it hasn't been diluted with heteronormativity, becoming the type of event that inspires former sorority treasurers to try a new shade of eyeshadow, their "yaaas kween!"s echoing through East LA. But the Rhonda of the early aughts was well worth romanticizing—she offered us partying, but made it profound. It makes sense that Rhonda taught me about pansexuality—she was an ingenue, honored to be the issuant of so many firsts. Her dance floor felt like a gender-bending embrace, the closest a person could get to being inside a disco ball. After we went once, we were hooked.

A discerning drag queen named Phyllis Navidad always worked the door, and every month my friends and I sought her stamp of approval (or at least something better than side-eyed disdain). We obsessed over what to wear, yet never got the acknowledgment we craved—no matter how great we looked, we were still inevitably Rhonda's worst-dressed. The average attendee's outfit pushed both buttons and boundaries—the outfits were so fierce, the people who wore them so bold, that my cis friends and I recalibrated our definition of fashion. We gazed on in admiration, joining the raucous applause as people strutted by: hairy chests adorned with nipple tassels, naked breasts popping out between suspenders, the timeless

---

* To clarify: There are infinite genders. The "third gender" is a myopic way of thinking about anyone who identifies outside the men/women binary. I was wrong and ignorant. Told you not to trust me!

combination of earrings with a full beard. Gender norms were checked at the door with the rest of the coats—you could show up with some, but you'd have to leave them outside.

Rhonda's nights were so full of color that my memory of the Rotterdam warehouse now seemed rewritten in grayscale. I hadn't equated clubbing with being fabulous or being brave, but through her, I learned it could be both. I found inspiration from everyone there, but always felt guilty about this—why look up to someone for being themselves when being themselves shouldn't have been a challenge to begin with?

And yet it felt impossible not to marvel at the crowds. My teachers were queer people who styled lace-front wigs with lingerie. Queer people who wore a size-fifteen shoe, but still deemed it worthwhile to dance for hours in a heeled boot three sizes too small. Queer people who knew better than anyone that, when it comes to gender, the same things that brought you pleasure could make you hurt.

When I was twenty-five, I moved to New York—a decision I'd made for my marketing career, but also because even I had to admit that the LA partying had gotten out of hand. One day I was walking through the Financial District—an image my California self would've considered "très chic" but my New York self considered "annoyingly far from the F train"—when I got a Twitter notification about the news.

A gunman had opened fire inside a gay nightclub in Orlando, Florida. Forty-nine people were dead. Fifty-three people were wounded. Countless others had been there and now would deal with the trauma of this night for the rest of their lives. My stomach felt heavy. Standing in the middle of the sidewalk, I gripped my phone, frantically looking around, hoping to meet the eyes of someone who might be able to commiserate. The streets were packed, but people kept walking as if nothing had happened. Maybe they hadn't heard. Or maybe they had, but it hadn't affected them—they could just keep going about their day.

It had been a massacre, a hate crime, and an event that the media became obsessed with, printing details gruesome and personal alike. In the weeks that followed, we learned that 90 percent of those killed were Latinx or of Latinx descent, and we saw news outlets continually overlook that fact—the hate crime hadn't only been motivated by queerphobia, but by racism too.

We also learned the victims' names—saw the joyful content they'd once made about coming out and finally being able to be themselves. As I watched one video of a son joyously dancing with his mother around their kitchen, a Portuguese word came to mind: saudade—feeling melancholy and nostalgic for something you love, but also feeling grateful for having experienced that love at all. The cycle was pain and beauty and pain again. Though these people had managed to free themselves in their minds, their bodies were still under attack. I'd thought nightclubs were the places where everyone was supposed to be their freest—I'd even thought LGBTQ+ safe spaces were hardly needed anymore, as being queer was more widely accepted than ever before. I'd been ignorant. Privileged. Very much both.

I pored over all press coverage related to the event. It was a morbid fascination, but I couldn't stop—I longed for intimate moments with every victim, to imagine us laughing together while waiting for a drag queen to start her set. Consumed by videos and stories, I descended into guilt about my obsession. Tragedies happened every day—why had this one pulled me in? I felt solidarity but also distance, and told myself I wasn't gay enough to mourn so deeply, as if these people were my kin. Though I sensed my own queerness, it remained a shark's shadow beneath the surface—a threat I'd never acted on, far from dictating my life or probability of staying alive. I went to gay nightclubs by choice, not because I needed a venue to finally unlock myself. I felt like a fraud—any connection I claimed to queerness now seemed hard to grasp, like a rainbow that would soon evaporate into the clouds.

But there was one thing I couldn't shake: my profound connection to the spaces themselves. That hackneyed comparison between nightclubs and churches stems from truth—in terms of worship, safety, and refuge, gay dance floors had given me more than any cathedral ever could. These bars proved that having glory holes didn't disqualify you from being a holy space—on the contrary: they were temples and then some, offering forgiveness, providing confessionals, and granting everyone permission to show up exactly as they were.

With Pulse, that sanctity had been violated, but that didn't take away its legacy. So many lives had been lost in Orlando, and at the same time, there were also so many lives these spaces had saved. Whether or not I was queer, whether or not I "belonged," gay bars had been my escape. I barely knew who I was just yet, but somehow they'd managed to save me too.

Next came the revelation that life was short. Shorter than I'd thought, especially for queer people, who happened to be all the people I liked and all the people who seemed to like me. I started thinking, hard, about my own sexuality—I felt compelled to act on it, to honor the little voice inside me that said I might be hiding something.

I already knew I owed this to myself, but now I owed it to these fallen siblings too. I needed to put my queer desires into action. And I knew exactly where to start.

I scheduled a trip back to LA, making sure it fell across a weekend when Rhonda was in town. Most of my close friends had already outgrown the club scene and the multiday hangovers it induced, but a friend of a friend named Franco gleefully suggested I tag along with him. Franco knew everyone and, fortunately for me, often forged intimate bonds with acquaintances. He was the type of person you wanted to pour your heart out to—when I bashfully texted him that I was interested in exploring my queerness, he told me he had someone for me to meet.

The euphoria hit as soon as we got past Phyllis, but then I remembered Orlando, and saudade tempered the night. I drank it away, sipping slowly but feeling my liquor fast. Before I knew it, I was buzzed on a bench, talking to one of Franco's friends.

"Franco is the best, right?" she shouted over the muffled bass coming from the next room.

"He's the BEST," I slurred.

"I'm not even mad at how he introduced me."

"Um, remind me what he said?" I was relieved she'd brought up introductions, considering I'd already forgotten her name.

"You don't remember? He called me 'Lauren the Horny Lesbian'!" She bit her bottom lip, then scooted toward me until our thighs touched.

A woman had never flirted with me before—if Lauren

had been less forward, I might not have picked up on the signal. Neon lights moved across her face, illuminating her long blond hair and delicate features. She projected a sense of toughness, the kind of confident veneer that one puts on after being bullied in middle school. She wore baggy clothes, swallowed by a sweatshirt, and though I liked her style, I didn't yet understand how to receive masculine energy from someone who presented femme, someone who seemingly strived for the same beauty standards I held myself to. We had questionable chemistry, a layer of staleness between us, but I was willing to ignore it if she was.

"Franco knows I'm trying to hook up with a girl tonight," I blurted. I'd said it by accident, but Lauren didn't seem fazed. She tilted her face and I moved toward her for a kiss, hoping we'd meet in the middle. She moved forward an inch before pulling back.

"Maybe if you take my number," she purred, turning over her hand for me to place my phone in her palm. The line could've been smooth, but her delivery felt calculated, a ploy to leave me wanting more. I still gave her my phone—she saved her contact and sauntered away, disappearing into the sequined crowd.

A few drinks later, I texted: Remember me? ☺

Hi Jen, she wrote. I'm home now. Come over?

Address? I asked.

I paid my tab and grabbed a taxi to Echo Park. The driver sped through the hilly neighborhood, making me nauseous, but eventually pulled up in front of a narrow duplex painted cornflower blue.

As soon as I opened the door, Lauren kissed me, hurling her body against mine. My posture stiffened in her arms, surprised—after a lifetime of wanting to try this, was it really happening this fast?

"Let's go to my room," she insisted, grabbing my hand and leading me up a spiral staircase. We couldn't have climbed more than one flight, but in my memory, the steps seemed endless. I felt like Rapunzel (less Disney, more Brothers Grimm): trapped, scared, and en route to the top of a tower. I gulped, assuming any fear was due to nerves. I reminded myself that I *wanted* to be here. This wasn't a punishment; it was a prize.

Lauren jumped onto her bed pulling me down with her, both of us tumbling onto the heather-gray sheets. Her room smelled like Axe body spray, channeling flashbacks to high school hookups with boys where we got caught by their moms.

"You know I've . . . I've never done this before," I cautioned. My mouth felt dry.

"Franco told me. But no worries." She stroked my hair. "It's a good thing. I like knowing I'll be your first."

I smiled, grateful she'd framed my inexperience as desirable. "What do we do, then?"

She hoisted herself onto one elbow, then rolled her body on top of mine. "You? You lie there." She lowered her hand, running her finger underneath my waistband. "And I . . . do this."

I expected her to take off my pants, but instead she moved her hands to my shoulders, using both to pin me down. Holding me in position, she bent her knee and rubbed it against my inner thigh.

"Is this . . . sex?" I asked, 80 percent as a joke.

"We're not doing sex tonight," she replied, fully serious. "Tonight is just a taste."

She lifted her knee between my legs, jostling it back

and forth. This wasn't exactly the foreplay I'd expected, but I didn't hate it? Her brow furrowed with commitment—she had the focus of a student in a barre class who desperately wanted the instructor to say "good job." Her performance didn't exactly deserve a compliment, but that wasn't her fault—it was mine, considering I'd given her absolutely no direction. When I finally did speak, the words that came out were "Are you gonna go down on me?"—a critical question that I'd asked with the sexual tact of a TSA agent. I gulped repeatedly, waiting for her answer, not even sure whether I was ready for it to be yes.

"Not tonight," she said. "Like I said—just a taste."

Whatever we were sampling, the notes were off. She glared at me like she had a secret, channeling an Uber driver who'd shunned the Waze directions and claimed to know a hidden route. I wanted to give her five stars so as not to sabotage her career, but my mind wouldn't stop racing. I'd been looking forward to my first queer hookup, so why wasn't I having fun? People always said bi girls were just experimenting, but I was even bad at that. Maybe those other rumors were true—maybe bisexuality didn't exist. Was I lying to Lauren the Horny Lesbian? Was I lying to myself?

I may have been spiraling, but she remained steadfast. If I could make my body act aroused, maybe my mind would catch up? I took deep breaths, arching my back, pressing myself harder into her leg. I hoped this would have some kind of reverse-Method-acting effect—that going through the motions of pleasure might elicit the real thing—but no matter how much I feigned enjoyment, I couldn't turn off my brain. The most obvious way out of this seemed cowardly, but I didn't know what else to do.

To fake it with a woman, specifically a lesbian, would require an Academy Award–winning range I had not yet demonstrated—the community-theater-grade performances that had swelled the pride of so many men would certainly not pass here. Aiming for subtlety, I stayed quiet, wrapping my arms around her, gradually digging my nails into her back. I flexed my legs for a few seconds, then loosened my grip, feigning a whole-body release.

"Did you cum?" she asked.

"Yep," I lied. Faking an orgasm always hurts you more than it hurts the person you fake it for—it's a self-imposed roadblock to the bliss you deserve. Faking it with men had always been shameful, but now I'd done it with a woman? Pitiful. I deserved to be straight.

Lauren either believed me or she'd suspended her disbelief. Sitting up tall, she grinned like the Joker. "Spend the night! You know . . . if you want."

I told her I had a flight to catch and started searching for my socks.

In the car back to my hotel, I lowered the windows, letting in the cool California night air. The driver had on KCRW and "Over" by Maya Jane Coles pumped through the speakers. Hearing a song I equated with warehouses made me feel like a hypocrite—a disappointment to the club scenes that had reared me, an insult to Rhonda and her gorgeous crowd. I'd expected this night to finally validate my sexuality, but it had done the opposite—here I was, doubting myself even more.

I figured that if a woman couldn't get me off, I couldn't possibly be bi. Today I recognize that this logic had many fallacies—for one, orgasms don't define sexual attraction; for two, I'd never let a lackluster encounter with a man convince me that I wasn't straight (including the guy who couldn't cum unless *Bourne Identity* was on). I'd self-inflicted a double standard and had expected my first hookup with a woman to somehow "prove" my queerness to myself.

I now know that no sexuality requires proof, and that you don't have to hook up with anyone of any gender for your identity to be legit. I also know that bad hookups don't always have a deeper meaning or implication about your sexuality— they can even happen with someone you love. Many factors can influence your level of enjoyment (e.g., the person you're hooking up with, whether that person puts on music, the extent to which that music is Dave Matthews Band because it "reminds them of their first kiss").

But back then, one uncomfortable night was enough to psych me out. Since I didn't have a foundational faith in my queerness, I took these results to be conclusive: I was straight. The revelation felt bittersweet—yes, it meant abandoning a part of myself, but knowing for sure (or thinking I did) was such an immense relief.

I still went to gay bars and queer nightclubs on occasion, usually dictated by who was DJing, or another superficial reason I could use as an excuse. Inside, I made an extra effort to be conscious of my place. Though these venues remained sanctuaries, I now felt somewhat removed from their power, as if they catered to a religion that had refused to let me in. Each time I went I couldn't get out of my head—I shifted on my feet, questioning whether I belonged. I put my queerness on pause and recommitted to my heterosexual life. It would be years before I'd try again.

PART II

I WANT YOU TO LIKE ME (EVEN THOUGH I DON'T LIKE YOU)

CRUSH ON A COUPLE

THOUGH I SPENT most of my twenties thinking I was straight, that didn't stop me from desperately trying to have a three-some. Threesomes felt safely heteronormative—a quirky straight fetish rather than a queer urge; a quick, easy way for a gal to please her man. Porn reinforced this idea: girl-on-girl hookups usually transpired for the pleasure of the viewer (rather than for the pleasure of the women themselves) and typically functioned as foreplay before a holy cis man and his penis arrived. Most onscreen threesomes positioned women as objects for male consumption, implying that female queerness could only exist in reference to the male gaze.

But I hadn't thought about any of that—I just thought it sounded fun.

In hindsight, it's ironic that I thought of threesomes as a "straight thing" considering they're inherently queer (find a group-sex configuration that only involves one straight couple and you'll win the Nobel Prize). It's even more ironic that "obsessed with threesomes" functions as a common stereotype about bisexuals—one that feeds the perception of us as greedy, slutty unicorns (that's my name, don't wear it out!). But because of monosexism and bi erasure, bi people don't even get to reclaim this trope and call it our own. Imagine a world where hookups involving more than one gender were a sine qua non of multisexuality—where it was normal to think: *I can't wait to sleep with all of these people. I wonder if I'm bi?*

Maybe this is why, for most of my life, my threesome aspirations didn't phase me. I just thought they made me a straight girl with a wild side, rather than confirm that I was very queer indeed.

In the movies, threesomes transpire effortlessly, when three hot people find themselves in proximity to a bubble bath (happens all the time). But for me, orchestrating one took serious work.

My first attempt was in 2013 when I lived in Los Angeles. Tinder had just been released, but it didn't take long for me to hate it—using the app to find single men soon devolved from "great toilet activity!" to endless ennui. Straight dating meant enduring a steady stream of dudes who wanted to be actors and "didn't think the timing was right." People seemed to find each other replaceable, probably because we *were* replaceable—swipe one of us away and a new one would grow in our place. Every date felt routine, as did the emotions I felt afterward: I was either desperate for the guy to text me or I'd already forgotten his name.

But going out with a "straight" couple, I thought, might be different. I wouldn't meet the same awkwardness as when I'd hooked up with Lauren since there would be a guy around. My imagination wouldn't run wild picturing our future, since the two of them would already have future plans of their own. A threesome would give me another chance to touch a woman's body, and it also seemed like the ideal form of meaningless sex: There wouldn't be room to get emotionally invested. "What's love got to do with a little ménage?" Fat Joe had once asked. Eleven years later, I answered.

At the time I lived with a Craigslist roommate whose grueling job involved managing production of the Oscars. I spent days searching for interested parties, often groaning about this laborious task, equating the stress of my sexual prep work to my roommate's career (no wonder she and I barely spoke). Today, you can hardly open a dating app without being confronted by open-minded liberal couples—they're like stomach gurgles in a two p.m. meeting, almost impossible to avoid. The prospects still aren't perfect—maybe you've seen the meme that says "every couple looking for a third looks like this" over a photo of Grimes and Elon Musk—but at least they're abundant. In 2013, it was a different game.

The couple profiles I did find gave off strong catfish vibes (black-and-white portraits and suspiciously low-res thirst traps), so I set the bar high and went out with the first two people whose photos had faces in frame. I messaged with the woman, a quirky twenty-four-year-old who looked like the early 2010s equivalent of Ella Emhoff. She sent more pics of her partner—a cute lanky guy with freckles and a Jewfro—then suggested a location: the jazz bar next to Canter's Deli. I was thrilled. If things went well, we would sleep together. If things went *really* well, we could grab rugelach for the road.

We slid into a big round booth, butts squeaking across the cherry-red seats, and I spit all the game I had. I complimented Ella's LCD Soundsystem tee. I asked about Freckles' job. I suggested grabbing rugelach for the road. I was crushing it, somehow the best version of myself—charming, carefree, and for once in my life, a good listener. The bartender even bought me a drink—he'd seen a single woman sitting with a couple and figured he'd cut in. Ella and Freckles seemed to appreciate that a stranger had fawned over me, and suggested I continue flirting with him. It became a game: I'd walk to the bar and bat my eyelashes, then return to our booth with a free vodka soda and a story. The three of us lingered until the bar closed. After that, outside under the streetlamps, I kissed them both, one at a time, and they said they would text me soon.

But they didn't. A few days passed, and I kept checking my phone. I wasn't insecure so much as confused—I couldn't figure out what went wrong. Just as I was about to reach out and ask, Ella texted me:

Sorry we didn't call, she wrote. We discussed it and we aren't sure we're ready for this yet. Great meeting you though! Maybe we can connect again someday. ☺

I sighed, annoyed that I'd been thwarted by their strong communication skills. Guess it was back to square one.

✳

After moving to New York, I tried again. I talked about threesomes to anyone who would listen, which meant I often brought them up on dates with straight guys. This was a dark era for my self-respect—a time when I used the MyFitness-Pal app on a daily basis and still thought music festivals were fun—so it checks out that I conflated being fetishized with being adored. But for as much as I talked about threesomes, I rarely brought up bisexuality by name. Years later, I learned how porn may have contributed to my staying closeted: Apparently videos that feature women hooking up with other women rarely get categorized as "bisexual." Instead it's almost always categorized as "lesbian." This is because porn categories aren't intended to reflect the sexuality of their actors, but to serve as reference points for the presumably cishet dudes at home watching. "Bisexual" *does* exist as a category, but if you look it up, you'll notice it again centers around the male viewer's sexuality, returning results for videos featuring one cis woman and two cis men.* (This arrangement is sometimes called the "devil's threesome," though I'm pretty sure that term now exclusively refers to Satan, Lil Nas X, and the pole.)

Eventually one of my dates mentioned an app called 3nder (today known as Feeld), which then had the tagline "Trios Made Easy." I downloaded it (to use without my date—sorry bro), then crafted a bio: "Writer who loves typography, vegan food, and doing whatever you say ☺." Before Joey could point out that the emoji was trying too hard, I got my first match. The couple looked like they were from the Midwest—the woman had a fake tan, and though I didn't love the inauthenticity that conveyed, her boyfriend seemed down-to-earth enough: his shaggy hair had Zac Efron vibes, and he wore a T-shirt featuring the Smiths.

---

* Yet another fact I learned from bi activist Shiri Eisner. Their book is called *Bi: Notes for a Bisexual Revolution*—do yourself a favor and read it already.

Looove the Smiths ☻, I said. Fortunately he didn't ask me to name a single song, and the three of us arranged a date.

We met at a Williamsburg bar that I knew to attract an obnoxious crowd—it was the kind of place that played exclusively classic rock and referred to itself as a "haunt" on Yelp. There were tables in the front and billiards in the back (the bar equivalent of a mullet), and since I arrived before my dates did, I grabbed a pilsner and snagged a bench facing the door. As they walked up, I glimpsed the girlfriend's orange skin from the window, marveling for a moment at how mismatched their partnership seemed. But the second they walked in, I got tunnel vision—I couldn't take my eyes off the guy.

He must have felt chemistry too, because as soon as they sat down, he leaned toward me and asked about my favorite font ("Apercu, no question"). I practically melted, and we talked all night—if his girlfriend hadn't been there, it might've been the best first date I'd ever been on. I enjoyed myself so much that I didn't even think to include her in the conversation. She never complained, but about twenty minutes in, I noticed her scrolling through her phone.

After a few drinks, we stood up for a round of pool. By this point I was coming down from my starry-eyed flirt session—it was clear that the only way I could go home with him was by going home with her too. As she held a cue and studied the table, I walked up beside her and put my hand on her arm. She squirmed away, then snapped, "Pro tip, sweetheart: On your next date like this, don't ignore the girl."

✳

A few months later I got up the nerve to try 3nder one more time, now equipped with some critical feedback that I felt ready to apply. Soon after logging on, I got a match and a message from a guy whose profile name was Boy, saying that he and his girlfriend, Girl, loved vegan food too. Given the context, one common interest was more than enough, so we made plans for a drink.

They chose a bar that toed the line between luxury and lowbrow—it smelled like leather and cheap cigarettes. I spotted Boy and Girl near the back, each perched on a stool on the same side of a high table. I ordered a Maker's on the rocks, hoping to seem impressive.

"We've got a cool girl on our hands!" Boy joked, not knowing how much this made me melt.

When we clinked glasses, I awkwardly attempted to meet both of their gazes, darting my eyes back and forth. They didn't look like their pictures—they looked better. This couple was radiant, glowing with anticipation of their impending adventurous night.

Girl did most of the talking, and based on my past experience, I knew to pay attention. Luckily it was hard to look anywhere other than her chocolate-brown eyes—and she had a legitimately fascinating job.

"Photojournalism is decent, I guess." She shrugged. "I mean, yesterday I took portraits of a bunch of naked people in Times Square, which was fun?"

"She's the shit, right?!" Boy asked. He wanted to show off his partner's greatness, but he was too late—I already understood.

Boy and Girl had a lot in common: They were each petite,

Iranian, and wearing a wedding ring. They told me they'd spontaneously gotten married in Prospect Park last month, and they still looked like newlyweds: sparkling eyes, a bounce in their step. I imagined their wedding had felt like an authentic celebration of love, rather than a pageant for their families or a stunt for the gram.

Eventually I asked if they'd done this before—they said yes, once, and the experience had only fueled their fire as a couple, awakening them to each other in a whole new way. I hung on their words, amazed that a love like this was possible. Had they fought or broken up? No—they'd had a dreamlike, low-maintenance wedding. My chest felt weightless, and I realized: I had two crushes! But I had no understanding of polyamory, so I didn't know what to make of this—was such a thing even allowed?

As if sensing my uncertainty, Boy and Girl reached across the table, each holding one of my hands. I gulped. They were inviting me to transcend my role as spectator of their relationship and become part of its fabric. This wasn't just a one-night stand anymore—something about it felt real.

We walked three blocks to their place. The apartment had the quaint optimism of people starting a life together, the walls covered with photos and travel souvenirs. I felt like a tourist, wandering through their romance without a map, ready to get lost.

We lingered in their kitchen and Boy handed me a Mason jar filled to the brim with red wine.

"So," I said between sips, wiping my mouth on the back of my hand. "What now?"

Girl answered by walking over and kissing me. I kissed back. After a few minutes, Boy joined us, and once the make-out had run its course, they each grabbed one of my hands again and towed me to their room.

The next two hours were a blur—the beast with three backs, three tongues, and six hands; the taste of salty skin; an acrid musk of body lotion and BO. I could go into further detail about the sex, but I don't want it to seem like I'm writing this essay just to brag (that's what the author photo is for, babe). The only aspect worth mentioning is that Boy and Girl were incredible communicators—they constantly checked in, asking questions like "How does that feel?," and it seemed like they actually wanted to know. If they hadn't been so attuned to my pleasure, I might not have been so attuned to theirs. I realized that if that first couple I'd met in LA hadn't told me about their uneasiness, our sex would've been awful, like being lost at sea.

Afterward we stretched out on the bed, exhausted. Boy lay on my left while Girl lay on my right, and I switched my gaze between them before staring wistfully at the ceiling. "You're incredible," I said to neither one in particular, hoping that might communicate that the compliment was directed at them both.

I jumped back into my jeans—they'd asked if I could spend the night, but since I had work the next day I decided against it, even though I longed for a leisurely morning in their bed. Rubbing the heel of my palm against my chest, I told myself to be grateful. Wasn't this the best part of being a tourist—the fact that you could leave?

But on the ride home, my imagination played out our life together, the same way it often did with single men. I found myself picturing coupley scenes but with three people: Boy, Girl, and I strolling through a museum; the three of us headed on vacation, taking up a whole row on the plane. I wondered which room in their apartment I'd take (or would we share?) and began planning the speech I'd give my parents (there was zero chance my dad would ever pronounce "throuple" right). When I got home, I considered putting on *Vicky Cristina Barcelona*, but ultimately heeded my promise to never watch a Woody Allen movie again.

The next morning annihilated me—commuting to Manhattan while hungover is the last unwritten Greek myth. After the subway ride, it seemed like years had passed, putting me safely in the chill period of contacting them (even though it was only nine a.m.). I sent the wittiest text my whiskey-soaked brain could come up with: Do you get to sleep in today, or are the naked people in Times Square begging to have their stories told? I spent the afternoon making excuses to check my phone, each time seeing only my message and the same gray "Delivered" underneath.

The rejection felt dull, impersonal, and painfully obvious. Of course they didn't need me—they were busy being in a relationship with each other. The dangling question mark in my text reminded me that I'd gotten my hopes up—it felt like finding spinach in my teeth after a long day.

Getting shut down by two people could've hurt twice as much, but the pain felt eerily familiar. Maybe that was because I'd really had only one crush—I'd fallen for both of them, not as individuals but as a unit, attracted to their sparks, their honesty, and the strength of their bond.

Maybe I didn't want Boy and Girl as much as I wanted what they had. That night, when I finally got home from work, I opened Tinder and started to swipe.

THE MEN
WHO GHOST ME

THE ONLY THING the men who ghost me have in common is that they ghost me. Beyond that, no two are alike—they come in all shapes, sizes, and states of unprocessed trauma. Sometimes I picture them as a collection of figurines, the variety of which would surely stun at a Sotheby's auction. But then I remember that ghosting is defined by absence, so here I am, left staring at an empty shelf.

You'd think a disappearing act would take skill (or at least a few hours of YouTube tutorials). Yet somehow even the laziest of these suitors are veritable Houdinis, stealthy and silent, effortlessly vanishing into thin air. Like true professionals they never look back, leaving me to play stagehand and close down the show. What do I do with all these props—the text threads that could've stretched to the moon, or the aphorisms they once said in bed that I can't manage to forget? ("The secret to tattoos? Keep getting more." "Your first coffee of the day should *always* be hot.") Each time I hang around, waiting for them to reveal how their illusion worked, but eventually realize it wasn't a trick. (Even if it had been—a good magician never tells.)

Does it make me complicit if I know what I'm getting myself into? By now I can sense who's going to ghost—I know to be suspicious of the ones who send voice memos, have cool jobs, or go down on me too well. But can I listen to that intuition? Can I quit while I'm ahead? Of course not. I'm like a child who only learns by doing, yet she does plenty and somehow never learns.

I have to ask myself if I'm making these mistakes on purpose. I have to know that these men are just vessels for the emotions they leave me with, and that I'm more addicted to the feeling of longing than any one person I think I long for. At least I'm rarely "in love" with these people—does that help? Sigh—even I know it doesn't. Not loving doesn't keep me from staring at my phone, hoping the next text comes from their name.

Sometimes I draw a flawed comparison between ghosting and BDSM's dominant/submissive dynamic. Despite the fact that BDSM relies on positive things like aftercare, boundaries, and consent, the analogy arises for an obvious reason: Ghosting treats you like shit and leaves you wanting more. I'm never sure whether or not I enjoy it, but I must, because I keep coming back.

✳

The director in town for a shoot takes out his phone to show me a rough cut of his mediocre sitcom. I can't hear the dialogue over the din of the bar, but I laugh anyway—we're here after two days of furiously app-texting about *The Bachelor*, and since I'm still high off the quality of that banter, I'm inclined to indulge him. After two drinks we close our tab, then fuck at his Airbnb for three nights in a row. He prefers silent sex, so I keep my mouth shut, and even though I walk home at two a.m. each time, I still convince myself he will move to New York for me someday. A year later I see his mediocre sitcom on TV. When I text my congrats (send with effect: confetti), he replies haha yay! and our rapport turns over in its grave.

The journalist who claims to be afraid of dating a sex writer asks lots of questions. I soon realize he isn't afraid of me but of death, and he wants a sex writer to immortalize him. Drunk on power with Steno pad in hand, I promise I'll profile him à la "Frank Sinatra Has a Cold" and the callback to journalism school gets us both wet. I ask what he wants his legacy to be—instead of answering, he grabs my hand and we sprint toward his place. The only other time I see him move that fast is when we try for a quickie at mine during his lunch hour and he can't get it up. He panics and bolts, leaving me naked on the couch, and we never speak again. I assume he had concerns that I'd make impotence his legacy—founded concerns, apparently, because here I am.

The barista boy squeezes my stomach during sex, and it makes me fall in love with him. Though I'm in love, I'm also devastated—having my imperfect body worshipped forces me to confront that this isn't how it's always been. When the boy's name disappears from my recent texts, I vow to beg all future lovers to knead my belly like dough, but I never do—I am too self-conscious, both about liking it and about having fat to grab. If anything, I swing back toward the opposite: If hands even come close to my stomach, I immediately shove them away.

✳

The app founder I meet in Mexico City tells me to get on all fours and finger myself. I say, "That's all threes," and he says, "Shut up," and we both break character, collapsing into laughter on the bed. I fall asleep at his place by accident and marvel at his apartment in morning light—teal walls with built-in sneaker displays, the coolest place I've ever woken up. I tell him I'm in town for another week and he mumbles, "That's great," while looking at his phone. Days later, I muster the courage to ask for the café he recommended, but my messages stop going through. Getting blocked is like falling in love— you never forget your first time.

✳

The sheepish coworker who slouches over his desk wants me to punch him in the face. This comes after weeks of Gchat flirting—at first I resist, hesitant to shit where I eat, but he wears me down with homemade GIFs and questions about my favorite words. When he finally asks me out, he uses my *least* favorite words—"would," "maybe," and "might"—all in the same text. It's like talking to a paper towel, but a handsome one who tells me I'm "enigmatic" and says he can't believe I'm real. We get Ethiopian food which leads to hands touching which leads to me riding him which leads to the $64,000 question: Would I be so kind as to knock him the fuck out? I demure, though this is just a tactic to seem innocent—I know the story will be worth it, so after a minute I ask how hard. He responds by quoting Tyler Durden, and I clarify, "You want me to hit you as hard as I can?" to which he nods: "I want to go to work tomorrow with a black eye." I wind up and strike, falling short of a shiner, hurting my hand more than his face. The next morning I shake out my wrist at my desk, hoping he'll walk past with a sly smile: "You okay, Jen? Carpal tunnel's a bitch." But instead he spends the day avoiding my gaze, staring at his computer so intently you'd think he actually liked his job. I wonder what I did wrong—forget to wear rings? Hold up a mirror to his shame? In any case, this damage can't be fixed.

He drifts away but never leaves, another demon stuck in my head. I exorcise best when I exercise, so I decide to sweat him out. Ironically (and—let's be honest—intentionally) I choose a kickboxing class. The studio plays Outkast's "B.O.B." and lets us go gloveless, so twice a week I step under the hot lights and pummel the leather bag until my knuckles bruise. I always picture his face, but the rationale behind the image shifts: On the bad days, I'm hitting him because he likes it. On the good days, I'm giving him what he deserves.

THE POWER DYNAMIC

(Content Warning: Mentions and description of substance abuse; sexual assault)

IN 2013, FIVE years before several men accuse Kevin Spacey of sexual assault, millions of Americans binge Netflix's *House of Cards*. A particular moment sticks with me, wherein Spacey speaks directly to the camera and quotes Oscar Wilde: "Everything in the world is about sex, except sex. Sex is about power." Spacey isn't speaking as himself but as the (murderous bisexual) character of Frank Underwood—it's as if to say, "I'm not a creepy old man, but I play one on TV."

At the time I don't know the truth about Kevin Spacey the Person yet, so I'm able to stomach—even be moved by—Kevin Spacey the Actor's words. Oscar Wilde's words feel like scripture to me, giving shape to a truth I've carried with me my whole life. I knew sex was the key to power long before I experienced either sex or power, and long before I knew how much people could abuse them both.

*

I first wrap my mouth around a penis over a decade prior. It's
eighth grade—I'm acned, optimistic, and eager to please. The
penis belongs to my new boyfriend Luke, who lives in a town
called Nashville about thirty minutes away. Luke identifies as
a redneck: He owns chickens, drives a Ford F-150, and goes to
the shooting range every weekend. Eventually I'll recoil at the
thought of him (especially fifteen years later while watching
footage of a Trump rally and seeing either him or his exact
doppelgänger standing in the front row). But at fourteen, I'm
certain: I'm in love, and I'm about to prove it.

My obsession with blow jobs began when I was still
thirteen—when Becca gave one to her boyfriend of three
weeks during a group outing to *Final Destination 2*. They huddled in the last row at the theater, their grunts echoing while
the rest of us stared ahead, taking in all the creative ways to die.
At the sleepover afterward, Becca reported that the BJ happened "super-fast," which we all agreed meant she was good at
it. I clenched my teeth and felt flooded with jealousy, craving
detailed instructions so I could do this too. I smuggled several
bananas into my room and Becca walked us through logistics:
Open your mouth. Breathe through your nose. Under no cir-
cumstances can you show your teeth.

Over the next few months, I thought about blow jobs every
day. While watching movies in class, I rehearsed techniques with
my tongue behind closed lips, like a dancer miming through
choreographed steps. I felt propelled by a carnal curiosity—I
had a hunch that holding my own in the bedroom would grant
me godlike access to the world, and I could pull the sword out
of the stone if only I managed to give good head. Years later, I'd

learn from writer Andrea Long Chu that perhaps this hunch was assigned to me at birth, right along with my sex: "*female* is distant cousins with over two dozen English words, including *fecund, felicity, fennel, fetus, affiliate,* and *effete,* as well as *fellatio,* from the Latin *fellāre,* meaning 'to suck a dick.'"

Today, I am to go down on Luke in a one-room wooden cabin that belongs to someone's parents, the type of modest structure a five-year-old might draw if told to sketch a house. The place sits right by the roaring highway that runs through town (we would've picked somewhere quieter, but for sexually active teens, this is as good as it gets). At least it feels quaint like the rest of Nashville—the town's main strip teems with bed-and-breakfasts, antique shops, and ice cream stores, and the air smells like cinnamon candles every time of year. My grandma comes here for weekend vacations—a wholesome backdrop for my sexual debut.

Luke and I enter the cabin with timid steps while our friends loiter outside. Someone yells that they'll be timing us, and I realize we each have different KPIs: I win if the clock is short; Luke wins if he lasts. It doesn't occur to me that sex should be something for mutual enjoyment—right now it feels like a competitive sport, and Luke's friend with the cell phone stopwatch is our biased referee.

After shutting the door, Luke hits play on a boom box and reclines in a rocking chair. I kneel in front of him like a woman in church, unzipping his pants and holding his cock in my hands, surprised by the tenderness of something that's supposed to be "hard." The act itself takes eight minutes, a number I figure out years later after calculating that a two-minute song by the Clash repeated exactly four times. But in the cabin I can tell by the smug look on Luke's face that he's lasting a while—a bad sign for me. I move faster, and when bitterness explodes on the roof of my mouth, I swallow without a second thought.

Two weeks after this, Luke calls me to break up. It's nonnegotiable—he's already moved on and has made out with someone else. I weep onto the receiver but remain focused, asking for feedback—if, at least, I gave good head.

"Eh," Luke says. "I'd give it a four?"

I cry harder. He suggests I learn to use my hands.

✳

Because one of our friends has a big mouth (pun intended), this incident floats back to my hometown—it's my first piece of juicy gossip and it earns me the title of "slut." I effortlessly sustain this honorific through high school, thanks to a group of Christian cheerleaders one grade above (all of whom proudly identify as Republican). They devote their lives to two things: God, and making sure I know what kind of girl I am. They trash-talk me to the boys I like and graffiti my name in bathroom stalls next to pencil-drawn dicks. They torture my friends and me, yet still flash us smiles in the hall, grinning like their teeth are smeared with Vaseline. The bullying doesn't break us—in fact, it hardly strikes us as bullying at all. For the life of me, I can't understand why "slut" is not a compliment.

One night the cheerleaders call Laney in a panic, explaining that one of them had unprotected sex and now needs help purchasing the morning-after pill. (It's not that they can't afford it—it's that they're too embarrassed to show their faces at our small town's local CVS.) We answer the call as a group and consider hanging up on them, but know we'll get off more on the superiority of being kind than the thrill of being rude. Vigilantes in American Eagle jeans, we make a U-turn and go straight to the pharmacy, then drive to the mansion where they're having a sleepover. We pull up to the end of the long driveway and find one girl waiting on the curb. She walks to the car, grabs the box, and mouths "Thanks" before she sprints back inside.

✳

During high school, I do my research. Oblivious to the gulf between porn and sex ed, I study whatever short films I can download on KaZaA—my favorite is called "Oral Sex Training Video" and though it's just teacher/student role-play, I learn from it nonetheless. I gravitate toward scenes where women seem ecstatic and in command, and stare at them in awe—they seem fearless and ever enthused.

I imagine how oral sex might feel—comforting, like being filled with warm laundry from inside. Luke's point begins to make sense: If a hand is lubed up correctly and moves in harmony with one's lips, it might successfully pass as an extension of a mouth. The more I think about it, the more sucking dick strikes me as poetry—an elegant, erotic art form when done right.

From pop culture and the cheerleaders, I've learned that giving a blow job is supposed to be degrading; it's not an action to aspire to. Admittedly, its name doesn't advocate well for itself: "blow" suggests huffing and puffing, "job" implies hours of thankless work.* "Giving head" is flawed language too—it suggests altruism, selflessness. As if the best part of gift-giving isn't watching someone open the present you so brilliantly picked out.

Even as a teen I see past this branding issue and wonder: Why are blow jobs so bad? No one talks about the fact that filling an orifice can make you feel whole. And then there's the misguided assumption that manipulation must be a precursor—that because a blow job is submissive it's inherently a nonconsensual act.

My adolescent brain already doesn't buy this. Forget Becca's warnings—teeth give us power. They give us control, even when we're on our knees. Teeth offer protection too—in case of emergency, we're just one jaw hinge away from a life-altering strike, a heroic escape. At any given moment we can channel Lorena Bobbitt, not as the punch line the media makes her out to be but as the woman I will later learn she is: a survivor of abuse pushed to her limits, acting in self-defense (but not exactly mad about revenge).

*

A few months into freshman year, a sophomore named Cole Craig leans on my locker and invites me over after school. His parents are gone for the week, and he has "lots of vodka" in case me and my friends want to "get weird." Cole Craig

---

* Comedian Jacqueline Novak touches on this (and other penis-related etymology) more eloquently than I ever could in her brilliant one-woman show *Get on Your Knees*. A favorite moment is when she addresses "erection," saying the word feels "a bit architectural for what's going on there—no one's going in that building. It's not up to code."

has two first names and acts like it—he's cocky (pun intended again) but has the charisma to match. He grins at me, puka-shell necklace gleaming under the fluorescent hallway light, and without hesitation, I say I'm in.

My friends all have choir practice, but Laney decides to skip. I'm relieved she's the one joining—she's adventurous and always down to try something new. Neither of us knows yet that we're bisexual—we barely know bisexual is a thing we can be. All we know is that there's something we don't understand about ourselves just yet, and we have a hunch that growing up fast might help us figure it out.

Cole lives walking distance from our high school. When the bell rings, Laney and I trudge through a neighborhood dotted with replicas of the same cream-colored house. A lime-green bra strap peeks out from under her tank top—it's attached to her favorite push-up, the one covered in autographs from a ska band we saw in Indianapolis together. My dad drove but let us wait in the meet-and-greet line by ourselves, and when we got to the front Laney lifted up her shirt. The band, three burly men in their twenties who should've known better, shrugged and uncapped their Sharpies, while Laney stuck out her chest with pride.

We know we've arrived when we hear muted hip-hop, and we follow the sound into the backyard. The space seems optimized for adult parties—picnic and ping-pong tables, complete with a hot tub in the middle. Cigarette smoke wafts through the air, and I notice the music emanating from a speaker disguised as a rock—"I need a down-ass chick that'll roll with the clique," raps someone that Cole will later tell me is Juicy J. Four boys we've never met before lounge on lawn chairs, each dressed like a cartoon bully in a huge T-shirt and baggy pants. I notice Cole is slightly cuter than the others, but beyond that it's tough to tell them apart.

Cole gestures to us from the picnic table, a shepherd herding lambs to the slaughterhouse. He tosses the contents of a small paper cup down his throat, and Laney and I nod at each other, as if doing it together will make it hurt less. We sip the clear liquid like soda, not yet aware that its taste is something to avoid.

I look at Laney, relieved that she also seems to be holding back puke. We've never tried alcohol before, so if you told us that by the time we turned eighteen we'd be drinking it almost daily and in excess, we'd sneer at you in disbelief. But whether we can picture it or not, that vodka-soaked world becomes our reality—for the most part we'll manage to stay afloat, but we won't be surprised when we learn that bi women experience increased rates of both substance abuse and sexual assault. In some devastating way these statistics will validate us, our traumas reassuring us that yes—we're worthy of the bisexual label we're leaning toward. But as teens, all we know is that we're hungry to experience whatever comes next—maybe it'll help us understand who we are.

"Again?" Cole asks, lifting the handle of Kamchatka. We nod.

Time gets fuzzy, and a million things seem to happen at once—the loosening up, the invincibility, the clothes dropping to the deck. Before I know it, the sun disappears and the sky turns a brilliant sapphire, a jewel-toned jolt of energy that feels like permission to give in. We climb in the hot tub and onto Cole's lap, and he perches us on opposite knees like two ventriloquist dummies. I notice Laney's stringy auburn hair hanging over her boobs—she'd look like Ariel if there wasn't mascara all over her face.

"It would be mad hot if you both went down on me," Cole goads. "You know—at the same time."

"No way!" We giggle. We know we shouldn't want to do this, but we don't want him to stop asking either. In any case, how are we supposed to know if this is right—if this is what we want? The act seems simultaneously sour and erotic—is a teenager really the best judge to decide which of those feelings should win?

"At least make out, then." Cole knows we'll be game for this and also knows where it might lead. Laney and I lock eyes, then wade into the center of the tub. Surrounded by the smell of Aussie hair products and chlorine, I taste her tongue, its papillae like a coral reef, and suddenly we're immersed in wetness from bodies and mouths and water too. I let myself enjoy the feeling and so does she. We keep making out of our own accord, and for a moment I forget we're not alone. I get the sense that I'm here on a mission, tasked with uncovering something new, and my thoughts flail around in my head like an arm searching for a sleeve.

The kiss gives us momentum, so Cole only has to ask for his original wish three more times before he gets it. Laney and I each put our mouth on one side of his dick, sliding up and down while boys around the backyard watch.

"All right, Cole!" one of them shouts.

I take this as encouragement—at least Laney and I have been noticed for our commitment. Applying Luke's critique, I use my hand, and Laney—a quick learner—follows suit. Cole grunts and groans and after ten minutes decides he's done, blaming something called "whiskey dick" even though we drank vodka. I wipe my mouth, disappointed that we couldn't make him finish, and stew in the sense of failure (the guilt and confusion won't hit for years).

"You girls did great," Cole assures, patting us on the back. He climbs out of the hot tub to grab towels, at which point Laney and I nod at each other again, a telepathic reminder that we're a team.

Laney and I stay close friends, but after that night we start making our own separate mistakes. We err alike but in different rooms, usually following whatever course of action our hookup has determined for us, unsure how to define consent when we ourselves aren't sure what we want. We wonder if it's okay not to know—can we decide later, or is that a decision in itself? Some people say "consent culture" means they're expected to "read someone else's mind." But what about me, Laney, and all the others who can hardly read our own?*

The flailing that began in the frothy water continues, a story that threads through beds, backseats, and house-party bathrooms. We seek out countless sybaritic nights, each drenched in a pride that turns to shame when it dries. We say we look out for each other, that we're always a phone call away. But we both know this kindness is merely a gesture—we can barely handle ourselves.

Over a decade later, when we gain the vocabulary to describe our traumas, we still rarely use the r-word—it feels so dramatic, a term that doesn't (or couldn't) apply to us. Instead

---

* For answers to this question, read Katherine Angel's *Tomorrow Sex Will Be Good Again*. She writes that consent is far from enough, especially for women to enjoy sex: "The rhetoric of consent too often implies that desire is something that lies in wait, fully formed within us, ready for us to extract. Yet our desires emerge in interaction; we don't always know what we want . . . [This] must be folded into the ethics of sex rather than swept aside as an inconvenience."

we use phrases like "bad sex" to gloss over the details, and everyone knows how to infer. Rather than process these events, we numb them—at first the liquor helps, but soon enough it leads to more pain. We find ourselves drinking and fucking and drunkenly "fucking"—a traumatic bisexual loop.

In our late twenties, we manage to confront our own histories and find our rage, but soon realize our anger exists less because of the horrors themselves and more because of their mundanity. By this point we've tolerated and accepted the fact that "not okay" things happen every day. We recognize that Cole Craig essentially coerced us, and sure: He should probably rot in hell. Yet for both of us he's a blip, background noise—his existence and wrongdoings rarely cross our minds. I hardly think about that night at all, and when I do, the sting isn't because of what happened as much as because it was so unremarkable. I haven't even told my therapist, and I bet I never will.

The other memory that sporadically surfaces is the kiss. There's an ickyness in recalling that we both enjoyed it a little—in confronting that this was our first time hooking up with a girl. For years Laney and I remain equally perplexed by our own sexual orientations— we refer to ourselves as bi over drinks and in private text threads with ease, but never claim the label in public. "Bisexual" is another word that feels dramatic—we're not sure if we deserve it. On top of that, it's impossible to separate our queerness from Cole Craig's backyard—to know if we're attracted to women because of the male gaze or in spite of it; to determine whether our impulses stem from lust, objectification, a feeling of sisterhood, or all three. It's hard to tell if we lost our agency, or if, as young women, agency was never really within our reach.

Our realities had been shaped by gender roles, stigmas, and personal histories—frameworks that paved the way for us, whether we understood them or not.

In my thirties, I finally call myself a bisexual. But I still can't shake these questions; can't determine which parts of my desires are truly my own. No matter where bisexuality takes me, a pivotal chunk of my queerness will always remain submerged in the past, beneath the roiling water of a hot tub, center stage.

THE NEON SWEATER

*(Content Warning: Descriptions of sexual assault,
mentions of police brutality)*

THE DAY AFTER Trump was elected I cradled a terrified three-month-old golden retriever in my hands. At the time I worked at a media company, a publisher known for list content featuring cute cats and dogs, and that day, our office managers had found the most on-brand way to help distressed employees cope: They'd filled a conference room with therapy puppies that we could hold while we wiped our tears away.

My puppy trembled, its body vibrating like a tuning fork, and I wondered if he too felt the fog that had fallen over New York City. At twenty-eight and single, this felt like the closest I could get to staring into the eyes of a child, a creature who didn't ask to be brought into this world.

Either the dog or the news made me realize that writing lists like "16 Things You Should Forgive Your Succulents For" wasn't going to leave this planet better than I'd found it. I set down the puppy, then went straight back to my desk and applied for new jobs. I sent my résumé to Planned Parenthood, Global Zero, and every other nonprofit I could think of, and the next day I took an interview with an old friend. He presented an opportunity that wasn't at a nonprofit, per se—he ran the creative department at a PR agency—but said he focused on "marketing with social impact" and that he could double my salary. I didn't yet comprehend the irony of using both the greater good and capitalism as bait, or what it said about my own ignorance that I fell for it.

Quickly my day-to-day revealed that this promise of social impact work had been a lie. I was assigned to projects for cable companies, packaged goods, and technology updates people didn't need. I wanted to quit every day, and I felt that way for two years. At the risk of sounding like a Lifetime movie, the only thing that kept me from leaving was a friend.

When we met, Eden was three years my junior, though I immediately registered her as cooler than I would ever be. She looked like Marcie from *Peanuts** with a bob and a Bushwick flair: a film buff, a video game nerd, and an incredible chef (the only person I've ever met who actually owns a sous vide). Eden was heavily influenced by the dualities of the South— raised in Atlanta, she grew up amid the legacy of the civil rights movement and the Reagan conservatism that weaponized it. Though her family valued traditions like cotillion balls and Sunday suppers, Eden's social justice bone steered her toward Southern grassroots activism, where she encountered the works of Fannie Lou Hamer, John Lewis, and SNCC. Her

---

* Google Marcie if you need a visual reference, and also if you need to read a bunch of think pieces about her queer relationship with Peppermint Patty.

political journey crept steadily toward the left, but consistent with the contradictions, her progressiveness regressed around men—she'd moved to New York for her boyfriend, a hedge-fund guy who promised her a nice life with a big kitchen, and occasionally I caught her slipping into fantasies about a huge wedding.

Outside of work, Eden lent her design talents to the Women's March (though she left after the event's first year, saying the org was "more committed to coddling white women who bought T-shirts than to radical action"). But in 2017, attending a protest with corporate sponsors felt like a productive way to be mad, and every woman I knew intended to go. One day while gathered in the office bathroom, Eden and I discussed our protest signs: She planned to write "Believe Black Women" on hers, and wanting to build on that sentiment, I showed her a "TRUST WOMEN" graphic on Instagram—"This could be cool too!" Eden eyed me askance in the mirror, genuinely confused about why I'd brought this up. Eventually she spoke, playing dumb on my behalf: "But that would be a different thing . . . right?" I agreed even though I didn't understand, then rushed home to figure out what I'd missed. I soon realized what I'd done was a classic display of white feminism—I'd been #AllLivesMattering, using womanhood to do it.

Though Eden had gently corrected me, I didn't want to reveal any more of my ignorance—if we were going to stay friends, I needed to step it up. Yes, maintaining a friendship with another white person was the wrong reason to start anti-racism work. But by the same coin, my motivation shone a light on how effectively Eden had used her own privilege—she did what white people should do, and held me, her problematic white friend, accountable for growth.

I threw myself into unlearning, but I always felt a few steps behind. Eden reminded me she was still learning too—despite all the reading she did growing up, her radicalization had happened just two years prior, when Michael Brown was killed by police. Years later, I learned that even though reading about anti-racism is a necessary step, it doesn't always translate to action, and it definitely isn't a means to an end. As Lauren Michele Jackson writes for *Vulture*:

> "Anti-racist" suggests something of a vanity project, where the goal is no longer to learn more about race, power, and capital, but to spring closer to the enlightened order of the anti-racist. And yet, were one to actually read many of these books, one might reach the conclusion that there is no anti-racist stasis within reach of a lifetime.

Regardless of there not being an end point, Eden was a sponge for information with a passion to share it—once while wasted at a work happy hour, she randomly shouted, "JEN! Did you know MLK was assassinated by the U.S. government? Coretta Scott King brought a civil suit in 1999, and the jury found the government GUILTY. That literally happened— google it. Oh, we're getting another round? Modelo, please!"*

Our conversations leveled up from there. I thought of Eden as a teacher, but she directed me to the people she'd learned from, insisting she was not the authority—just a white

---

* There's plenty of reading for more deets on this, but I'd recommend starting with the 1999 *New York Times* article "Memphis Jury Sees Conspiracy in Martin Luther King's Killing," which states the jury found "Loyd Jowers as well as 'others, including governmental agencies'" responsible.

woman relieved to have someone else in the office who cared. Any time we got an actual work assignment, we spent ten minutes on task before switching into study mode: I shared something I'd learned, then she suggested a podcast,[*] book,[†] or article[‡] to build on it. Whenever I thanked her for these recommendations, she grew uncomfortable, making it clear yet again that she was not the original source. Sometimes Eden put forth facts that were hard for me to accept, which inevitably sent me into a spiral—I ruminated on the ideas, objected to them, then finally started to understand. I'd never had a friendship that was simultaneously so effortless and illuminating,[§] let alone one that so routinely passed the Bechdel test (unless we'd had a few drinks).

After I'd been at the PR agency for a year, Harvey Weinstein got the public shaming he deserved. The #MeToo movement, started by Tarana Burke in 2006, now spread across social media—it seemed like people were finally listening to survivors. Yet many people (cough men cough) continued to ask ignorant questions, burdening women and other trauma survivors[¶] to relive their experiences and shoulder the labor of education. For Eden and me, doing labor around racial justice was mandatory, since neither of us experienced racism directly. But we did experience sexism directly, and grew evermore exhausted when we wound up explaining gender 101 to

---

[*] NPR's *Code Switch* and *Scene on Radio*'s "Seeing White."

[†] *Between the World and Me* by Ta-Nahisi Coates; *Assata: An Autobiography* by Assata Shakur; *The Cooking Gene* by Michael W. Twitty; and *Bad Feminist* by Roxane Gay.

[‡] Ijeoma Oluo's "Welcome to the Anti-Racism Movement—Here's What You've Missed," which Eden referenced to me over and over again.

[§] This illumination was often painful, as confronting one's own role as an oppressor should be—as the writer and educator Rachel Cargle (@rachel.cargle) says, "Anti-racism work is not a self-improvement exercise for white people."

[¶] Many of whom were, in fact, men.

our male colleagues. Yes, we told them, we walked home with our keys between our knuckles; yes, we put our hands over our drinks; yes, we both had been sexually harassed. As annoying as these conversations were, Eden reminded me that we still had enormous privilege, with salaried day jobs that let us slack off while we took on these teaching roles.

When the news broke that comedian Louis C.K. had dangled his dick in the faces of multiple women, Eden and I headed straight for the gray office couches, a spot where we could hide from the four horsemen of the apocalypse (aka our four male creative directors, one of which saw #MeToo as an opportunity to win a Webby).

"Listen," Eden said once we were safely alone, "I hate the prison system. I don't think it works. I think it's racist and punishes you for being poor."

"Right," I agreed. I'd never considered this before, but it made sense.

"I'm not even sure what justice looks like," she continued, "but I know prison is not it. And all that said, I don't know what to do with these men! If I'm being honest, I want to lock them up. I want to send them to an island where we never have to see them or think about them or look at them again. I want them to suffer FOREVER." Her cheeks grew red and blotchy—I'd never seen her this worked up before.

I too hated these men—they were despicable abusers; their actions had effectively ruined the lives of multiple human beings. But for some reason, I couldn't bring myself to wish them off to an island or to pray that they'd disappear. Of course, it wasn't my job to decide what these men deserved—their punishment should've been determined by those they'd hurt. But as it was, the only real punishment the justice system offered was jail, and for the first time I considered how unproductive that seemed. Prison left so many questions unanswered: If we cast abusers out to the metaphorical (or literal) sea, what would happen when they inevitably came back—would they just exploit their power again? Could people be redeemed? Was it worth society's time (and money) to try? I realized how embarassing it was that I'd only now considered the prison system's efficacy—where had my energy been for millions of incarcerated Black people, Indigenous people, and people of color? How gross that I'd started asking these questions only when pondering the fates of abusive white men.

A few months later, a woman under the pseudonym "Grace" wrote about an uncomfortable, though arguably consensual, encounter with comedian Aziz Ansari. To process and procrastinate, Eden and I headed to the same gray couches, where she read out loud to me from a relevant think piece called "Consenting to Normal" by Hyejin Shim. Eden's face lit up, eyes racing through the text, and I realized this was the first time I'd borne witness to her own learning (she typically did this work on her own time—read the books, paid the sources,* and showed up the next day, already smarter than me).

"This essay is incredible," Eden gushed, and sent me the link. The piece argued that we need to reframe the entire way we think about sexual violence—as long as we see it through a binary lens (e.g., consensual/not consensual, legal/illegal, okay/not okay), the burden will still fall on survivors to definitively say "no." Shim pointed out that even the affirmative

---

* Send money to Black people you learn from on the internet!

consent model was far from survivor-centric: "Why is it that in so many purportedly 'feminist' opinions and re-writings, Ansari's actions remain unchanged, while Grace is the one who must be stronger, better, smarter, faster?"

"Damn," I said, but Eden didn't look up. Instead she read a different line out loud—a quote Shim had included from Indigenous writer Kelly Hayes: "We exceptionalize both 'good' and 'bad' people to spare ourselves the labor of interrogating normalcy—the very space in which most harm occurs."

I squinted. "So . . . what are we supposed to do, exactly?"

"Everything." Eden smiled. "We have to fix it all."

✳

Six months later, I was still single, Trump was still president, and Harvey Weinstein's trial still hadn't begun. People had gradually accepted the normalcy of this new era—collective outrage quieted to a hum, growing loud again only when news broke of anti-trans legislation, a heartbeat bill, or a xenophobic idea that would imminently be written into law. Injustice felt like dull, constant back pain: Unless our sciatic nerve was acting up, we simply learned to live with it.

I found myself growing nostalgic for the carefree drug-filled nights I'd loved before realizing I should care about other people and the world, and decided to return to a venue called Nowadays in Queens. The space felt like a hip greenhouse, hot-pink lights refracting off giant ferns, and the dance floor never got too crowded. Before entering paradise, all attendees agreed to a strict code of conduct: No racism, no transphobia, and no touching anyone without clearly expressed consent.

That night I went with some mutual friends, including Zack, a guy registered in my mental Rolodex as "that shy hot dude you talk to at parties sometimes." When our groups mingled, we somehow always found ourselves in a corner together, me usually breaking the silence by asking for music recommendations and details on upcoming sneaker collabs. These conversations clearly flattered Zack, giving him a chance to show off how much Hypebeast he'd read lately, and his eyes always went soft with gratitude, his social anxiety set at ease.

We'd spent about a year running into each other, but under Nowadays' rosy glow, I noticed his gaze lingering on me—his interest felt bigger and brighter, more romantic somehow. When our group moved to the dance floor, Zack and I stood in the back, inching closer together until we kissed.

"Took us long enough," he whispered. Interpreting that remark as a confession of enduring interest and thus a sign of safety, I thought, *Why not fall into this?* and pressed my forehead into his. I alternated between his mouth and my drink—he tasted like Altoids and the room smelled like smoke. We made out for hours, techno booming around us. Our friends shot dirty looks, suggesting we should get a room, and eventually we took the hint.

Zack's apartment was just as well put together as his outfits—the living room felt effortlessly minimal, decorated with a pearl-white couch, a silver side table, and a shag rug so fluffy it could've been snow. It seemed like one of those Instagram apartments that no one could actually live in, because who would possibly trust themselves around so much white decor?

He played Jorja Smith through a built-in speaker system,

and after checking my pants for dirt, I sat on the couch. We held beers as a formality, and I bobbed my head along with the song, telling him he had great taste.

He glowed. "Maybe I could make you a playlist this week."

"That would be nice."

In 2018, a playlist had about 30 percent as much game as a mixtape once did, but 30 percent was enough for me. We fucked for hours, alternating between the couch and the rug. He touched me like I was made of silk, sliding his fingers across my body, his hands learning all of my curves. In his arms, I felt powerful, feminine, and soft.

I didn't want the sex to end, but when it did, I checked the couch and rug for stains, relieved we hadn't left one. *What kind of person has sex like THAT in a room like THIS?* I thought, unsure whether I was judging him or myself.

By then it was four a.m., and Zack asked me to stay the night. A bed did sound nice—certainly nicer than a forty-five-minute Lyft back to my place. I followed him to his room, and we climbed onto his mattress—it was pressed against the wall, beneath a window to the black night sky. Looking up, searching for stars, I stretched out underneath the sheets and shut my eyes.

It felt like only one hour had passed before I woke up to Zack pulling me toward him. At first it seemed sweet, like he wanted to spoon, so I pressed my ass backward, grazing the tops of his thighs. He must have taken this as a signal for something else, because his hands moved down to my underwear and tugged. I tossed his arms aside and muttered a groggy "Not right now" before falling back asleep.

A few hours later, I opened my eyes to an azure sky in the window above, then registered that Zack's hands were on my body again. He was trying to flip me over to face him, and I clearly hadn't woken up as quickly this time.

"No," I insisted, pushing him away with slightly more force. "I'm too tired."

I felt his hands retract, and though I was annoyed that I'd had to tell him twice, at least this time he seemed to listen. I drifted back to sleep.

The third time I woke up, I saw a baby-blue sky—it was dawn. But instead of seeing the window from below, I was now staring directly out of it, my eyes suddenly level with a tree branch outside. I could tell I was sitting upright, and also that I'd gotten here fast. I felt dizzy, like I'd just ridden the Tilt-A-Whirl. Had someone swung me into this position? How could I be here when I'd just been lying down, asleep?

Disoriented, I looked down at Zack. His eyes were shut—he didn't seem wide awake, but he wasn't asleep. He'd pulled me on top of him, and now fumbled between my legs, tugging my underwear out of the way to put himself inside.

My body shook, suddenly filled with shock and fear. Before I could figure out how I'd misjudged my connection with Zack to this degree, I had to determine what to do next. Regardless of who'd started this (though that had been him—duh), it was now up to me to make it stop.

In my tired stupor, I ran through the options:

OPTION 1: REACT APPROPRIATELY (ideal)

Goal: GTFO ASAP.

How It Works: Scream, "What the fuck are you doing?!," then call yourself a Lyft. Block his number. Cancel him on Twitter. Ruin his life.

Pro: He gets what he deserves.

Con: You look like a *teensy* bit of a bitch in front of a guy you thought you liked.

OPTION 2: REACT "LIKE A LADY" (not ideal)

Goal: Escape, but in a chill way!

How It Works: Politely dismount and make an excuse for your abrupt departure.

Pro: You can still date him (even though he assaulted you).

Con: You can still date him (even though he assaulted you).

OPTION 3: DO NOT REACT (*EXTREMELY* not ideal)

Goal: Cause the least amount of drama.

How It Works: Do nothing. At least you can control your attitude while it happens—feel free to get frigid or to fake an orgasm to pass the time. Once it's over, you can leave. Or you can stay for breakfast! (That is—if you're invited.)

Pro: You'll expend zero effort—this is the glorious path of least resistance.

Cons: Everything. All the cons. But especially the fact that you'll soon start to consider yourself complicit in your own sexual assault. It won't be your fault, of course, but it's certainly going to *feel* like it is. Are you sure you can handle that right now?

He was inside me already—every second I delayed a decision felt like giving him permission to stay. *There's still time to pick Option 1!* my brain shouted. But my body, too tired to fight, chose Option 3.

I remained on top of him, glancing around as if someone might show up and rescue me. A minute passed and my shoulders relaxed. The birds outside chirped. I heard myself moan.

When I got home on Sunday, I threw myself into a frenzied fit of productivity—I got a head start on work, ran six miles, and did a week's worth of meal prep (for the first and last time in my life). But whenever I slowed down, I noticed the shame again, like dishes in the sink I'd hoped would wash themselves. Rationally I knew I wasn't responsible for the way I had (or hadn't) reacted—when someone puts you between a rock and a hard place, it's not your fault if you can't tunnel your way out. But I felt guilty for not protecting myself, and for making a sound designed to convince him that he'd actually done something right.

After my errands, I fell onto my bed, using my phone's selfie camera to stare at my puffy face. I studied the dry spot next to my lip, traced the yellowing spots beneath my eyes. I looked pathetic. *Has #MeToo really taught you nothing about self-respect? About speaking up? And you couldn't even make it to the mirror to confront your spinelessness? Great—you're lazy too.* I was victim-blaming, which is never okay, even to yourself. But acknowledging that didn't make me stop.

In stillness, regret consumed me; yet at the same time, I knew so many other people had been through similar or worse assaults—mine had not been remarkable in any way. It wasn't the first time I'd had nonconsensual sex,* but it *was* the first

---

* There's no such thing as "nonconsensual sex" because nonconsensual sex is rape. As Carmen Maria Machado writes in her *New Yorker* piece about *Promising Young Woman*, "Rape does not go away when you refuse to say it. Euphemisms are death."

time it had happened after my own dawn of unlearning—the first time that I knew better and had been cognizant enough to stop it. Until the #MeToo movement, I'd carried a shameful secret: I harbored a tiny bit of disrespect for survivors who'd been broken by assaults like my own; people who treated these violating acts as anomalies rather than inevitabilities, who sought support groups and seemed triggered by the news. My twisted logic was that, if I'd been able to deal with these realities for so long, why couldn't they? Even before #MeToo, I must have known this perspective was disgusting—people were entitled to have their own feelings about their own experiences (and it wasn't even a matter of entitlement, considering none of us could control our trauma responses in the first place). But I struggled to find compassion for others' outrage toward something that I'd seen as "just a part of life." In reality, I was probably jealous of anyone strong enough to confront their past—they reminded me that I hadn't really done that yet. Seeing other survivors speak out forced me to reflect: If their assaults had been unacceptable, maybe mine were unacceptable too.

I didn't tell anyone what had happened with Zack—I was far too ashamed. Even though I'd done nothing wrong, I couldn't stop thinking that I'd had some stake in the events, and so at the height of a movement about speaking out, I stayed quiet, feeling like a disappointment to the cause.

But fortunately, that Monday at work, Eden didn't ask many questions about my weekend. We had a different topic to discuss: alternatives to police. We huddled together, once again sheltered by a glass conference room while we discussed the ills of the world.

Recently the news had been full of disgusting stories of

white people calling the cops on Black people just for existing, and though this phenomenon was by no means new, the media attention was. White people had called the cops on Black people for waiting at a Starbucks, for golfing too slowly, and for refusing to pay for plastic utensils at Waffle House. The latter incident involved police brutality—officers threw a woman named Chikesia Clemons to the diner floor and threatened to break her arms. Black people, Eden told me, were (and are) three times more likely than white people to be killed by the police. Calling 911 didn't ensure safety for everyone—and for Black people, it often did the exact opposite.

According to sitcoms, cops helped everyone—they were good guys who ate donuts and rescued cats from trees.* But by now I'd watched Ava DuVernay's *13th* and had learned how deeply the prison system was rigged against Black people—while white men had a one in seventeen chance of incarceration, the odds for Black men were one in three.

"If we shouldn't call the cops, what should we do?" I asked.

Within seconds, Eden found a blog post by a writer named Aaron Rose titled "What to Do Instead of Calling the Police." My cheeks grew hot; I was embarrassed that I'd thought the question was so complex when answers were just a quick Google search away.

The post focused on tactics of bystander intervention, specifically ways to deescalate if a conflict arose. But big picture, the post pushed readers to think beyond carceral solutions, directing us toward resources about transformative and restorative justice. While the legal system asked, "What laws has

---

* I'm grateful for Natasha Rothwell's set in 2020's *Yearly Departed*, which features a eulogy for TV cops. She says TV cops never failed to make her laugh, citing the time one said, "We're gonna treat everyone equally," as "the funniest shit I've ever heard."

this offender broken, and how can we punish them?," these approaches centered the victim, asking, "What harm has the offender caused, and what can they do to repair it?"

Restorative justice, we learned, involved bringing affected parties together to discuss how the person who'd caused harm could make amends. These conversations were heavily structured, designed to engender empathy, helping each side see the other's humanity again. After all parties connected (which often took more than one conversation), the offender apologized. But rather than the kind of bullshit "I'm sorry" that the word "apology" connotes, restorative justice pushed offenders to acknowledge the harm they'd caused, expressing true remorse and setting an action plan toward change so it would never happen again. The victim then decided if the apology was good enough—if not, the offender tried again.

Transformative justice meant applying these humanity-driven ideas at scale, examining the root causes of conflict and the systems that put them in place. Both approaches seemed slightly idealistic,* but they exposed what needed to be done, and offered a more nuanced, less racist solution than prisons, police, and courts. I gazed upward and felt my face brighten—maybe a better future did exist.

The primary challenge seemed to be that enacting this kind of justice put the onus back on the victim, forcing them to eventually "forgive" their offender (and most likely relive their trauma along the way). Even I knew that piling work onto survivors was a hard no—someone who'd suffered from abuse (or any crime) had already been through enough. But

---

* It may have *seemed* idealistic to me, but, as the end of Shim's "Consenting to Normal" addresses, many groups are already doing this work—Philly Stands Up, generationFIVE, and Safe OUTside the System, to name a few.

fidgeting in my swivel chair, considering how to deal with Zack, I could understand why a survivor might actually see this approach as a blessing rather than a burden. Fighting violence with incarceration was like seeking an eye for an eye, but what if there was an option that could bring healing to all parties? What if you could actually witness your abuser evolve?

Until recently, I'd assumed the state's disciplinary system worked—that it helped us give offenders "what they deserved." But I'd never taken a step back, never considered how the sheer existence of prisons stripped victims of any ability to decide what justice actually meant to us. Since prisons were the only viable option, we were fed dreams of revenge—the idea that "justice" looked like forcing our abusers to spend the rest of their lives in regret, whether inside a cell or dealing with the repercussions of a criminal record outside of one. Not only was this a lie—out of every 1,000 sexual assaults, only four would be incarcerated—but it made no sense: Just because someone went to jail or had their voting rights witheld didn't mean they were healed. Prisons conflated accountability with vengeance, but these alternatives promised something more: rehabilitation, redemption, and a future beyond social death.

I thought about Zack, wondering what I wanted. Ideally, a time machine—a chance to not spend the night, or at least to choose something other than Option 3. Since that wasn't possible, I felt torn—he deserved to suffer, but I also craved a more tangible, longer-lasting accountability. Galvanized by these ideas, I decided that talking to Zack would make me feel better. At minimum, it would let me imbue my assault with political significance. And at maximum, it would give Zack the opportunity to teach me something radical: that people could actually change.

I considered using restorative justice principles, but quickly realized that having this conversation by the book wasn't going to work. Most conflict resolution guides had hundreds of pages outlining the importance of trained facilitators and community support. It didn't occur to me that there may have been a reason these conversations had so much structure, and that by deviating from that structure, I wasn't really practicing restorative justice at all. The only thing I knew for sure was that I felt empowered again, and I wanted to confront Zack ASAP. Fuck it—I'd do it alone. What could possibly go wrong?

✴

As excited as I thought I was to have this conversation, I kept stalling, and before I could text Zack, he texted me. He sent the sparkle pink heart emoji followed by a link to a playlist. I tapped the Spotify link and the chirpy pop of Easyfun filled the room. Exasperated by the contrast of the music and my emotional state, I groaned.

For the first time, it occurred to me that Zack didn't realize he'd done anything wrong (they rarely do). Why else would he be contacting me with such an innocent text? I had to confront him now—for myself, yes, but also to ensure that his ignorant ass never did this again.

Despite being emotionally tormented, I didn't want to seem "crazy" (perish the thought!), so I engineered the most casual confrontation I could. I asked a mutual friend to play middleman and invite both Zack and me to a concert in Bushwick the following week, hoping a crowded public place would give us some much-needed nonchalance.

The night of the show, I craved the confidence that came from a great outfit, so I put on my best sneakers and a new sweater. It was tennis-ball yellow and hugged my curves perfectly, like the top half of a Sexy Highlighter Halloween costume. On the way out the door, I caught myself wondering whether Zack would like my outfit, which made me wonder if I only wanted to "confront him" so I would get to see him again. I couldn't tell whether I was strong for attempting my own version of alternative justice, or weak for being unable to cut my abuser out of my life. (In reality, I was neither—just a survivor, trying to cope as best she could.)

Across the crowd of concertgoers, I noticed Zack immediately—his striped shirt stood out, since everyone else wore all black. Ugh, he looked good. I tensed up at the sight of him, my shoulders lifting an inch toward my ears. After weaving through the mob, he hugged me, oblivious to the thought that I wouldn't be thrilled to see him. I struggled to match his warmth since I felt like a covert supervillain—I had the nuclear codes, the ability to ruin his night.

In hindsight it's obvious that a crowded concert was a terrible environment for this conversation—my desire to seem carefree had led me into a trap. I waited until our group inevitably moved to the bar next door, but even that was packed like a hipster clown car. The place gave off an intentionally-under-construction vibe, like it was too avant garde to have finished walls. People danced under wooden rafters, and everyone got an armpit in their face.

I bought a Topo Chico and a vodka shot, then snagged a bench seat, planning to thumb through my phone as the crowd trickled out. But before I could even open Instagram, Zack sat down, squeezing into the sliver of space beside me, his thigh touching mine.

"You've been distant tonight," he said, narrowing his eyes.

The statement was clearly a question—he studied my face like it was a lamp he couldn't figure out how to turn on.

"I know, I just . . ." I sighed. I should've asked him to coffee instead. Three strangers scooted past us, their bodies annoyingly close to our bench, and one accidentally spilled beer on my shoes. I broke Zack's gaze to glare at them.

"Do you want to go somewhere we can talk?" he suggested. Apparently he was hyper-attuned to my comfort now. "My place?"

I clutched my stomach almost instinctively—the thought of returning to his apartment filled me with dread. I didn't want to see his bedroom window or beautiful living room again. I could call him tomorrow—start over; try the coffee thing. But he was right there in front of me, wide-eyed and sincere. I wanted to do it tonight, but the bar was still swarming with people. I sighed, and decided I'd rather make a mistake than a scene.

"Fine. But just to be clear, we're only talking."

"Of course," he replied, and I believed him.

We took a car to his apartment, sitting in silence on opposite sides of the backseat. After climbing his stairs and seeing his furniture again, I gulped. I sat on the spotless couch, my neon top emitting a glow (cheerful aura, come through!). Zack started to grab drinks from the fridge, but I stopped him: "Not for this." He nodded, then sat down, leaning toward me.

"What's on your mind?"

"Honestly, I . . . I'm not feeling great about last time." I crossed my arms.

"Okay. Say more." He swallowed so hard I could hear it. He was listening—like *really* listening, ready to receive.

"I . . . just . . . don't feel like . . . I don't know," I sputtered.

My heart thumped beneath my sweater. Zack's eyes were still wide, his mind still attuned.

"I don't feel like I wanted it," I blurted. "In the morning. I think I said no." I couldn't stop the words from coming—they were like blood spurting from a wound. "I don't think it was consensual. I stopped you multiple times. And actually—it's not 'I think I said no,' because I *did* say no. And you still tried to fuck me. You tried to fuck me while I was asleep. Three times. I said 'stop' three times. Well, technically I said 'stop' twice. But the last time I only pretended to enjoy it, because I woke up on top of you, and pretending was easier."

Instantly I felt lighter, like I'd tossed a trash bag down the garbage chute and would never have to smell it again. I straightened my spine.

"Wow," Zack said, shaking his head. "That's awful. I'm so incredibly sorry I made you feel that way."

"Whoa, there—it's not just that you made me *feel* some way," I insisted. "Don't act like my emotions are the problem. You did something bad. You . . . you know. Don't make me say the word." Naming the act would make the trauma too real (apparently I'd forgotten that making trauma real was the task at hand).*

"I won't." He shifted his body toward me, then picked up my hands, sandwiching them both between his. "But honestly, thank you for telling me. I'm so sorry. I feel terrible. You should never have to feel like that. It will never happen again."

"Okay. Uh, great." My heartbeat slowed. I couldn't believe how well he was taking this. I looked at the floor again and, on the way, caught a glimpse of his six-pack through his shirt.

---

* As usual, I should've listened to Carmen Maria Machado.

NO, my brain shouted. *Don't do this, Jen.*

But he looks so good! my brain replied. *And he's so nice—he just took accountability!*

Accountability? Psssh. That was just an apology, and an apology without change is just manipulation. True accountability requires action. And even if Zack became a literal saint, it wouldn't mean you had to sleep with him again.

I know I don't have to. But what if . . . I want to?

Ugh, FINE. My brain sighed. *Go ahead. But fool you twice, shame on you.*

I snapped back to reality and realized Zack was staring at my lips. "Is it okay if I kiss you?"

Instead of saying yes, I kissed him first.

After that, everything happened fast. In an effort not to overthink, I focused on the physical sensations: He traced his finger down my chest, as if wiping dust off the side of a fridge. Our lips touched. Clothes fell. And just like that, we'd done it again. Somehow it felt as good as the first time.

As we lay on the rug, I rested my head on his chest. I couldn't decide how to feel. I wasn't exactly a feminist warrior for sleeping with my abuser, or for "facilitating" that joke of an accountability conversation. But was I glad to have slept with him? Annoyed at myself? Guilty? Pleased? I had no idea. My eyes started to shut but I jerked them open, looking at the clock on his microwave: four a.m. Again. Seeing this, I sprang to my feet and fumbled around for my clothes—I had to get out of there, no matter how tired I was. But just as I found my sweater, Zack said the magic words.

"You're welcome to spend the night."

I glared at him, balled-up neon in hand. "I . . . shouldn't."

"I get why you wouldn't want to," he continued, bashfully

patting his hair. "But it's late, so if you want to stay, you're invited. Either way, I get it. And either way, I promise—it'll never happen again."

"I'm so tired." I yawned.

"Your call." He tossed his hands up. "If it makes you feel better, you can even sleep on the couch."

I didn't process that *he* should've offered to sleep on the couch—I heard only what I wanted to hear: Zack had made a mistake, I'd called him on it, and he'd taken some version of accountability. He seemed to feel truly sorry—as much as someone could feel sorry the same night they learned they'd done something wrong.

I felt drained, the evening's intensity catching up with me. Even if I did call a Lyft, I wasn't sure I'd make it to the car. Staying was the safest option—I could leave first thing in the morning. And even though he'd offered it, the couch seemed awkward. I dropped the sweater, put on my bra and underwear, and followed him into his room.

Could people change? I fell asleep thinking they could, smiling ever so slightly at the optimistic idea. But when I woke up hours later, morning light peeking through the trees, my body suddenly on top of Zack's again, I realized I was wrong. Or maybe I was right, but I'd been trying to take too many shortcuts—maybe true change did require a facilitator, a hundred-page manual, and the strength to tell your friends.

At least this time, I managed to choose Option 1—the option that meant shedding dead weight from your life rather than living with regret. I shouted, "WHAT THE FUCK ARE YOU DOING?!" and leapt off the bed. Zack seemed half asleep as I hurriedly unplugged my phone and stormed into the living room, picking up my clothes with one hand and calling a Lyft with the other.

My car arrived in two minutes. As I laced up my boots, I caught a glimpse of the couch. It was still bright white, except for the spot where I'd sat the night before, which now was covered with a massive neon splotch. I rubbed my eyes to make sure it wasn't gunk left on my lashes, but the color didn't go away.

It wasn't until I was halfway home that I realized: My new shirt had stained his perfect home; his perfect couch. I gasped.

This wasn't exactly restorative justice. It wouldn't single-handedly abolish the prison system. It wouldn't grant anyone large-scale liberation.

But in some small way, it was revenge.

KNOTS

IT IS MARCH 2017, and according to my Instagram, I am a bad bitch. I've filled my grid with memes encouraging women to reclaim our sexual prowess; to take pleasure into our own hands.

One says: BE A SLUT—DO WHATEVER YOU WANT!

Another quotes Nicki Minaj: I DEMAND THAT I CLIMAX. I THINK WOMEN SHOULD DEMAND THAT.

And, of course, Audre Lorde: WE HAVE BEEN RAISED TO FEAR THE "YES" WITHIN OURSELVES.

I caption each with a feminist affirmation and/or fuck-you: YOU'RE NOT INTIMIDATING—THEY'RE JUST INTIMIDATED or THERE'S NO SUCH THING AS ASKING FOR TOO MUCH 🖤

I post each of these while I'm horizontal, shit-faced on my couch, my fingers covered in orange dust from a bag of

Ruffles Cheddar and Sour Cream. I call this position Warrior 4 (Breakup Recovery Posture), and the Instagrams are part of it—as a brutal affront to the women's rights movement, the only reason I'm sharing empowering memes right now is to convince my ex-boyfriend that he made a mistake.

That ex is Ian, the guy who dumped me two weeks ago. Ian was the first boyfriend I'd seen as a partner—he seemed responsible enough to copilot a life with, and though I never cleaned my shower and didn't understand how insurance worked, he made me feel like I might be responsible enough too. He was, regrettably, a finance bro, but at least he was the kind who voted for local Democrats and claimed to be in touch with his feminine side (because he had a sister and stepped foot inside a Zara once). On weekdays, he slicked back his hair, his vibe somewhere between used Cadillac salesman and Draco Malfoy. I overlooked the sleaziness because he had a good heart and always championed my passion for social change. Only later did I realize that he saw my activism as a cute hobby—when I hosted a consciousness-raising for women to share their struggles obtaining birth control, he called and said, "Knock 'em dead, ladies!" like we were selling Mary Kay.

If I'm being honest, at least part of my interest in Ian had to do with the fact that he was rich.[*] I told people my favorite thing about him was his ambition, but anyone close to me knew "ambition" was code for "ability to fly me to Ibiza in Delta Comfort+." We met in college, and when we finally started dating five years later, we were long-distance

---

[*] Another brutal affront to the women's rights movement.

the entire time—he had a big-shot job at a start-up* and right after we'd first kissed, he'd temporarily relocated to Shanghai. But thanks to his money and corporate access, the distance was easy, and we made it fun. We saw each other every month, meeting in destinations like Cambodia and Hong Kong. We always fantasized about future travel plans, with the tacit understanding that he'd be the one to finance those dreams.

Ian described our relationship as "easy" and "low-maintenance," which seemed like the highest compliments a girl could get. I patted myself on the back but also felt an underlying fear—deep down, I must have known that our dynamic revolved entirely around his needs and hinged on the assumption that I wouldn't complain. Sure—in my heart, I wanted a partner who lived in the same city, who would prioritize me, and who didn't legitimately like the Chainsmokers. But I knew that, in exchange for keeping these truths to myself, I'd get to live out a Cinderella fantasy (if Cinderella felt guilty for not hating capitalism enough).

The extravagant trips held me over for a year, but after that I needed more. One night, I decided to fight for myself—I FaceTimed Ian and insisted he talk to his boss about coming home. "I don't care *when*," I explained. "Just give me literally any concrete date." I didn't want to seem demanding (god forbid!), and figured this plea was open-ended enough to count as a compromise.

But alas.

---

* I won't name this start-up but will say that they later had quite a few PR disasters, and I watched each unfold with popcorn in hand.

"I'm never gonna be able to give you enough," Ian responded, shaking his head, and within minutes he was choking back tears. He seemed legitimately upset by the thought of losing me (which I loved), but not upset enough to ask his boss for the information. Realistically I would've suffered through a few more months of not knowing, but Ian said this wasn't fair to me (he was the expert, after all). Ladies, is it asking for too much to want to live on the same continent as your partner? Apparently so. Ian also explained that he'd used our relationship as an escape, a way to avoid assimilating into Shanghai by keeping one foot in New York. I, the long-distance girlfriend, had been his excuse to look at his phone instead of the new city around him. Yet even now, two weeks after our breakup, he's still watching every Instagram story I post within seconds—seems like that digital detox is going well.

Aside from curating feminist memes in hopes my ex-boyfriend might see them, my post-breakup life consists of two other pastimes: (1) going on dating apps, and (2) getting drunk. Ruffles aren't the most substantial meal, so tonight the wine hits me hard. In a blur, I message a man from Tinder and we set plans for Sunday.

A Brooklyn tiki bar at five p.m.—it's a date.

＊

His voice is the first thing I notice. It's syrupy and confident, sultry and masculine—the kind that, even just when saying "Hey" from across the bar, slips past your ears and shakes your pelvis awake. The second thing I notice is that he's wearing a T-shirt, which bums me out. It's not that I need my dates to wear button-ups (that's Ian's style, and thus even worse), but it's always disappointing to confront that I, the woman, had to put more effort into my look. Though my lace-up boots barely qualify as heels, I did spend at least thirty minutes on my makeup—twenty minutes longer than usual. I want to be annoyed, but then he says more words, and I forget any patriarchal vendettas against him.

"You must be Jen." Each syllable hits me like fresh air. His name is Elias, and I say I've never heard this name spoken aloud outside of a church. He says it's Hebrew, actually, but he's a Catholic-school dropout. Now noticing his beard, I say he looks like the Bed-Stuy version of Jesus Christ.

"I'll take it." Elias smirks.

He walks toward the mahogany bar, orders for us, then waits for our drinks. As he stands I ogle him, gaining a more intimate understanding of his beard—it's long enough to convey his own maturity, but short enough that I could kiss him without getting a rash. His shiny brown eyes remind me of marbles, and when he looks at a fluorescent flamingo on a nearby wall, I find myself getting jealous of the bird.

After fully taking stock of his appearance, I realize I have no recollection of him from the app—his messages, bio, and photos are a blur. I could check my phone to review our conversation, but something tells me not to—this feels like a rare opportunity to make a first impression in real life. Online dating means your curated profile will always precede you, yet this night had managed to evade preconceptions; it had no existing script. After a year of structuring my relationship around time zones, itineraries, and logistics, not to mention being Ian's distraction from reality, here's a chance to take someone as he is, and to invite him to do the same to me.

Elias returns with the drinks. We sit on two barstools, our

knees knocking together. To keep things analog, I ask get-to-know-you questions, and though they're just an excuse to hear him talk, I learn a lot: He's South African, rides a motorcycle, and is currently doing a PhD on street art at Cornell.

"I love Banksy," I blurt, then frown. "Oh god, so basic. Please don't walk out."

Elias laughs. "Banksy's all right."

I mime wiping sweat from my brow. "Phew!"

We spend an hour talking about how street art deserves more critical acclaim. I'm grateful to be an armchair scholar, and I regurgitate things I learned from the brochures at—yes—Banksy's MOCA exhibit in LA years ago: Street art brings high culture to the masses. Street art subverts everything—cities, global power dynamics, and everyday objects themselves. And most importantly, street art works within the confines of ephemerality. The form itself is a study in non-attachment—any mural could get painted over at any time.

"I like to say graffiti is best served hot," Elias tells me, sucking a drop of stray tequila off his finger.

"That's a sexy line," I reply. "But you already know that, don't you?"

He grins.

Next I ask about his favorite piece, and Elias brings up 5 Pointz in Long Island City. I know the space—a warehouse that would've blended into the surrounding factories if artists hadn't covered it with Technicolor murals and huge-scale tags. Elias tells me that countless hours went into those walls and artists finally thought they had a canvas that might last. But one night in 2013, the building developer decided to whitewash the warehouse without warning, demolishing the work for good. Now the 5 Pointz tragedy had become part of the broader street art legacy. It served as a reminder that all graffiti (and all things, tbh) were impermanent, no matter how certain they might seem.

Elias tells me he makes ends meet by supporting the legal team fighting for those artists and what was taken from them. Regardless of how I feel, or will feel, about the justice system, this is a noble pursuit, and it turns me the hell on. He gets another round of drinks, and when he returns, I'm buzzed enough to ask: "Remind me, what did we talk about on Tinder—was it street art?"

He raises an eyebrow.

"I was, er, kinda drunk when we matched," I elaborate. "Just trying to figure out how you convinced me to come here and talk about your dissertation for two hours."

He laughs. "Hold up, though—you messaged *me*."

"I did?!" I recoil, then remind myself that it's 2017—I'm allowed to text first.

"It was pret-ty forward," he says à la Larry David, then smirks.

"You seem like you know something I don't."

Elias studies my face, as if unsure whether to say what he's going to say next. After a few seconds, he gives in. "You said, 'I want you to teach me shibari.'"

"*What?!*" My mouth drops open. Shibari is the Japanese art of rope-tying, a kink I've seen on Tumblr and have fantasized about—heavily—before. It involves using rope to tie someone's arms behind their back, and often includes hoisting that person from a rafter, suspending them in the air. I loved how it looked, but also how it positioned the tied-up person as the center of attention—exactly where I wanted to be. "Well, that was presumptuous of me."

I lean back on my barstool, hoping this body language will trick him into thinking I'm hard to get.

Elias shrugs. "Not really. I mean, my profile literally says, 'Message me if you want to learn shibari.'"

Now I raise *my* eyebrow. I always assumed that guys with BDSM-related mentions in their bios were desperate catfish, almost worse than men who posed with an actual fish they'd caught. But Elias seemed great, and in retrospect, how fucking refreshing that he'd been forthcoming about what he liked. I made a mental note to never kink-shame again.

"How much do you already know about it?" he asks.

"Not much. I've always wanted to learn more, but every time I google it, I wind up getting turned on by the pictures and the rest is history."

"I know the feeling." He laughs, then spreads out on the barstool, fitting both of my legs between his. "If you're curious, I'll show you."

I glance down, then glance up. He's holding me like Suzanne Somers with a ThighMaster—ready to squeeze.

"You'll show me?"

"Yeah."

"Then consider this a consultation." I put on my best corporate role-play voice. "I'm interested in your services but need more detail. What does a typical session look like?"

"Thank you for inquiring, ma'am," he replies. "First I would lean across this barstool and kiss you. It would be wet, but I wouldn't use my tongue."

"Uh-huh." I lean further back to offset how much I want to lurch forward.

"Then I would ask if you want me to tie you up tonight. And you would reply . . . ?"

I know my lines. "Yes. I do."

"We'd take my bike back to my place, the engine vibrating between our legs."

I've never wanted to ride a motorcycle before, but suddenly the thought of it practically makes me drool.

"At home, I ask you to take off your clothes, then get on the bed. In tabletop position."

"Is this the part where—"

"No talking." He lifts his hand, like I'm a dog who'd better behave. "This is the part where you let me take control."

My blood rushes between my legs—it takes every ounce of my discipline not to strip down, straddle him, and fuck him right here. I bite my lip as a performative act of restraint (visual reference: fuckboy emoji). Without breaking eye contact, he brings his hand to my face and tugs my lip out from under my teeth. Then he presses a finger to my mouth, as if to say, *"Shhh."* I shiver in ecstasy, trying to tune out the perky Dolly Parton song that just came on.

"As I was saying," Elias continues, "you're on the bed. I come up behind you, put my hand on the small of your back. I glide my palm up your spine, and once my hand is between your shoulder blades, I press you down, face-first. Your makeup smears all over my sheets.

"You moan, but the mattress muffles the sound. Your ass is up, and I keep one hand holding your back down, so I can spank you with the other—hard. Then I tell you to stay there, to keep that ass up for me, and you do. I get the ropes—one black, one red—and lift your arms, one by one, behind your back. I thread the black rope in and out, underneath and over again, wrapping it tight so you can't wriggle away.

"I tie the red one around your chest, looping it around

until your tits have their own little frame. There's rope between them so each one sticks out, two pointy presents just for me.

"I flip you over and onto a pillow so you can lean on your arms behind your back. Then I work my way down your body, starting with your mouth. I kiss you. I kiss your neck. I suck each one of those tits. I kiss your stomach. I kiss your hips. And finally I spread your legs. Like this." His hands, I notice, are massive and flat, and he slides one into the snug space between my thighs. Once it's there, he makes it into a fist—this causes my legs to jut outward, knocking into his, and both our bodies lift like we're in a car that just went over a speed bump. I gasp—this feels so good, it's hard to believe he didn't actually enter me. I lean forward, anything to be closer to his face. He meets me in the middle, his beard mere inches from my skin.

Ah, I think. *When Ian said he could never give me enough, this was what he meant.*

"Do you want to come over now?" Elias asks. Still silent, I nod. He leads me out to the curb where his motorcycle's parked, and I realize our reenactment starts here. My mom always warned me about riding one of these, and the nerves must show on my face.

"You ready?"

I make a so-so gesture, then he hands me a helmet. I snap it on. "How 'bout now?" My shoulders relax, I nod. He's already so mindful, and it occurs to me why that's so important: Because submission relies on the element of consent. I can already tell that the most intoxicating part of our night is the fact I've opted in—I've made a conscious decision to surrender, a calculated choice to release. Consent isn't just mandatory—

it's integral to pleasure, providing a bungee cord so both of us can fully let go.*

He swings his leg over the chassis and I awkwardly do the same, then scoot forward and wrap my arms around his chest. The wind blows in our faces for six blocks. I take deep breaths, trying not to think about crashing or what might be happening to my hair.

We climb the stairs to his apartment, a studio filled with glossy art books and a birchwood canopy bed he built himself (because of course he did). Within seconds, his play-by-play proves accurate: He presses me onto the bed. My makeup smears. He gets the black rope first, then the red, then flips me onto the pillow, kissing down my body in a line. He takes each breast in his mouth as if it is, indeed, a gift. Finally, the moment I've been waiting for arrives: He spreads my legs.

When he enters me, I gasp like I did at the bar, but this time it's loud enough for his neighbors to hear. Our movements sync up, our rhythm aligns. The climax strikes me like a lightning bolt, arcing through my body before release.

After I finish a few more times, he unties me. I tilt my chin down and peer up at him. "How do I follow that?"

"You don't," he replies.

I sigh, both relieved and delighted, shocked it's taken many years of my life to feel this good. I stare up at the bed frame, studying the woodgrain. I wonder if we'll see each other again or if, like the walls of 5 Pointz, it wasn't meant to last.

---

* Lina Dune (@askasub) writes that BDSM communities have a saying: "You can't give away power you don't have." Dune also points out that this power exchange can only occur when the submissive person allows it to happen, so maybe submissives have had the power all along.

The chemistry we had that night does seem to be gone forever—we sleep together several times over the next few months, but the excitement dwindles and it's never the same. We stop using the ropes. I start contributing in the bedroom, occasionally reverting to my Ian-era practice of giving head without asking for anything in return. Sometimes Elias and I go out to dinner, but whenever there's a lull in conversation, I'm far more relaxed about looking at my phone.

The more routine our relationship gets, the more I recognize that Elias was a rebound—an incredible rebound, but a rebound no less. It's likely that I played a similar role for him, and neither of us felt used because we were both using each other, working through our respective demons as a team.

We stop making an effort to hang out and our hookup cadence slows until it fades away. I don't see or hear from him until months later when we run into each other at a Williamsburg bodega and agree that we should grab a drink.

That night at a wine bar he asks what's new, and I tell him I'm trying to date women—for real this time. Aside from Ben and the occasional one-night stand, I keep my sexuality close to my chest—I mentioned it to Ian only once, in passing, and we never discussed it again.

"You're bi?" Elias perks up. "Same, actually."

"Seriously? What a pleasant surprise." I know some women claim to be turned off by male bisexuality,* but for me, it's always had the opposite effect. I see queerness as an indicator that someone is in touch with themselves, and Elias has al-

---

* Wanna hear some bullshit? In 2015, one third of Pornhub's gay male porn views came from women. And yet bisexual men still experience stigma, largely perpetuated by women—a 2019 study in the *Journal of Bisexuality* found that straight women rated bi men as less sexually and romantically attractive than straight men. Sigh.

ready proven that to be true. I rock back on my chair, relieved I'm not with Ian—having dinner on a yacht, wishing I could go home with one of the waitresses instead.

"It makes sense that you're bi, you know," I say between sips of wine. "Explains why you're the best sex I've ever had."

His cheeks flush. "Well. It takes two."

Outside the bar Elias kisses me, deep and wet, like it was back then. I long to feel the rush of blood I did that first night, but instead I feel preoccupied. I have a busy day tomorrow. I want to work out. And honestly, I'm just so damn sick of dating men. A few months ago, I probably would've just gone home with him and mentally checked out during sex. But Elias was the one who taught me that I deserve more. And honestly, he deserves more too.

"Soooo . . . you wanna come over, or . . . ?"

I take a deep breath and shake my head.

He nods, processing this. Our time is up.

"We did good, Jen." He pulls me into a hug.

"We sure did," I reply, face brushing against his beard.

Elias flags down a cab and puts me inside. As the car pulls away I stare out the window, trying to figure out how I feel. I'm proud for honoring the "yes" within myself, even though tonight that looked like saying "no." At least things ended before they got stale—best served hot, indeed.

PART III

I WANT TO BE QUEER ENOUGH

OUT OF THE WOODS

(Content Warning: Discussions of transphobia, racism, and police brutality)

CONGRATS ON MAKING it through the most male-dominated section of this book! For a minute there, maybe you wondered whether I, your bisexual narrator, was actually (gasp!) straight. I wouldn't be mad if that thought crossed your mind—sure, it's a tad biphobic, but an attraction to men can be disorienting. And if anyone understands that, it's me.

When I was in my mid-twenties, my interest in men constantly made me wonder if I was gay enough to come out. (Should I call this an insequeerity? Sound off in the comments!) I was waiting on some kind of external validation—any confirmation that I was, in fact, bi and had the right to say that out loud. But I was trapped in a loop: Since I rarely spoke about my sexuality, no one knew to give me said validation, thus I rarely spoke about my sexuality ... and repeat. To make a very straight reference and quote Chuck Klosterman, "The beginning is the end is the beginning."

I desperately wanted to be a "queer person," but in hindsight, I don't think I knew what that meant. I lacked imagination and couldn't conceive of queerness beyond individual sexual identity; I had no concept of collective liberation. I didn't understand that even on a personal level, queerness is not an end point but a practice—a process of self-interrogation to hold us accountable for growth and push us toward a better world.

I also later learned that being white and queer means sitting at a unique intersection of oppression and privilege. In a post-Trumpian era that fetishizes "diversity," white queer people (like me) are often viewed as marginalized, and though this isn't wrong, per se, it's not the whole story.[*] As Billy-Ray Belcourt writes, "Queers who ride the advantageous waves of whiteness slide smoothly into the depths of the normative"— white queers are markedly less oppressed than Black queer people, Indigenous queer people, and other queer people of color, facing lower risks of incarceration,[†] unemployment,[‡] and homelessness.[§]

---

[*] This reminds me of gender politics in the wake of #MeToo, when white women (also like me) were seen as victims of sexism, yet we still benefited from significant race-based privilege. At that cultural moment, white supremacy was not the system under fire, so when the world promised more women in leadership and equal pay, white women often advanced first, our successes once again arriving at the expense of Black women, Indigenous women, and women of color. This became known as "white feminism": an empowerment-driven politic that focused primarily on helping white ladies get ahead. (For more on this, read Rachel Cargle's essay for *Harper's Bazaar*, "When Feminism Is White Supremacy in Heels"; or read Kimberly Seals Allers's piece for *Slate*, "Rethinking Work-Life Balance for Women of Color.")

[†] In 2019, queer youth of color (specifically Black youth) had an increased risk of criminalization.

[‡] Black trans people had a 26 percent unemployment rate (twice the rate of trans people overall and four times the rate of the general population).

[§] Forty-two percent of Black trans people have experienced homelessness in their lives.

If I'd had a better grasp on these truths and had realized I wasn't the center of the world, I might have gone easier on myself while figuring out my sexuality. I might have recognized that queerness isn't about individual answers as much as collective questions. I might have understood queerness as a lens to help us envision the future: Did we really want to be "equal" by measure of a racist, sexist, monosexist society, or can we, perhaps, aim higher?

*

But at twenty-five I couldn't be bothered to think about anything bigger than myself. I'm sure part of this was white individualism, but another part of it was just lack of perspective—to recognize how queerness could benefit the greater good, I first had to understand how (or if) it benefited me.

Bisexuality made this complicated. I didn't feel straight but knew my actions suggested otherwise, as I'd already constructed my entire personality with the goal of impressing men: I listened to trap music, taught myself Settlers of Catan, and once spent $[redacted] on a shower curtain designed by Dave Eggers. But regardless of my target audience I felt confident, and for what seemed like the first time ever, I liked myself—I finally knew how to dress for my body; I'd developed the acumen and independence to go on a weeklong international vacation alone. I'd stepped into my womanhood and found power in that. Coming out didn't make sense unless I had somewhere to go.

I knew plenty of queer men, but the only out woman I knew was my coworker, an Australian lesbian named Claire. Though I didn't realize she was gay until she told me, she often came to work in garb that should have tipped me off, her wardrobe an ever-changing mix of flannels and Doc Martens. She loved to take up space, and I don't think I ever saw her cross her legs.

We worked at a media company (the one with the post-election puppies) where our desks faced each other's, and we shared the job title "Creative," which was a euphemistic way of saying we produced sponsored lists. We couldn't exactly be proud of a writing career with outputs like "Which Tide© Liquid Detergent is Most Compatible with Your Zodiac Sign? (QUIZ)" but we were internet nerds. What other workplaces had conference rooms named after famous cats, a "GIF of the Day" contest, and a week where staff were allowed—nay, encouraged—to take meetings wearing a Snuggie?

Our company loved showing up for social causes (idea: maybe start by paying your employees a living wage?), so when they announced that they'd sponsored a Pride float, the whole office was expected to attend the parade. At ten a.m. on a Sunday, I joined Claire at a bar—we spent the morning chugging whiskey gingers and tossing rainbow confetti around Sixth Ave. I felt honored to "show up for equal rights," though I didn't realize that an event full of cops and corporations was anything but progressive. I definitely didn't realize that the pursuit of equality was inherently a flawed mission, since it encouraged us to chase milestones that were only important because straight people had deemed them so. The hype around legalizing same-sex marriage even kept most LGBTQ+ people from looking at any underlying issues—it distracted us from questioning marriage as an institution or unpacking social reliance on monogamy itself. Years earlier, in 2010, activists and allies had begged to repeal "Don't ask, don't tell." What might have happened if the energy spent fighting for inclusive military policies had instead been used to critique the concept of war itself?

Years later, I learned a catchy word to describe this phenomenon: homonormativity. (At least it's slightly catchier than, say, "neoliberal hegemony of the queer community at large.") Professor Lisa Duggan popularized the term, writing, "We have been administered a kind of political sedative—we get marriage and the military, then we go home and cook dinner forever." Her point was that if we only focus on equality, we'll only end up achieving assimilation. While that's still a form of progress,* there's a blatant cognitive dissonance in associating "queer liberation" with access to straight white institutions.

But on a personal level for me back then, assimilation sounded like the dream. I'd managed to conquer the straight world, at least to some degree (read: I couldn't keep a boyfriend but I got laid a lot), and finding my place in the queer community felt like the next frontier. Claire and I had lunch together every day, and I listened intently as she taught me about media beloved by lesbians—cult movies like *But I'm a Cheerleader*, Sapphic shows like *Xena*, and innovative songwriters like Joanna Newsom. Claire's green eyes lit up when she talked about lesbian bars—she told me there were only so many left in the country, and that New York was lucky to have even a few. Mainstream media often portrayed WLW a specific way (rich, white, femme†) but if you looked back at Manhattan's lesbian

---

* It's especially important when we're talking on a global scale—as of 2019, seventy-two countries still criminalize homosexuality and eight still punish queer people by death.
† Yet again this relies on homonormativity—as Sherrie Inness writes: "By emphasizing that lesbians are beautiful, well dressed, and born to shop . . . writers build up an image of lesbians as being 'just like us'—or, in other words, 'homosexual = heterosexual.'"

bar scene through the '70s, '80s, and '90s, you'd see a wide range of music, styles, and clientele. From Bonnie & Clyde, a bar on Washington Square Park frequented primarily by Black women, to Sahara, whose name was thought to poke fun at NYC's lack of gender-expansive spaces (a desert, if you will), it was clear: There were so many ways to be gay. I was impressed, but I wasn't sure yet which of those ways applied to me.

Claire talked about New York's few remaining lesbian bars* as if they were safe houses, describing the West Village's Cubbyhole as the bar equivalent of a hug. But there was limited space in Manhattan, so much of the lesbian scene spilled over into weeknight takeovers at Brooklyn bars. Claire and her friends attended a party (cleverly named "Misster") every Wednesday at a spot called the Woods. I lived a block away from that bar (with Erin, who had moved to New York to "find herself" but was always out of town) but hadn't been inside before, so my mind immediately painted the picture of a Brooklyn Lilith Fair—acid and crocheted bikinis as far as the eye could see. As evidence that Claire suspected I was queer, she always invited me to tag along.

I'm not sure what scared me more: the nakedness of being new at something again, or the fear of enjoying the new stuff too much. Regardless, each week I turned her down and found myself at home, wondering what I was missing.

Fortunately I've never been great at resisting peer pressure, and the embarrassment of getting FOMO about a place two hundred feet away eventually caught up with me. The next time Claire extended the invitation, I said yes.

---

* This discussion came years before the COVID-19 pandemic. As of October 2020, there were only fifteen lesbian bars still standing across the USA. ☹

*

We agreed to meet at the Meatball Shop, a restaurant with multiple New York locations that desperately wanted to hide its true nature as a chain. The Meatball Shop played a formative role in my early New York years, probably because it tried as hard as I did: It was the metropolitan version of mall dining culture, mediocrity that relied on kitsch as an excuse to charge double the price. But that night, I took comfort in being surrounded by poor font choices; in having the structure of an entire menu focused around one food. I was already anxious, tapping my foot—the fewer decisions I had to make, the smoother things would go.

I wore a silky button-up and high-waisted jeans, and had just started applying pink lipstick at the table when Claire walked in, dressed in all black, her freckled skin flushed from the cold. We ordered cocktails with enough sugar to qualify as desserts and sat at a tall table near the front.

"You ready?" she asked, setting her elbows on the table. "Big night for you."

A bead of sweat ran down my back. "Sure," I replied. "It's a roomful of women. How hard could it be?"

Most of Claire's friends were meeting us at the bar, but one of them, Rob, joined us at the restaurant first. Rob also worked with us, but I didn't know him well. He intimidated me—the kind of gay man who knew his worth almost as well as his show tunes trivia, and who expected others to accept his judgmental comments graciously, as if he'd done them a favor. Hands in the pockets of his peacoat, he greeted me with a nod. After peering at my outfit over his dark-rimmed glasses, he turned to Claire and said, "Huh. Wouldn't have guessed."

I gulped. I could hardly disagree—next to Claire, I looked like an uptight mom who was just passing through, quickly grabbing a meatball while en route to the Starbucks next door. I scolded myself, knowing I could've dressed much gayer—I should've shown less cleavage, worn my hair up, or gotten a tattoo sleeve on the way here.

The anticipation ramped up on our walk to the bar, but when we stepped inside, the scene struck me as surprisingly unremarkable: rustic décor, a long bathroom line, and a Top 40 soundtrack full of songs you've heard before but can't name. The women seemed approachable, casually sipping beers, open-mouth smiling, as if being here meant they could finally relax. For the first time I considered that, when given space to flourish, queerness could be understated. A mediocre diner. A shitty bar. A way of life.

In contrast to the crowd, I was a ball of stress—I felt like I was onstage performing, desperate to overcompensate for Rob's perception of me. I would eventually realize that the thing making me so uncomfortable was "femme invisibility," a tendency for femme-presenting queer people to be overlooked and invalidated, even within queer contexts. I'd learn that even though the issue transpired in spaces where men weren't usually present, it still stemmed from sexism—butch lesbians were often perceived as more "valid" because of the arbitrary value patriarchy places on masculinity.* But at the time, my own femininity felt like an enemy, impossible to reconcile with my yearning to be gay. In the long term, it seemed

---

* It's important to note that butch people experience a whole different kind of invisibility, usually at a broader social or cultural level. As Kerry Manders writes, "femmes often 'pass' as straight, whether they want to or not—[butches] are nonetheless maligned and erased for our failure of femininity, our refusal to be the right kind of woman."

like I had only two options: stifle my girlie side or keep feeling erased.

Claire and I ordered PBRs plus a tequila shot. While we waited, I attempted to imitate Claire's effortlessly masc body language, widening my stance and leaning against the bar. I stood awkwardly, trying to seem chill while being the exact opposite, and noticed women laughing with one another; the bar felt like a gathering of old friends. There was something unintimidating about this place, and that was exactly what made it so intimidating. I was afraid to fully fall into myself, because what if I did that and still didn't belong?

"Jen!" someone shouted, and I turned. It was a friend of Erin's named Amber, a beanpole-thin white girl I knew well because I'd often gotten stuck talking to her at parties. She described her own style as "model off duty" and I remembered her once saying that she proudly identified as "basic"—a term that was essentially a synonym for "straight." To my knowledge, she was straight: Amber had a tendency to ramble about boy drama, and though I'd indulged her in the past, I didn't want to do it here. I tried to avert my gaze before we locked eyes, but failed. Amber waved, then skipped across the room.

"Oh em gee! What are you doing here?" she chirped.

"I'm just . . . hanging with my coworker," I said, deepening my own voice to offset the sunny tone of hers. It suddenly occurred to me that standing next to Amber might actually make me look queer by comparison. I inched in her direction.

"I'm here with my coworker too!" Amber squealed, pointing to an androgynous-looking brunette. Then Amber leaned in and whispered in my ear, "I think she's super cute."

My mouth fell open before I could stop it. Had Amber the

walking Madewell ad just effortlessly communicated that she was . . . bi? Why was this so easy for her?

Before I could process, Rob walked past us.

"Hey, love," he said to Amber, looking her up and down. "You're stunning. I adore you."

"Thanks, babe!" She giggled. "Oh em gee, do you watch *Girls*?"

"*Do* I?!" he replied. As they hit it off, I turned back toward the bar. While waiting for another beer, I started to spiral— no one was paying attention to me, which meant that either: (1) they didn't think I was cute, or (2) they all knew I wasn't gay enough to be here. "Fancy" by Iggy Azalea came on and I considered hitting the dance floor (most offensive line in this book), but then I glanced up and saw Amber, somehow already across the room, kissing her coworker on the neck.

"I'm gonna go to the bathroom," I mouthed to Claire. She gave me a thumbs-up while her gaze stayed locked on a Vanessa Hudgens look-alike, and I slipped out of view. The bathroom line had gone down so I ducked in a stall and wiped off the last of my pink lipstick, then walked out of the bar and went home.

✳

By now, most queer people know that we must get rid of toxic in community [sic]. The sentiment may have been born on *SNL* (thank you Bowen Yang and Sara Lee), but I'd argue that it makes a great, real-world goal—and accomplishing it might be within our reach.

My optimism kicked in five years after that night at the Woods, when I encountered the work of Cuban writer José

Esteban Muñoz—his most famous text, *Cruising Utopia: The Then and There of Queer Futurity*, offers a radical reframe of queer politics, framing our fight through a lens of "utopia." Muñoz explains that for him, and many marginalized LGBTQ+ people, "the present is not enough." This doesn't mean avoiding the reality we live in—just that building a better future requires imagination. For transformation to occur, we must believe in magic; we must have faith in the "concrete possibility for another world."

Though Muñoz published *Cruising Utopia* in 2009, it was no coincidence that I stumbled upon it during June 2020. This was Pride Month, yes, but it also happened to be a critical moment for racial justice, after the murder of George Floyd sparked global protests against police brutality. Memes and infographics circulated, reminding us that Pride was not canceled but had actually returned to its roots: "The first Pride was a riot," "All Black Lives Matter," "Not gay as in happy—queer as in fuck the police."

The movement took over mainstream media (about time), but most of the coverage centered on cisgender Black people (for example, the *New Yorker*'s commemorative cover featured only cis Black victims, even though police violence disproportionately impacts Black trans women). So mid-June, a group of queer organizers began planning an action called Brooklyn Liberation to dedicate intentional space for the fight for Black trans lives.* It was inspired by a powerful 1917 NAACP protest called the Silent Parade, when ten thousand attendees

---

* In 2021, the organizers hosted another action focused on standing up for trans youth in the face of an onslaught of transphobic legislation. Speaker Anesu Nyatanga asked the crowd to close their eyes and picture their liberation dream, but I kept mine open—I was already there.

wore white and marched down Fifth Avenue without saying a word.

The action took place on a museum lawn in downtown Brooklyn. Though quarantine-inspired agoraphobia was strong, the massive turnout proved that the urgency of this fight was stronger. There were more than fifteen thousand people there that day, making it the largest trans-based protest in history. Not everyone was silent, but almost everyone wore white.

Because of this staggering number and uniform dress code, every photo of the event looks breathtaking (the aerial ones will give you goosebumps). A micro-community had assembled to fight for Nina Pop, Brayla Stone, Dominique "Rem'mie" Fells, Riah Milton, Layleen Xtravaganza Cubilette-Polanco, Tony McDade, Yahira Nesby, Brianna "BB" Hill, Muhlaysia Booker, Bee Love Slater, Bailey Reeves, Pebbles LaDime "Dime" Doe, Bubba Walker, Kiki Fantroy, Tracy Single, Denali Berries Stuckey, Brooklyn Lindsey, Zoe Spears, Chanel Scurlock, Tatiana Hall, and so many other Black trans people whose futures were wrongfully stolen from them, stolen from us, stolen from this world.

"Let today be the last day that you ever doubt Black trans power," declared speaker and organizer Raquel Willis, and the crowd erupted, chanting: "Black trans *power* matters." Of course Black trans *lives* matter too, but that day reinforced that asking for the minimum has never been enough.

A protest cannot—and should not—be a utopia, especially if that protest came into existance because too many lives had already been lost. But there was something utopi*an* about the community that formed that day, as if harnessing our collective energy had granted us a communal third eye—the ability to glimpse a future we hadn't been able to see before. On paper, we wanted to burn everything down. But in reality? We . . . still wanted to burn everything down. The difference, though, was that in reality destroying the status quo wouldn't be an act of anger. It would be an act of compassion. Setting normativity ablaze meant creating space to start anew.

Once the march began, the crowd spilled onto Eastern Parkway, stretching far out of view. Protestors carried signs advocating for alternatives to police, echoing the internet's recent demands for a solution beyond reform.* Part of me still wondered if abolition was realistic; I doubted society's ability to reimagine "justice." But maybe my outlook needed reimagining too—as Mariame Kaba wrote for the *New York Times*, abolition suggested "a vision of a different society, built on cooperation instead of individualism, on mutual aid instead of self-preservation."† The crowd kept flowing, and I found myself fixating on one woman's cardboard sign, my eyes tracing the lines of her Sharpied words: "You say love is the answer. We say abolition is love."

Muñoz's work suggests that we should hold both community and futurism as core values, and our queerness should strive toward justice for all.‡ I had learned that getting outside of one's self was the first step—the irony was that in setting

---

* People had been sharing resources on Instagram to reinforce that a copless future was within our reach. An example case study: Dallas ran a program where they dispatched social workers in response to certain 911 calls involving mental health emergencies. Though it was only a test, the program helped curb reliance on the city's overcrowded prisons and dropped hospital admission rates by 20 percent.

† Kaba also rightly points out that hesitancy around the term "abolition" is common among white people, or anyone for whom community has never had to play a survivalist role: "When people, especially white people, consider a world without the police, they envision a society as violent as our current one, merely without law enforcement—and they shudder."

‡ I also love the way queer organizer Adam Eli (@adameli) phrases this idea: "Queer people anywhere are responsible for queer people everywhere," full stop.

our own egos aside, individuals would benefit from community progress too. It goes without saying that the revolution shouldn't revolve around comforting a bisexual white girl at a Williamsburg lesbian bar. But if, to paraphrase Audre Lorde, none of us is free until all of us are, then a revolution that centers Black trans power might wind up freeing me—and all of us—just the same.

These days when I don't feel "queer enough," I try to remember that queerness isn't a box to check—it isn't even tied to a goal. Queerness exists as a vehicle—an engine that stokes our curious brains, conjuring new ideas for what tomorrow could become. Queerness has the power to launch us into Muñoz's "collective futurity," a world where community remains fundamental to everything we do. If we can shed the weight of individualism, we can achieve so much more than assimilation. We can soar past "equality" until that concept is far behind us, just a tiny blinking star.

BISEXUALITY IN MEN: A RETROSPECTIVE

From: **Jen**
To: **Ben**
Date: **October 1, 2018, 11:09 a.m.**
Subject: **That Essay I Mentioned**

Hiiiii thanks again for chatting this out w/ me on email. Didn't want to do it over text since this convo requires a certain degree of seriousness from both of us. Plus sometimes it's nice to have an overwritten gmail exchange that dredges up the past, just so we can feel something 🖤

Soooo like I said, I'm writing an essay about that time we dated, lol. It's supposed to be a personal story that also sheds light on issues impacting bi men, and after doing an in-depth review of my exes, it turns out you're the only bi one I still talk to. I know this is semi-triggering and neither of us want to relive our uncomfy lil relaysh. But we'd be doing it for something bigger than ourselves, so maybe we can both take one for the team?

Lmk your thoughts. Also, how was the date with dutch girl?

Xx

-

Jen Winston
@jenerous | she/her

_____

From: Ben
To: Jen
Date: October 2, 2018, 9:45 p.m.
Subject: RE: That Essay I Mentioned

Tbh I thought the date went well but she just texted me that she's still hung up on her ex—some guy who lives in Berlin ofc. Ugh. At least she was honest? Whatever. I have a date with a Brazilian guy on Thurs so we'll see how that goes.

Def down to help with your essay. Glad you're writing it too—people don't talk abt bi men enough (aka ever) and it sucks. Like remember Edward, that guy who ghosted me last month? Idk if I told you this, but I confronted him for disappearing and he said my bisexuality had freaked him out. I'm used to women reacting like that but it still surprises me when gay guys do it :(

Lmk what you need!

-Ben

_____

From: Jen
To: Ben
Date: October 3, 2018, 11:06 a.m.
Subject: RE: RE: That Essay I Mentioned

Sorry about Dutch girl bb, but sounds like you saved yourself months of wondering what she wants. And now Joey Jamie and I don't have to come up with theories of why she's not texting back so you also saved us that emotional labor <3 thank u <3

As for the essay, I have it structured as a summary of our "romance" w/ stats and stuff woven in. Rough plot would be:

1.) Us as roommates
2.) How we got together
3.) The ~threesome~
4.) Our fall from grace

I could def use your help with more deets and specifics about #3. I don't remember much—just have a vague recollection that the night didn't go very well for me lol.

Send over what you remember? Also fuck Edward xoxo

-

Jen Winston
@jenerous | she/her

From: Jen
To: Ben
Date: October 4, 2018, 2:41 p.m.
Subject: RE: RE: RE: That Essay I Mentioned

Omg sorry for the double email (first day at the internship vibes!) but I just found part of an old essay and it made me lol. I submitted this to Modern Love in 2015—truly shameful that I a) wrote it b) shared it c) thought the New York Times would be interested, lmao.

Honestly it's hilarious (I describe the kiss as "electric") and also fairly emo since I wrote it right after we broke up. Sending in case you need a good laugh or something to jog yr mem as you start to think about *us*:

> One Wednesday in February, meteorologists across the Northeast U.S. warned of a treacherous incoming blizzard. Though it barely ended up even raining (duh), the threat of snow sent New Yorkers into a frenzy—we locked our doors and grocery-shopped like the apocalypse had arrived.

My roommates, Ben and Jamie, and I already knew our offices would be closed the next day, so we treated the night like an adult sleepover—playing board games while alternating between hot chocolate and wine. Jamie started joking about blizzard Tinder dates and all three of us took out our phones. Eventually she went to bed, leaving Ben and me alone on the couch.

Ben was a scruffy Jewish guy from Pittsburgh who'd been one of my best friends for the last seven years. We were incredibly close, having shared many vulnerabilities—I'd seen him drunk-cry (endearing), he'd seen me drunk-eat (legally qualifies as Public Indecency in most states). Recently I'd developed feelings for him, and now that we were alone, I wondered if he'd developed them too.

"Show me your matches." He scooted toward me, pretending he wanted to get a better view of my phone. Our legs touched and my heart started pounding, seemingly desperate to escape my chest. I held up my screen, revealing a profile: Tina M., 2 miles away—a woman who had also liked The Onion on Facebook.

"She's cute," Ben said, but he wasn't looking at her—he was looking at me. Unfortunately for Tina M., she was just a pawn; an excuse to justify why we were sitting so close.

Ben and I had a bond that my other friendships lacked. We were both bisexual, and often wrestled with how to exist in that identity—we wondered which words would best explain it, and how we could put it into action. All I knew was that Ben seemed like the only person in my life who understood my sexuality. He embraced my urges, even encouraged them—he'd been the one who'd suggested I include women in my Tinder settings in the first place.

"Good call," I cooed. But before I could swipe right Ben kissed me, and I dropped my phone to the floor.

> I'm still not sure why that kiss felt so electric. Maybe it
> was the thrill of secrecy, Jamie having just gone to bed.
> Maybe it was our shared sense of queerness—we knew
> we had a powerful connection, but couldn't articulate
> where it stemmed from. Or maybe it was the onslaught
> of logistical questions that hit after you hook up with
> your roommate: Do we call ourselves a couple? Whose
> room do we sleep in? Should one of us move out?

Lol. We both know I couldn't "coo" if my life depended on it.

I liked you a lot apparently? Feels weird to think about now.

–

Jen Winston
@jenerous | she/her

_____

From: Ben
To: Jen
Date: October 5, 2018, 11:58 p.m.
Subject: RE: RE: RE: RE: That Essay I Mentioned

LOL. But other than the coo, feels pretty accurate to me?

I remember that threesome with crystal clear vision, lol (though
that's prob because I was the center of attention, tehe 🤚)

It was spring, right after that blizzard thing. We'd only been
dating like 3 months but had decided to open our relationship—
the rule was that we were free to hook up with whoever, but
I was gonna focus on men and you were gonna focus on
women since neither of us had really experimented as much
with our bisexuality as we wanted to. Tbh I'm proud of us for
even attempting that—it was a fairly progressive arrangement.
We thought we could have it all, friendship & love & sex with
everybody. I think we both were too scared to do the self-
discovery thing alone.

So I went to Metropolitan in Williamsburg and met this guy Jay.
You were out of town for something . . . maybe in Barcelona on a

girl's trip? Actually, yes—wasn't that when you bought molly and were so proud of yourself for pulling off an international drug deal, but later you found out it was just speed? lmao.

Anyway. Jay was medium hot, wearing a baseball cap. His body looked like a mannequin, but not the chiseled kind—more like the relatable low-budget ones in souvenir shops.

He bought me a drink and we made out while the TV behind us glowed with a graphic fisting porn scene. (Swoon!) I invited him home but he had a ride so we made plans to hang out again. When I said I had a gf who was out of town, Jay said he'd always wanted to have sex with a girl but hadn't met any women who were down to fuck a gay guy. I told him I knew just the girl—said that you loved queer men and that your dream was to be Eiffel towered ("she wants to go to Paris" lol). He was down so I got his number and told him we'd call.

The next weekend, you and I got a hotel on the Upper East Side near Jay's place. (We didn't want to bring him back to the house—Jamie didn't deserve that.) It was a shitty Marriott that we booked with your Dad's credit card points, so we pretended it was our anniversary and they upgraded us to a suite (that was still shitty). Oh maybe you remember this: we smoked a joint right when we got there and it set off the fire alarm which almost got us kicked out. Off to a great start!

After that we grabbed dinner and chugged some wine (okay, two bottles) to calm the nerves. We asked Jay to meet us at the restaurant but by the time he got there we were soooo sloppy. He seemed super nervous, kept fidgeting and stuff, so we had like one cocktail before we all came back to the hotel.

Ok I gotta run but I'll send more tomorrow. Should we track down Jay's email and loop him into this chain for old time's sake? jk

—Ben

From: Jen
To: Ben
Date: October 6, 2018, 8:55 a.m.
Subject: RE: RE: RE: RE: RE: That Essay I Mentioned

This is already embarrassing and we haven't even gotten to the sex yet lol. Honestly I'm scared bc these memories are already bringing up some complex shit for me. I think I forget how ~real~ our relationship was bc I've forced myself to tone it down in my brain so we could get back to being friends. And can't believe I didn't manage to sleep with a woman during that time lol—she's serving complete and utter self-sabotage!

But enough about moi—there's so much to say here re: bisexual men! It's interesting—Jay comes from the gay (but questioning) POV, you come from the bi POV, and I come from the POV of a girl, just standing in front of two boys, asking them to fill all her holes. <3

Maybe I also come from the POV of a woman who finds male queerness attractive. People fetishize bi women, but sort of do the opposite to bi men—maybe "revile" is the right word? Ugh. I'm still so sorry about that bullshit with Edward bb.

Also the media always makes bi/fluid men look bad. OMG—remember that ep of Insecure when Molly found out the guy she was dating was bi? I feel like the episode was literally called "Stay Away, He's Gay!" You know I love Issa and I'm not saying Molly's reaction wasn't realistic, but society could def benefit from some cute & affirming portrayals of bi men.

Tbh seems like ppl are scared of male bisexuality bc it threatens masculinity. Masculinity as a concept is supposed to be all decisive and sure of itself (eye roll). But as you and I both know, bisexuality is associated with confusion, fluidity, multiple options, etc—and all of those are seen as "feminine" (or at least not masc). That means bi men are embracing their "feminine" side in multiple ways. The gender binary is SHAKING.

Bi men are the fucking best—y'all have the potential to be traitors to the patriarchy and smash that shit from inside! Ok now im hyped so i g2g lol byeeeeee

—
Jen Winston
@jenerous | she/her

From: Ben
To: Jen
Date: October 6, 2018, 9:10 p.m.
Subject: RE: RE: RE: RE: RE: RE: That Essay I Mentioned

Lol. I agree with all that. And don't worry, some complex shit's coming up for me too.

I def remember that ep of Insecure. Cis women (even liberal ones) have so much biphobia toward men, and nobody talks about that! I've heard the fear comes from HIV stigma but it's also def related to the misconception that all bi guys are actually gay. Either way it sucks.

Also there aren't many bi male role models. Like I've matched with male celebs on dating apps (c-list but still) and I see them publicly say that they're either gay or straight! It's like come onnnnn. I'm not trying to control how anyone identifies but if ppl with platforms could be open about fluidity it would make things easier for the rest of us.

Ok—back to the threesome. To spoil the ending, the sex wasn't that great—I'm p sure I'm the only one who came *flips hair*

At the hotel everyone took off their clothes. You made out with Jay and he fingered you for a min (seemed like he did ok?) and I just kinda watched. Then we passed him back and forth before he focused all of his attention on me. He and I made out for a while, and I'm not sure what you were doing. Maybe texting? Lol.

When he first started focusing on me, you took the hint and got out of bed. Actually I vaguely remember you keeping yourself occupied by, like, fingering yourself? Oh man, your readers will love that—they'll be all, "you go girl, get yours!"

But at one point you were so uninvolved that I think you went to the bathroom to give Jay and me some space haha. Eventually he and I finished, then he went home, and you & I woke up hungover the next day. The end!

On second thought, maybe you shouldn't write this story because it could reinforce some negative bi stereotypes—since Jay wasn't into you, it might seem like he was gay all along. I know that's not true but people are pretty narrow-minded and might interpret it like that. If you do write it, make sure you call out that it's common for men who ID as either straight or gay to actually be bi, but to just be super uncomfortable admitting that. Then because of that discomfort, out bi guys end up getting hostility from both sides—and not even in the Eiffel tower way, smh ☹

—Ben

From: Jen
To: Ben
Date: October 7, 2018, 10:03 a.m.
Subject: RE: RE: RE: RE: RE: RE: RE: That Essay I Mentioned

Oy. No wonder I blacked this out. I wanna say #NoRegrets, but like . . . some regrets?

But your point about reinforcing stereotypes is so interesting. Maybe Jay even had some internalized biphobia, so he focused on you bc he was more comfortable with men? Sort of reminds me of that threesome date I went on where I accidentally ignored the woman—that reaction was def more related to my own internalized shit than to her as a person (though she did have a v bad fake tan).

Or idk, maybe I'm just looking for excuses about why he ignored me. In retrospect, my takeaway from that night was pretty biphobic—remember how I spent the next day all bitter, telling Joey that Jay was "definitely gay"? It was def easier for me to assume that someone wasn't attracted to women than to accept that he was rejecting me for me.

That's consistent with my personality—as you know I was (am) awful at taking rejection. (Though being rejected during the middle of a threesome was a new level tbh.) I def didn't take it well when you broke up with me, which by my calculations was only . . . a few weeks after that threesome? Lol you asshole.

Of course idc—you did you what you had to do, and like you said: the feelings just weren't there. But god, I'm sorry I was such a mess—slamming doors, throwing shit, writing long emails about how I could never forgive you for dumping me (I guess dramatic digital correspondence is in our blood).

With three years of hindsight, seems obvi that we aren't a romantic match & I'm honestly super grateful you did the dirty work of ending things. I was forcing this—I just wanted it to work so badly. In a way, I'm still surprised it didn't—I thought a friends-turned-lovers arrangement was GUARANTEED to be a success. But I felt neglected. You felt stifled. I lost myself. You realized we didn't want the same things, and you were right.

I was also prob extra emotional bc you were my first bi partner, you know? I've heard lots of gay men feel a bond with the first dude they hook up with—that person becomes their shepherd into gay life. Maybe we had something like that? I've always known I needed someone to bring me into the WLW world—still do tbh—but I didn't realize how much I needed someone to help me understand my bisexuality specifically.

TL;DR: we had similar ideas of queerness but different ideas of love. (Did that sound too Dawson's Creek?)

Ok, last thing: It's kinda interesting to think that, to our friends and everyone else, we prob just seemed like a regular straight couple. I literally JUST NOW wrapped my head around the fact that our relationship was actually a "queer relationship"!!!! I've been trying to have one for years, not realizing I'd already had one! Just shows how deep all this bi erasure stuff goes.

Anyway—appreciate u. Grateful 4 u. Glad we're friends again.

-

Jen Winston
@jenerous | she/her

From: Ben
To: Jen
Date: October 7, 2018, 8:18 p.m.
Subject: RE: RE: RE: RE: RE: RE: RE: RE: That Essay I Mentioned

Thanks for saying all that. I appreciate you too. (Alexa, play "I Don't Wanna Wait" by Paula Cole)

I def agree about the bisexual shepherd thing—glad that somehow worked out even though neither of us knew what we were doing.

Specifics aside, I think our relationship had to happen and then had to end in order for us to stay friends in the long term. Plus isn't it a common queer thing to be friends with your exes? Kind of validating tbh.

Lmk how the essay turns out! Also I forgot to tell you—the date with that Brazilian guy went super well, and I also just matched with this Jewish girl who seems rad. Gonna text you about her now—need help figuring out what to say. ☺

—Ben

DO I MAKE MYSELF QUEER?

SOME PEOPLE COME out through a text. Some come out through a heartfelt conversation. Some claim they never needed to come out because, at their fifth-grade talent show, their passionately choreographed dance to P!nk's "Don't Let Me Get Me" did it for them.[*]

When I finally got up the nerve for the big reveal, I wanted the method to do my journey justice. So I made the announcement the most intimate way I knew how: through a branded Instagram Live in partnership with Quiznos! Jk— but it was through a #NotSponsored feed post.

It was early 2019, and I was thirty. By this point I knew for certain that I needed to label my sexuality—if I didn't explicitly name my queerness, it seemed too slippery, like a bar

---

[*] This was Joey.

of soap that would fly out of my hands. The word "bisexual" gave me something external to hold on to, an "oh shit" handle I could grab as the earth shifted beneath my feet.

Though my close friends knew how I identified, I still hadn't told the holy trinity: my parents, my coworkers, or social media. Every time I tried, I got caught in a paradox: Talking about bisexuality felt performative, but staying silent felt like self-erasure. I knew I had the right to be myself, but since I'd spent most of my life reaping the benefits of straight privileges, shouldn't I avoid taking up space?

Ultimately that dialogue didn't matter, because my motivation was not the idea of "being my most authentic self." My motivation was to get laid by someone other than a man, and coming out was a way to kick my own ass in gear, forcing me to date outside my comfort zone. I'd been on a handful of dates with women before and had adjusted my app settings to include all genders, but whenever chemistry seemed to get going it quickly faded away, and I found myself screwing a guy again. I didn't really put up a fight since dating men let me avoid interrogating myself. The longer I stayed in hetero land, the longer I could overlook the internalized homophobia I'd stuffed deep down and ignored. (Now that I'm openly queer, being stuffed deep down and ignored is my kink!)

Heteronormativity controlled my brain like an invisible fence that buzzed when my thoughts crossed a line. Marrying a nice guy? Inside the fence. Making love to a woman by candlelight after a rousing viewing of *Tell It to the Bees*? Outside the fence. On the bright side, at least I could blame my conditioning for making me so bad at flirting—if I tried to hold eye contact while talking to an attractive femme person, years of Indiana public school education swirled through my head, insisting that I shouldn't feel these butterflies while thinking about a GIRL. (Note that this was the same quality schooling that portrayed all Native Americans as white kids in headdresses and insinuated that Robert E. Lee was a hero.) Today I know that most queer people deal with this shit, but back then I looked at confident gay and lesbian Instagram influencers with envy. I assumed they hadn't faced any of these hurdles because they'd had no choice but to overcome them, having no "straight" attraction to hide behind.

Though my hetero programming* was strong, I thought coming out might be able to silence it, pushing me into my truth. I've always found it helpful to announce my intentions publicly—maybe I can blame my ADHD for this, but if I want to accomplish any goal of any kind, I have to tell a minimum of three people. I struggle to prioritize things if I keep them to myself, and that's especially true when said things are hard. For example, once I went to a kung fu class and left determined to spend the next year getting great at martial arts. I dreamt about someday surprising my friends—the vision was to keep my practice a secret so I could show up at a rustic brunch and casually chop the reclaimed wood tabletop in half. Adamant to accomplish this, I downloaded fifteen Bruce Lee movies, watched countless YouTube tutorials, and shopped for sashes online. But I didn't thrive as much in my second kung fu class (we did cardio, ugh), and since no one knew about my ambitions yet, I had no one to keep me on track—my fantasies and motivation simply trailed off. To this day when I log into Netflix, the "Continue Watching" section taunts me to finish *Enter the Dragon*.

---

* Imagine a robot voice repeating: "MUST. CONSUME. PINOT. GRIGIO."

Combine that aspect of my personality with the dopamine rush of getting likes (a high I'm clearly not above chasing), announcing my bisexuality through the megaphone of social media seemed like the right choice for me. It did feel grossly millennial to ascribe so much weight to the internet, but something inside me said it might work—that my grid could serve as a contract I'd have no choice but to live up to. I needed to write my fluidity in stone (irony! cute) and an Instagram post was the closest thing I could get to an engraver—if I ever forgot who I was, I could scroll back through my feed and find myself again.

I drafted a long caption, listing the mental obstacles that kept me from coming out earlier: I didn't hate men (except systemically). I didn't want to look slutty (despite being slutty). I'd wrongfully convinced myself that coming out as bi would look like a cry for attention (even though everything I do is a cry for attention). Then I took a deep breath and hit share.

I braced for incoming criticism: *They'll think I'm faking it. They'll wonder why I "need" a label. They'll say I should be "pan" instead.*[*] I got a few annoying comments, but for the most part, people wrote supportive messages—notes of congratulations, accompanied by heart emojis and rainbow flags. Some people even shared that they were also bi and had struggled with similar bouts of overthinking—already I felt less alone.

Beyond that, my coming-out was uneventful, which was (and is) a testament to my privilege.[†] My parents weren't

---

[*] Just a reminder that bisexuality also includes all genders. ☺
[†] Much of the world considers "coming out" a Western concept in that it focuses on "confession" and that it centers the individual more than the collective, as people in Western countries tend to do. (Considering this is a personal essay collection about my sexuality, I'm not exactly proving this stereotype wrong.)

phased by the admission and weren't even mad that I'd told the internet before telling them (I guess when I'm your daughter, that's a reality you learn to make peace with). When we Face-Timed, my dad looked relieved. "At least this ups your odds of actually ending up with someone!" (He'd recently retired from the job teaching statistics, so I allowed him this one joke.) Even my coworkers didn't look down on bisexuality the way I'd expected. Most didn't care, which, in that context, was an ideal response. The ones who did bring it up said supportive things like: "I saw your post! Congrats!" A few said, "So happy for you! I'm bi too!"

To make a comparison that the queer community will probably banish me for (which, thankfully, they cannot do without Sarah Paulson's written consent), I liken coming out to using *The Secret*—naming your sexuality becomes a way of stating your goal, which brings you closer to the things you want. I'm not qualified to educate anyone about the law of attraction (that's what WitchTok is for). But I can say that when I told people about my sexuality they gave me resources, guest list spots, and the phone numbers of their single friends.

Queer people need to be choosy about who we'll be set up with: "Meet my gay friend, you have so much in common!!!" is a straight allyship tale as old as time. But when Sabrina, one of my best-dressed straight acquaintances, offered to set me up with a lesbian friend of her lesbian friend,* I obliged. I trusted Sabrina—she knew how to mix prints—and we ran in completely different circles, so at least her setup would be several degrees removed.

---

* This honestly could be the name of the aforementioned rustic brunch restaurant: "Lesbian Friend of a Lesbian Friend, New American fare coming soon to Park Slope!"

The lesbian friend of a lesbian friend's name was Gabby, and Sabrina described her as "a card-carrying member of New York's 'lesbian elite.'"* I didn't ask what kind of card or how one qualified for membership—I simply saw Gabby's photo, noticed she was a cute brunette, and texted Sabrina two letters: IN.

A few hours later, an unknown number messaged me: Hi Jen! It's Gabby—your friend told my friend that you're awesome.

I gulped. A woman texting me first? Sending a compliment? Presumably wanting to meet IRL? I had no idea what to say, but I knew that at thirty, I could no longer justify outsourcing my texts. I drafted a few potential responses in my Notes app, then settled on: Why would Sabrina lie like that ☺,† followed by: Nice to meet you too

There's a phrase often used to sum up the sad reality of heteropatriarchy: Women are afraid men will hurt them and men are afraid women will laugh at them. Obviously no amount of shame could ever justify violence, but I did empathize with the notion that women are intimidating, and having a group of them make fun of you would be an absolute nightmare. It felt especially stressful to put myself out there with a woman who was confident in her sexuality, clearly years ahead on a journey that I'd just begun. I pictured Gabby as Regina George and the lesbian elite as her Plastics, the three of them mocking me—the new bisexual who was probably only here for sport.

Still, I had to start somewhere, and I wanted to learn how to flirt. But as the week progressed, I found myself bored by our conversations—they were mostly small talk, Gabby sending a photo of her dog, me sharing mundane details about my

---

* If LFOALF gets picked up as a reality show for Bravo, Sabrina and I both demand royalties.
† Thank you to my friend Natasha for teaching me that the angel emoji always conveys the perfect amount of coy.

job. Based on my experience with men, monotonous conversations usually indicated you were actually considering someone, rather than treating them like fuckable trash (which is beautiful in its own right). Maybe we were getting the boring part of the first date over with? That way when we met, we could really jump in.

Eventually we did decide to meet for a drink. She suggested a Wednesday night, and I suggested, for some reason, a rooftop hotel bar in Dumbo overlooking the East River. The hotel had just opened and though I hadn't been to this location yet, Dumbo seemed like the perfect neighborhood choice. With its cobblestone streets and gourmet food courts, it felt like Queer Switzerland—neither gay nor straight.

I arrived and took the elevator to the roof. The May air brought with it a gentle breeze, announcing that summer was close. I felt optimistic until I turned a corner and saw the bar—it was packed with a Wall Street after-work crowd, men in suits and women in tight minidresses. My dreams of Dumbo as a neutral zone were officially dashed—apparently this bar was a club of the "models and bottles" variety, that marriage of capitalism and patriarchy that I'd learned to avoid back in LA. A remix of Gotye's "Somebody That I Used to Know" bumped through the speakers—not exactly the edgy queer hyperpop I'd imagined.

Call me Brendon Urie because I was Panicked! at the Rooftop*—I couldn't believe I'd chosen such an oppressively straight bar. I knew it was a harmless mistake, but it felt like proof that I wasn't ready for a date with a woman—the

---

* Fun fact: Brandon Urie has been open about his queer experiences with men and identifies as pan. We stan a multisexual emo king!

confidence I'd gained from the nice commenters dissipated, and I felt like a fraud yet again. For the first time it occurred to me that Sabrina might not have mentioned that I was bi when coordinating the hookup. Would I have to tell Gabby outright, or would this bar's cloud of Acqua Di Giò do the talking?

Before I could determine a game plan, I noticed Gabby paying for a martini at the bar. We were dressed like twins, each of us wearing high-waisted black pants, a jean jacket, and a graphic tee with the front tied into a knot. Since we both had brown hair cropped to our shoulders, we practically looked like sisters. I'd never really thought about what my "type" of woman was, but I realized it probably wasn't my mirror image (surprising tbh, considering the number of selfies on my camera roll).

But I owed it to Sabrina to at least try. I introduced myself and asked the bartender for a mezcal rocks, hoping Gabby might compliment my order. She didn't. An ODESZA song came on, because of course it did.

"Sorry about this place," I shouted over the music. We walked to a picnic table and sat down.

"Honestly? LOVE the vibe," she quipped. Sarcasm was a pleasant surprise—I decided I liked her.

"I swear I had no idea." I laughed. "The Miami location is gorgeous."

"Yeah? I heard it's expensive."

"Oh, I didn't *stay* there," I clarified. "Just lurked in the lobby trying to get free access to the breakfast buffet."

"I know the hustle," Gabby replied. We both sipped our drinks at the same time, and our silence gave way to the sounds of suited men cheering, women shouting "Wooooo!" for no reason. It was like a douchey rendition of John Cage's "4'33."

"So," Gabby eventually said. "Should we do the standard first-date thing and swap coming-out stories?"

"I guess we *could*." I shrugged, pretending I too had participated in this ritual several times before. "You go first."

"My story is, like, soooo average." She beamed, obviously excited to tell it anyway. "I was married, to, you know, a man. But then I fell in love with, you know, a WOMAN."

"Very *Carol*," I replied, proud of myself for having a lesbian media reference on hand. But under my pride was jealousy—secretly, I'd always hoped I'd find myself falling for a woman, but it hadn't happened yet—I presumed because no one had recklessly pursued me. Having someone else initiate a relationship would've taken the burden off me to "prove" my queerness—even coming out would've been less about living my own truth and more about succumbing to love. I often imagined it: I'd be in CVS, frantically applying Great Lash before work, when a Cate Blanchettian figure would approach and whisper in a sultry voice that I'd been holding my mascara all wrong. She'd adjust the wand then take my number and beg me to see her, remaining undeterred even when I told her about the boyfriend (aka powerful vibrator) that I answered to at home. Eventually I would leave him (it) to be with her—a princess fleeing her straight castle for a life of queer romance, clad in only nipple pasties and the Brooklyn moonlight. We would move into a brownstone the following morning and spend the next ten years arguing about who has to walk the cat.

But I was neither hot nor cool enough to sit back and let queerness find me. Ariana Grande could drive Lesbian Twitter wild with the simple lyric "I like women and men, yeah," but I wasn't a pop star[*]—women rarely fangirled over me on

---

[*] Though now AG and I both have a work called *Greedy* in our respective oeuvres, NBD.

their own accord. I had to play the offensive, to act captivated by Gabby's melodrama—at least this might suggest I would fangirl over her.

"What happened next?" I asked, wide-eyed.

"I . . . revamped my entire life." Gabby twirled a piece of hair, as if to convey that her metamorphism had been a breeze. "I moved into my own place. Went back to school. Got all new friends. Kept dating that woman for two years. Had the best sex of my life. Then had a horrible breakup. But que será, será!"

I searched Gabby's face for clues as to whether she still had feelings for her ex, but found nothing.

"Now we're super-good friends! You know how it goes."

I'd heard about this phenomenon—partially by living through it with Ben, but also because right after coming out I'd binged *The L Word*, which taught me that many lesbians stay friends with their exes.* I couldn't tell whether these friendships were legitimately platonic or just holding patterns until said exes got back together. *Maybe*, I thought, *bisexuals aren't the only ones who can't be trusted.*

"Oh, oh, I forgot the best part!" Gabby exclaimed. "When I went back to school I studied queer psychology, and now I run my own therapy practice where I support women who come out later in life."

"Wow, that's awesome. As a woman who came out later in life, I'd like to personally thank you for your service."

"Yes yes, let's hear your story now!" Gabby squealed. I didn't feel like we were on a date so much as thirteen-year-old girls giggling at a sleepover.

"I, uh, just came out a few weeks ago," I mumbled.

---

* It also taught me several lessons about how not to represent trans men.

"A few WEEKS?" She practically did a spit take.

"Yeah, like three, to be exact." I paused. "Wanna turn this date into a therapy session? You can send me an invoice."

She laughed, which I took as permission to exhale. "WOW. Congrats, though! Guess that explains why we haven't met before."

"I guess."

"Wait. Oh my god." She suddenly looked so serious that I thought the bartender behind me had dropped dead. Her stare had turned cold, but she grinned. "Do you know about the PARTIES?"

I didn't.

"There are SO many parties," she continued, peppy as a cheerleader. "Like, every single Wednesday. I think there's one tonight!"

"Ooh, great." I clenched my teeth, trying to hide my exhaustion. I didn't have the stamina to spend my thirties exploring yet another nightlife scene, especially one that took place mainly on weeknights. I'd already agreed to have a few drinks with her, which meant sacrificing sober sleep and showing up to work slower than usual tomorrow morning— wasn't that enough?

"Next week, we're going," she insisted. Our chemistry had progressed from gossipy teen vibes to drunk girls in a bathroom who'd decided to be best friends. There still was no sign of romance. "You're gonna LOVE being a lesbian."

Ah, crap. I'd been flying under the radar but now I had to correct her—if I didn't, I'd be lying. I took a deep breath to summon what little confidence I had and said through clenched teeth: "Oh, I'm actually bi, ha-ha."

Her face softened, then she reached her hand across the

table and placed it on my shoulder. Physical contact! Was this flirting? Maybe she didn't care about my sexuality. Maybe she even . . . liked it?

"Oh, sweetie." Gabby pouted at me, really sealing the "drunk girls in the bathroom" rapport. "It'll pass! After my ex and I broke up, I thought I was bi for about three weeks."

I almost got sassy and asked whether she meant her ex-husband or ex-girlfriend, but I didn't have the strength—the rest of her sentence stung. I knew I was bi. I was sure. Yes, just moments ago, the mere scent of cologne had made me question it, but I still knew in my heart—and I had my coming-out Instagram to remind me. My mind cycled through positive affirmations: Bisexuality was real. It wasn't a phase. For me, it was the verdict. The end point. I didn't yet have the vocabulary to name Gabby's dismissal as biphobic, but I knew it didn't sit right. It worried me that someone whose job was counseling queer women about their futures had tried to talk me out of my truth.

"Yeah, I'm pretty sure I'm, like, permanently bi though, ha-ha." I made my voice trail off in an effort to sound nonchalant. Hoping to change the subject, I brought up something I thought might distract her: "But I'd still love to go to those parties!"

"GREAT," she said. "In that case, I have a plan."

"Hit me," I replied, pleased that my own plan had worked.

"Well, first, let's be real: The two of us don't have much chemistry."

This was true, but admitting it? Rude. "Huh?"

"We don't." She shrugged.

"I mean, you're right." The honesty was a relief.

"So let's be friends. I'll be your mentor into the lesbian world. You're gonna love it."

"Can't wait." I pursed my lips. I didn't exactly want a lesbian evangelist as a teacher, and she'd already been dismissive of my sexuality. But at the same time, beggars couldn't be choosers—I'd never been so close to a queer-culture entry point, and I needed Gabby to be my guide.

"One sec." She picked up her phone and furiously tapped her fingers, channeling Kim Possible. "Okay. Yep. There *is* a party tonight, and we're going."

Before I knew it, we were in a Lyft.

Though Gabby's excitement had made these "parties" seem like off-the-wall ragers, this one turned out to be another lesbian night at a straight bar, similar to the one I'd been to at the Woods. I remembered what Claire had taught me about the scarcity of actual lesbian bars, and I wondered if I'd ever actually set foot inside one. (I'd also never been to a bisexual bar, but I didn't realize I was allowed to want that yet.)

Ironically, this lesbian night was happening at Union Pool. Union Pool was a converted swim supply store, notorious for its sloppy hookup scene. I'd been there only on weekends, when the bar was filled with twenty-four-year-old straight dudes, each eager to blow their internship stipend on a Lyft Line back to their place. I wish I could say I'd merely dabbled in the Union Pool scene but there was a three-month stint where I found myself there every weekend. Even though I'd once seen the bar as an after-hours paradise, I'd now describe it as something like "my personal hell."

At least being here meant that Gabby couldn't have judged my earlier bar choice too harshly. We showed our IDs and walked inside, and when the familiar bouquet of back sweat and cotija cheese hit me, the memories came flooding back. I wondered why I'd wasted my party stamina on garbage straight bars like this one—why I'd spent my good years playing Never Have I Ever, adjusting my Tinder preferences to a .01-mile radius, and making out with strangers in the photobooth until the staff kicked us out. Even though I was on the cusp of adulthood, queerness, and everything else I wanted, I felt too worn out to be back here. I'd grown into a stale version of my former self, too exhausted to give it my all.

"Come on—my friends have beers for us." Gabby gripped my wrist and towed me toward the patio. The outside, though packed, felt like a house party, the kind of gathering my high school self might have affectionately called a "kickback." In the fresh air, Union Pool's signature smell had been replaced by notes of Santal 33 perfume rising off of Brooklyn lesbians who casually sipped their drinks. You could tell a lot about a scene by its average footwear, and most people had on leather lace-ups or Common Projects sneakers, indicating tonight's vibe was classy—nothing like the other times I'd been here. On those nights, the brief had been simply "shitshow"— women knew to wear the suede booties from the back of our closets, the ones we could afford to throw up on.

Gabby brought me toward a group of effortlessly attractive women, all of them wearing military-green jackets and oversize sweaters. She introduced them one at a time: Jordan, the golden-haired programmer with a butch aura; Kiara, the quirky brunette with Pippi Longstocking–style braids; and Liz, the wiry Eastern European who didn't seem to know how hot she was, which only made her hotter (it took every ounce of feminism in my body not to hate her). They each gave a soft wave in acknowledgment of me and mouthed a kind "hello." I wanted to shout my questions—"What's my 'type'?" "Is bisexuality fake?" "How many times can you watch *Blue Is the Warmest Color* before you lose your attraction to men for good?"—but instead I just lifted my chin and uttered a trying-too-hard "'Sup."

Kiara, I learned, was also new to this scene, but had seemingly acclimated with ease. A month ago she'd come out as a lesbian, but already it seemed like she'd known this group of women for years. I realized so many queer people had a story like this: After coming out they didn't just get new sexual partners—they jettisoned their old lives and found new friend groups too. They committed to the lifestyle and reaped the benefits—it seemed clear to me now that you'd only get out what you put in. But I was still hesitant. For the most part I liked my life—I wanted to live my truth, but could I do that without bailing on my existing reality? I tried to picture myself abandoning my friends to hang out with a group of lesbians, but all I could think of was the time Joey went as Ellen DeGeneres for Halloween.* Would it be worth it to start anew? Or would that mean being even less true to myself than I'd been before?

Kiara monopolized the conversation—she was "stressed the fuck OUT" that the woman she'd gone out with last weekend wasn't texting her back. Gabby, Jordan, and Liz took turns advising what she should do, and though my experience crafting texts for Ben should've given me plenty of talking points, I felt seriously underqualified to give relationship advice in a lesbian context. Besides, even Kiara's problem made

---

* For Joey's sake, I should note that this happened before Ellen's hostile workplace allegations. (For Ellen's sake, I should note that everyone thought Joey was dressed as Boris Johnson.)

me jealous—what a milestone, to be far along enough in your queer journey to get ghosted by a girl.

Eventually Jordan went to the bathroom.* As soon as she was out of earshot, Gabby leaned in and whispered: "Kiara, what is happening *there*?" She tilted her head to the right, gesturing toward where Jordan once was.

"Gabby, she won't even *look* at me." Kiara sighed. "I'm sure you realized I don't even care about the girl from the weekend—that was just a distraction."

"I knew it!" Gabby bit her lip and smiled.

"Always a smart one," Liz said to Gabby, her voice suddenly deep, channeling *Zoolander*'s Katinka Ingabogovinanana. Eventually queer TikTok taught me that dropping into a low vocal register was a surefire way to let other women know you were flirting, but that night I saw it with my own eyes: Gabby giggled, straightened her spine, and batted her lashes.

"Ohmygod, stahhhp." She brushed Liz's arm.

So Kiara was into . . . Jordan? And Gabby was into . . . Liz? I'd barely been at this "party" an hour, and it already felt more dramatic than one of Jenny Schecter's short stories. I couldn't wrap my head around the group dynamic—was everyone friends, did they want to fuck, or was it both? I found myself missing the clean lines of straight life, where I could view all men as potential sex partners and not feel guilty about it.

Jordan came back from the bathroom and I studied her in-

---

* Union Pool was on *Complex*'s list of "Best Bathrooms to Have Sex In," and, unfortunately, I can vouch that it deserved this hype. I once met a guy and, upon realizing that he *also* knew all the lyrics to Hot Chip's "Boy from School" (fate!), I promptly dragged him into a stall so he could finger me (not Bathroom Sex but close enough). Naturally the stall lock was broken, so when someone opened the door on us, he casually withdrew his hand. We walked out like bandits, our hips pushing open the bathroom's wooden saloon-style doors, which were covered in a calligraphy-drawn warning: "One Person in a Stall at a Time!"

teractions with Kiara. I searched for chemistry, but all I saw was Jordan's gaze darting around the room, trying to avoid eye contact at all cost. It was hard to watch, so eventually I said goodbye to Gabby—"See you next week?" she asked; "Def!" I lied—and walked the few blocks home. I trudged past a plant store, a crepe restaurant, a church. The streetlights glittered, looking almost blurry, the way they would have if I'd just been crying.

At least for the first time in my life, I had a beautiful apartment to come home to. Joey and I had moved in a few weeks earlier—we bid the yellow-walled three-bedroom adieu after Ben won New York's housing lottery and Jamie decided to move in with her legitimately amazing boyfriend.* Joey and I knew we'd paid our debt to New York City real estate and deserved to level up, and after months of searching, karma did its thing and led us to this gem. It was in Williamsburg right next to the L train, complete with tons of natural light (!), a washer/dryer (!!), and separate bathrooms (!!!). Finally, we could live like adults.

I climbed the four flights of stairs (the only downside) and turned the key in the lock, opening the door to find Joey on the couch. The TV lit up the room and I noticed him clutching our favorite low-tier bodega snack: a bag of Garden of Eatin' tortilla chips and green salsa (mid-tier was LesserEvil Buddha Bowl popcorn, god-tier was Snyder's of Hanover honey mustard and onion pretzel pieces†). I felt a wave of relief.

Joey paused his show. He looked happy that I was home—

---

* For the type A readers keeping tabs at home, I did move out to live with Erin for a bit after Ben and I broke up, but once he and I were friends again, I moved back in. You can take the girl out of the windowless living room, but you can't take the toxic behavioral patterns out of the girl!
† Included this anecdote on the off chance that a Snyder's marketing exec will read it and want to sponsor me—if that's you, hmu!

he'd get to lean into the Gay Best Friend stereotype and help me find myself (always his time to shine).

"How was it?" he asked.

"The date? Oh, it was fine. After, like, one drink we decided to be friends, then she took me to this lesbian party."

"Whoa. Where?"

"Union Pool."

"Poor baby. No wonder you look sad."

I laughed. "No. I look sad because Union Pool was this lesbian party and I didn't fit in."

"Sounds like a classic coming-out arc to me!" He licked salsa off his thumb. "The real tragedy is those lost souls earnestly enjoying themselves at that place."

I sat down, pulling the chips toward me.

"Also maybe you forgot, but you're not a lesbian, Jen." Joey sounded like an overprotective mom—stern, which was out of character for him. He'd once told me that he rarely raises his voice ("being a bottom and all"), so I knew that if he did, I'd better fucking listen.

BAD AT SEX

IT IS ONE a.m. and I'm slightly buzzed, sitting cross-legged on a woman's navy-blue accent rug. Her immaculate bedroom sparkles, not a speck of dust to be found (a stark contrast to my own bedroom, where several Luna bar wrappers have been around long enough to qualify as decor). On the surface, I seem comfortable here—I'm sipping a Stella, singing along to Chance the Rapper. But inside, my brain and ovaries pulsate, both of them consumed by fear.

The woman's name is Ria and technically we're still on a date. Before we got here we drank micheladas at three different bars, where we talked about Hans Zimmer and budgeting tools (the conversation was riveting, I swear). Seeing as we've been hanging out for six hours things must be going well, but that thought doesn't calm me down. It's late. Sex is imminent. And I have no idea what to do.

The number one fear in the world is public speaking. People constantly regurgitate this fact, yet it's still shocking: The majority of humans are more afraid of being embarrassed onstage than we are of losing a loved one, having our browser history leaked, or getting a rideshare driver known for "great conversation." Personally I empathize since my biggest fear is also making a fool of myself—though I could care less if it happened in front of a crowd. I'm much more scared of messing up in front of one person—specifically this person: the first queer woman who seems to like me back.

Here's something that doesn't help: the fact that Ria is fucking hot—to put it mildly. She's hot because she's gorgeous (chiseled jawline, great boobs) but also because she's down-to-earth, a skater chick who has never been photographed without a beanie. (At the second bar, I coquettishly joked that she probably wears it to bed, hardly able to imagine a scenario wherein I might find out.) She's wearing overalls on a Sunday night and still looks like a model (because of course she does). At the beginning of the night, she told me that people sometimes describe her look as "LHB," meaning "Long-Haired Butch"—sure enough the description fits her perfectly.

We met months ago, before I came out, at a rooftop happy hour—we both showed up with our own friends but spent most of the night talking to each other. We made niche small talk about the internet days of yore—"Remember Harambe?"* and "What ever happened to Turntable.fm?"—and I was almost too enthralled to realize I had a crush. She wore jean cutoffs and a camera bag slung over one shoulder—I remember her toothy grin as she swayed on her feet, saying "duuuuude"

---

* I miss him so fucking much.

with such conviction that I wondered if it was supposed to be pronounced like that. I didn't know whether she was queer, but I did notice how she looked at me—her eyes scanning up and down, taking me in. When I think about our effortless chemistry, it's not lost on me that we met somewhere besides a lesbian bar. Sure, a work happy hour wasn't the most romantic setting, but at least it leveled the playing field—I wasn't the only one there who couldn't be fully themselves.

Still, we didn't exchange numbers—I wasn't sure how to initiate that conversation, and to my dismay she didn't ask. But a few months later we matched on a dating app and picked up where we'd left off.

Jen!! From the roof, right? she opened.

The one and only.

Omg. U gay?

I'm bi ¯_(ツ)_/¯

Close enough!

And it was. Two weeks of texting later, I'm sitting in this room that smells like a boutique hotel, and it seems obvious that it's almost time to kiss. Ria leaves the lights on, showing off her plump lips and perfect teeth alongside my red face and bloated gut. She joins me on the floor, sitting back against the bed frame and lighting a joint, then extending her arm to pass it to me. I inhale and scoot toward her, hoping she can't hear my heart pounding. It's only a matter of time before she finds out that I'm Bad At Sex™.

You can try to console me ("You're not as bad as you think you are, Jen!"), but I assure you—I am. Actually I'm worse. Because I'm already aware that I don't know and we both know I don't know what I don't know. Sure, many of the skills I learned sleeping with men remain relevant—things like advocating for my own pleasure and peeing after I cum—but technique-wise, I'm starting from zero. Frankly, it's a bummer: I worked to shed my gag reflex* and tirelessly did my Kegels,† but both of these accomplishments are now for naught. My experience with cis men has ostensibly become irrelevant (much like cis men themselves—ayo!). Right now, I'm tasked with what seems like the impossible: Getting another woman off.

I tell myself that I'm embarking on a new chapter and change is always uncomfortable. I've braved life-altering shifts before (e.g., moving across the country or trying a new milk substitute) but I've never faced any obstacle without sexual confidence. My experience in the bedroom has been my armor, or at least my (semen-filled) security blanket—you could strip away everything and I'd still have my dignity, all because of that one time I gave head with an ice cube in my mouth. (Though it did give me ice queen goddess vibes—for once, *Cosmo* was right.)

But now I have nothing. For lack of a more germane/less traumatic metaphor, I'm like Brie Larson's son in *Room*—a child who only knows the eleven-by-eleven-foot world they were taught. I've done basic research on how to finger someone (shout-out to wikiHow), but I also know queer sex isn't something I can google myself good at. Just like with any other activity, the best way to improve is through experience. As I learned from reading Malcolm Gladwell to impress men,‡ you gotta put in those ten thousand hours, right, bro?

---

* Though that's only if you don't count two weeks ago, when I threw up at a routine dentist X-ray. (Gramercy Smiles, please don't hate me—you're the most serious relationship I've ever had.)

† To clarify, this was not practiced as a sex trick but to stop my pee stream in a rush.

‡ Rhetorical question for my past self: Are straight people ok? (Rhetorical answer: No.)

But getting experience means taking risks, and Ria's far too important to be my erotic guinea pig. My mind runs through the list of things I haven't done: I haven't scissored, and knowing what we know about my masturbation style, not even Niels Bohr could run the physics to pull that off. I haven't made contact with many vaginas aside from my own. I've touched other people's only during threesomes, which limits the potential for critical feedback—in the heat of a group-sex scenario, no one is going to call you out on less than perfect dexterity. How was I supposed to know whether I did a good job?

At least threesomes made me feel comfortable—queer hookups seemed much less intimidating if a guy happened to be there too. Being alone with a woman raised other questions: What if I didn't like the sex—if it was Lauren the Horny Lesbian all over again? Or what if I liked it too much and realized I didn't need men at all? The latter question had followed me my whole life—the possibility of falling in love with another gender felt like a threat to the person I knew myself to be. Though I knew I wasn't a lesbian, queer sex taunted me like an ultimatum—as if eating pussy without a cis man around somehow meant no turning back.

Ria kisses me. She tastes like weed and spearmint Listerine, and I realize she must have swooshed some mouthwash when we first got to her place. My own breath tastes rotten (though the pickled onion from the michelada garnish was worth it), so her impressive personal hygiene serves as more proof that she's out of my league. Ria's skin feels like velvet. I remember the other women I've touched, and it occurs to me that smooth skin must be standard among this gender. How is it possible, I wonder, that all women can be so supple and soft? Does this mean *I'm* supple and soft? I doubt it, but a girl can dream.

We stand up and to my relief, Ria turns off the overhead lights, leaving us the flickering wick of a lone hinoki-scented candle. She removes her beanie, flinging it onto a dresser, and I perk up.

"Beanieless Ria? What a time to be alive."

"Har, har." She smirks and pulls me toward her on the bed.

While making out, we fumble our way under the covers. She unbuttons her overalls, shimmying them down to her waist, and though it's dark I can't take my eyes off her chest. Most of the women I've hooked up with have had relatively small boobs, and I hear a voice in my head saying, *You deserve to touch a pair of huge tits, Jen!* I don't "deserve" shit, so maybe the voice in my head is an incel? We can unpack that later. I put one hand on each, squeezing gently, the same way you'd check if an avocado was ripe. Her boobs are soft and perfect— better than I expected. For a moment I forget I'm trying to impress her—I zone out and smile, thrilled.

Not wanting to linger too long (wouldn't want her to think I was objectifying her!), I move one hand down her body, inside the bunched-up overalls. The lower I go, the more I sense impending doom—"Ladies and gentlemen, we're approaching the altitude where your captain no longer understands shit." Penises are easy to locate, usually just milling about in someone's jeans. But vaginas do the opposite, and navigating these angles is awkward at best—I already look like I'm grabbing a stuck bag of Combos out of a vending machine.

Only in recent years while perusing sex-positive Instagram did I learn that all vaginas are unique. Labia lips come in all shapes, colors, and lengths. Even clit locations vary from person to person. This should be obvious, but for a number of reasons (cough patriarchy cough), vaginal diversity had barely crossed my mind.* Still, because Ria and I have the "same parts,"† I'm ashamed that I don't intuitively know my way around. I could ask her what feels good, but what if that tips her off to how inexperienced I am?

I decide to wing it. Who knows—maybe I'm a natural, a pussy prodigy with an innate sense of direction? It's wishful thinking, but no—I'm the type who gets lost in a grocery store, and not even gay desperation can help me transcend that. I aimlessly rotate my hand, trying to assess the entry paths. I'm like a toddler on their first tricycle, doomed to ride in circles until rescued by their mom.

Eventually I find my way inside. I bend my wrist and face my palm inward, which unfortunately makes me think of the memes about Italian hands. But then something even worse happens: My entire arm falls asleep.

Ria must be able to tell that something's up—she pulls my hand out and sets it aside.

"It's fine," she says, though for the first time I hear a hint of annoyance in her voice. "Let me show you."

Now she slides her hand down my chest—it moves like it's on a track, easily finding its way to my waist. Somehow only now do I remember.

"Shit—I'm on my period."

Ria glares at me. Our eyes are less than an inch apart—I can feel her frustration in my bones. I regret how I handled this or rather, how I didn't handle it. I was so focused on

---

* Beyond worrying that mine would never be tight enough, of course.
† Yes, this IS a reference to Tatianna's spoken word on *RuPaul's Drag Race All Stars*—thank you for noticing.

hiding my inexperience that I forgot she might want to get me off too.

Though there's another reason my period slipped my mind: Being the modern progressive that I am (*goes to a farmer's market once*), I don't think period sex is a big deal. In the past, I've actually enjoyed it, both for the additional lubrication and for the knowledge that someone is willing to "go there" with me—there's something grotesquely satisfying about two adults who can acknowledge that menstruation is a natural part of life. In past encounters, I've noticed that cis men tend to have counterintuitive reactions to period sex: Men who consider themselves feminists often claim that the blood grosses them out, but men who demonstrate chauvinistic tendencies readily go all in without a towel.

But this moment is a first for me: I've never disclosed my period to someone who gets one too.

"Do you have a tampon in?" Ria speeds through the question. She seems unconcerned but also impatient. I feel like an imposition, an errand—something she just wants to deal with before she can fall asleep.

I nod, nervous about how she'll react.

"That's fine," she assures me. "I can use it."

Before I can ask what that means, she dives her hand inside my pants, moving fast, like a scuba instructor running low on air. Within seconds she locates the bottom of the tampon, then presses up, sending it farther inside.

"How's that?" she asks.

To my shock it feels amazing. "Whoa, it's, ooh—"

"Good?"

"Uh-huh. Yeah."

This continues for thirty minutes and somehow I cum

three times. Ria is a sexual MacGyver, able to transform a Tampax Pearl into a makeshift dildo (and it's not even a Super!). I offer to try to get her off again but she refuses, wanting to give us both a break.

"My gift to you," she says.

The next day she texts me.

Hey! Hope you got home ok. I had fun last night but I'm sure you agree that we should prob just be friends, lol.

I stare at my phone and blink. Nothing good ever followed a Hey-Exclamation-Point, and this is no exception. Though I know I feel embarrassed about the night at large, I'm not sure how I feel about her. But she wants to be friends and she's *sure* I agree, so I guess that settles it. Matching her indifference, I type:

Hey! Yeah def lol, thanks for last night and for sending this text. Down to be friends for sure. Still honored that I got to see Ria without a beanie ☺ I'm well aware that I've run this inside joke into the ground, but it's the only one we have.

Twenty minutes later she responds with a thumbs-up. I decide to find the silver lining. Getting rejected by a woman? Check.

BOUNDARIES: A FAIRY TALE

ONCE UPON A time (summer 2019), there was a Bisexual Girl who longed to stop dating Men. She was getting older, her once-perky tits starting to sag, and though Queer People exist at every age, she had foolishly convinced herself that her time to "act gay" was running out. She'd spent much of her life courting Men, simply because they were there (and also because they never gave her enough emotional fulfillment to feel satiated, so she stayed and begged for more crumbs).

After a one-night stand with an Intellectual who handcuffed her (yes, that one), she texted her Lady of the Bedchamber, Sir Joseph, to complain:

IM DONE WITH MEN

FOR GOOD

Sir Joseph had received this text many times before, and so he replied:

mmk lol

lmk how that goes

Unfortunately, Sir Joseph's cynicism was for good reason—within weeks, the Bisexual Girl became infatuated with yet another Man. This one was a mysterious political Speechwriter, full of contradictions—despite his professional rhetorical skills, he was terrible at communication. The Speechwriter took forever to text back, and though it was his cardinal flaw, alas, it was also the Cupid's arrow that most deeply pierced her heart.

The aloof Speechwriter elicited an insatiable hunger within the Bisexual Girl and, as true hunger is known to drive one mad, she fell for him quite hard. Although she'd sworn off Men, this one's emotional unavailability seemed to put her under his spell, convincing her that he was worth the digression. (The Speechwriter, it should be noted, was not special—she'd made similar compromises for many Men before, always somehow believing that she'd made a prudent choice.)

The Bisexual Girl told herself (and Sir Joseph) that she could hook up with the Speechwriter, but ONLY if it was just sex. She vowed not to get emotionally invested and to keep texting women and nonbinary people on the side.

On their first date, she wore tight jeans and strutted to the back of the bar, showing off while pretending to look for him. Within seconds, she received a text that said nice ass—he'd been seated at the counter, checking her out. From that moment on, she was nothing but putty, all the while thinking she was stone.

In the weeks that followed, their correspondences alternated between "u up?" texts, political commentary, and memes featuring cute babies (which, he performatively claimed, were his favorite kind). From this she deduced that the Speech-writer contained multitudes—he could fuck her for hours, rant about Piers Morgan, and also laugh at a toddler lip-synching to Big Sean. (In hindsight, the Bisexual Girl had an extremely low standard for "multitudes.")

But the baby memes alone activated her hormones—with every DM, her brain involuntarily reminded her that the Speechwriter would make a great dad. Against her will, she frequently considered his "father potential"—shuddering at the term, yet loving that he had so much of it.

They often met after midnight in his dimly lit bedroom where he worshipped every inch of her, making her tits feel perky once again. The trysts were delightful until one Saturday when they finished sex at three a.m., a time her aging body appeared to reject. Exhausted, she said, "I'm too old for this," to which the Speechwriter replied, "*You're* too old for this? I'm thirty-eight." Then, to her surprise he kissed her on the fore-head and whispered, "If one of my spinal discs slips, at least it was worth it."

The Bisexual Girl beamed. Being of sound mind and crys-talline sobriety, she took this statement for what it so plainly was: a marriage proposal. The next day while running errands, the Speechwriter texted her *that was fun*, and she stopped on the street and squealed. She sensed momentum, concluding that he would swiftly follow this text with something more—a mention of a five-year plan, a ring emoji, or at least another meme.

But over the next few hours, nothing came. Yearning for more, she clutched her amulet (read: phone) and had an idea: Maybe tapping the screen for other reasons could conjure the Speechwriter correspondence she craved.

She tapped and tapped but nary a text came. Nary a text in the morning, while tapping the crossword app on her commute. Nary a text at night, while tapping through Tinder on her couch. Nary a text on the weekend, even after tapping to post several thirst traps from her spin class.

Distraught, she sought counsel from her Lady—perhaps he would know what she was doing wrong.

Sir Joseph replied with wisdom that, in real life, probably took the form of a text: Talk to him bb. But as this is a fairy tale and fairy tales distort the mind, the Bisexual Girl remembers his advice like this:

> "You seem to like this guy,
> But you pretend that it's just sex?
> Unless you tell him how you feel,
> He'll end up like the rest.
>
> You clearly want to date him,
> To fall in love, or else.
> You should set some boundaries, luv—
> With him and with yourself.
>
> You have to talk out loud.
> You have to speak your truth.
> Tell him what you want and need
> So he'll stop using you!
>
> Of course this isn't foolproof.
> Of course this is a risk.
> But if you don't get what you deserve,
> At least you've dodged a bullet."

Indeed, Sir Joseph's poetic retort had the intended effect: It not only reminded the Bisexual Girl to set her own boundaries—it also hyped her up to enforce them. She would explain that she had started to actually like him and she was unsure how to proceed. She was open to taking his hand but she also knew there was a possibility that he might refuse her, considering that they'd never hung out during the day. The possibility of rejection loomed, but she was still riding the high of his orthopedic pillow talk. *We have a connection*, she reasoned. *It will be fine.*

She decided that she would wait until the Speechwriter inevitably texted her on Saturday at twelve a.m. (Yes, she could've texted him first, but she didn't want to do that, okay?)

And so on Saturday night, she donned her best velvet bell-bottoms, along with her fanciest underwear (nothing else was clean). She lounged around her house until nine p.m. when she left for a friend's birthday dinner in Bushwick. There she spent the whole evening clutching her amulet below the table, pretending to be checking the time.

Around midnight, just as the waiter set down the flourless chocolate birthday cake, the Bisexual Girl began to wonder if the Speechwriter was all right. Perhaps he'd been slayed by a dragon? Consumed by a beast? Or maybe his amulet just died?

But thirty minutes later, a love note appeared. It was more eloquent than she'd ever imagined: wyd rn?

She replied omw, then promptly paid for dinner and called herself a car. Channeling Sir Joseph's advice, she did affirmations on the way, trying to gather strength. "You are a fierce feminist warrior," she repeated, enunciating the words as she spoke. The incantation filled her with courage (unfortunately it also cost her Lyft rating one star).

When she arrived at the Speechwriter's apartment, she hugged him and sat on the bed. CNN was on in the background—the Trump-era equivalent of "setting the mood."

"What's wrong?" The Speechwriter peered at her with his huge green eyes.

"Uh . . . nothing." The Bisexual Girl crossed her arms. But something *was* wrong—her confidence had faltered. What had caused this—Anderson Cooper? Her thong riding up? Or perhaps it was the Speechwriter's gaze—maybe he had a power that she hadn't prepared for.

"Your body language is all weird," the Speechwriter said.

"No it's not." She uncrossed her arms.

"Yes it is. Do you wanna talk?"

She froze. She didn't *want* to talk, but she knew she needed to.

"Let's have sex first," she suggested.

The Speechwriter stood up, lifting his hand. "Listen—I can tell something is going on. And we're not sleeping together until you tell me."

The Bisexual Girl sighed—there was no turning back. She said something that probably came out like "I think I'm starting to . . . like you? Which means this either needs to evolve or stop" but that she remembers as:

> "I do not want to say it,
> And yet I know I must:
> I simply cannot keep
> Chasing you out of lust!

For I've developed feelings,
And I must come to ask:
Would you like to date me
Or leave me in the past?

It's one or it's the other,
Unfortunately so.
This is me setting boundaries:
I'm no longer your ho."

The Speechwriter drew his head back ever so slightly. He shut his eyes and took a deep breath, as if prepping for a yoga class. When he opened them, he smiled. He put his arm on her back like a father walking a child into the sunset, then spoke:

"I am so, so grateful
That you shared this here tonight.
If you'd kept it to yourself,
We'd surely have a fight.

But I am not exactly
In a spot to be tied down.
And so, I think it's best
If we stop fooling around.

I like you very much
And think we should be friends.
But I do not want to hurt you,
So this is how it ends."

Stunned, the Bisexual Girl nodded. Despite all the romance she felt, the Speechwriter had chosen to leave her behind. She'd always been terrible at boundaries and now she knew why: because setting them came with the risk that someone might actually observe them. She had already engineered her reality perfectly to her liking: a world where she had sexual agency; where there were no surprises; where the most agonizing confrontation was the opposite of confrontation— long, drawn-out ghosting that she'd dealt with a million times before. Setting boundaries meant threatening her sense of normalcy. It was like putting a block back on a Jenga tower— it might make the structure stronger, but it also might knock it all down. Was it worth risking the good things she had to gain the great things she knew she deserved?

Her heart knew the answer, and for as scared as she was of her destiny, she was proud of herself. This was the first time she'd actually advocated for her own needs, and Sir Joseph was right: She had, in fact, dodged a bullet. She wondered how many other "relationships" would've ended up like this had she spoken up. How many others were merely wasted time?

"Can we still have sex?" she asked the Speechwriter reflexively.

"I don't think that's a good idea." He walked her to the door.

As soon as she got in her rideshare, the Bisexual Girl cried and cried. She cried at the pain of being rejected (and at the shock of it, despite how many times she'd been hurt like this before). She cried because it was late and she was too tired to control her emotions. She cried because the driver was wearing an obscene amount of cologne and, my god, it reeked.

But she also cried with gratitude. She was grateful for

the Speechwriter—despite being an asshole for a few weeks, he'd been a gentleman tonight, someone who cared about her enough to stop using her, despite her desperate pleas to be used. She was grateful for Sir Joseph—he'd urged her to set this boundary in the first place, having been her knight in shining armor all along.

She stared out the window, watching couples walk past and considered that maybe she did want a relationship. It was hard to admit—the idea itself seemed patriarchal and embarrassing. But the Speechwriter's singing toddler DMs had shown her she was ready to become a domestic housewife (or at least a feral one).

The Bisexual Girl knew that most fairy tales included an enemy, and she wondered who her enemy was. Was it the amulet she'd used to post thirst traps? The prince she'd let herself pursue? The fairy-tale literary device that she'd gone all in on for some reason?

And then it hit her—the enemy had been right in front of her the whole time. It had duped her into suppressing her desires. It had convinced her that winding up with someone—anyone—was more important than listening to her own needs.

The enemy had always been fairy tales themselves. And for the Bisexual Girl, perhaps just realizing this was happy ending enough.

A FEW WORDS ON PLATONIC LOVE

THE PAIN ALWAYS strikes sharp when a friend in a relationship becomes a "we." It usually happens through written communication—a text or email RSVP to a group event: a road trip, ski weekend, or Zoom improv show you're forcing your loved ones to attend. You'll invite the friend by themselves, and they'll reply something like "We are so in!" At first you register their enthusiasm as positive, but seconds later, its context knocks you off-balance. You squint and reread: *We? Who's "we"?* For a moment, you wonder if your friend is just being obnoxious, using the pronoun in the royal sense. But then their intended meaning dawns on you and you just sit there, staring at your phone, alone.

"We" tends to be casual for the person who says it—it feels accurate to their reality, thus isn't given a second thought. But on the receiving end "we" can devastate, an accidental bullet unloaded into your gut. "We" tells the future, illuminating impending challenges: First your friend will stop wanting to stay out so late, next they'll be showing photos of their kids.

Beyond logistical headaches, there's also a sense of grief. You are, in fact, saying goodbye to your friend as a single human entity; farewell to them as you know them to be. English is far from a perfect language, but could there be a more perfect encapsulation for loss of individualism than this shift from one letter to two? The "I" character stands tall and defiant. It autocorrects itself to being capitalized, no matter where in the sentence it lives. But when transformed to "we," it shrinks down, both letters making themselves smaller to meet at the other's eye level. Sure, *w* and *e* are still unique—a consonant toward the end of the alphabet and a vowel near the top certainly make an unlikely pair. But no matter who these letters are by themselves, at this point they're nothing without each other.

When the "we" arrives digitally, it's manageable—at least you'll have space to process your feelings in peace. But if you're unlucky, it will come when your best friend sits you down and breaks the news: "I think we are moving to LA."

Four years earlier, Joey and I are both twenty-six. Every morning goes like this: He texts me a link while I'm half asleep, so I only think I see it. Then I wake up and definitely see it, but now I'm running late and don't have fifteen seconds to load an article. Then my commute is cold so I forget about anything else, and then I'm at work, paying attention to a different screen.

Acknowledge, Joey texts me two hours later. A few minutes pass and when I don't respond, he annoys me further by sending one single space. The blank text sits on my iPhone like a gray balloon, all full of helium with nowhere to go. Someday technology will allow Joey to react with two exclamation points, but with this early iOS, the only way he can show his impatience is with the space bar. I tuck my phone in my back pocket and step off to the bathroom, then duck into a stall and click.

He doesn't coddle me with trigger warnings so the headline takes me aback: "Fallen Construction Plywood Kills West Village Woman." I sigh but am not surprised. Yesterday he sent "Two Taxis Collide in Front of Williamsburg Bridge." The day before: "Woman Fatally Crushed by Midtown Elevator." By now our swapping of dire news has become a ritual, an ongoing exchange of existential dread. But we don't send updates on just any tragedies—only the ones we can see ourselves in. We cross the Williamsburg Bridge every day. The elevator was in an ad agency, much like the ones where we work. The plywood fell right by my office, and West Villiage Woman was on her phone.

These headlines give us license to imagine the worst, fixating not just on our own death but on each other's—I picture Joey in the headlines, he pictures me. I'm not sure why we do this. Maybe it's exposure therapy—if we imagine loss in all its gruesome detail, the pain can never catch us off guard. We can't stop disaster from coming for us, but at least we can kill the element of surprise.

The next week I finally have time to go outside for lunch. I see a construction site and once I pass it, I whip out my phone.

In west vil near plywood, I text, and Joey immediately replies with avoid scaffolding pls. I text back just did with a photo and he says good, then im doing an enema at equinox, then 426 First Ave, Apt 203.

Addresses are another ritual. Joey has always sent them without context, but gradually I've learned that they mean, "Here's where I'm hooking up in case you need to find my body." Each time I take a screenshot just in case and hope I never have to revisit it.

In any hypothetical death scenario, Joey and I stay realistic. We care about each other enough to admit that we will be pissed if the other person's memorial service inconveniences our daily life. It goes without saying that we'll attend (and give a profound eulogy at that), but if we have to cancel a non-refundable dermatologist consult to be there, we'll never let go of the grudge. In a few years, when we live in the beautiful fourth-floor walk-up together, we will watch an episode of *Fleabag* where Phoebe Waller-Bridge's character unintentionally looks stunning at her mom's funeral. Joey will tell me he'll look hot at my wake but will never forgive me if I look hot at his.

Joey's in luck, because when I imagine him in the headlines, I don't imagine myself as hot. I imagine myself as a human pile of crumpled tissues, smeared black eyeliner beneath the red circles that were once my eyes. I would continue texting him, wondering how long before my iMessages stop marking as delivered. I wouldn't send links anymore—just annoying cries for attention, a steady stream of spaces and that manipulative, understated word: Hi.

I also imagine myself as overwhelmed, knowing that my office wouldn't even give me bereavement days since Joey and

I are not dating, married, or related by blood. Micro-kitchen small talk will reach new levels of awkwardness: "Just the death of my best friend—no big deal. Kinda like losing a pet! Did you still need those files by noon?"

Because Joey and I don't have engagement photos or a relationship status on Facebook, most people don't even know how deep we go. They weren't in Vegas during that bathroom emergency, when Joey guarded the entire women's room because I had diarrhea while wearing a cream-colored dress. They weren't in that Santa Monica shopping center when he read the entire third book of the *Hunger Games* trilogy out loud to me, so we could experience the ending (and be underwhelmed by it) at the same time. They haven't seen our texts, though the conversations wouldn't mean much anyway—on their own, the blank balloons and URLs communicate nothing. It's an encryption concealing a language that no one else can speak.

As we grow into adulthood over the next four years, our bond strengthens. We hate the same things—Party City corporate emails, the word "shoppe," flying out of LGA. We date, but no matter how much we enjoy our suitors, it's understood that they're still in second place.

We develop more text rituals. We send the letters "SBP" when we're on a multilane road and are Surrounded By Priuses (it happens a lot, you'd be surprised). We send updates about the careers of everyone from Debra Messing to Rosalía to Chloë Grace Moretz. We start group threads with Ben then text back and forth like we're talking one-on-one, annoying him especially when we know he needs to work.

There are real-world traditions too. When we move in together, one of us buys what turns out to be a functionless bottle of leaky sunscreen, and over the course of several months, we take turns hiding it in the other person's room. We always spend my birthday hungover, eating garlic bread and watching a canceled TV series in its entirety.* We decide to go for a yearly bike ride around the perimeter of Manhattan (though we only do this once before giving up).

But the best tradition is Oscarpalooza, an annual challenge wherein we spend one January day attempting to watch as many Academy Award–nominated films as possible. We've kept this up for four years and have developed our own set of rules: Start early.† Bring granola bars. Acknowledge that the Oscars are a problematic institution and prioritize viewing work by Black and/or queer nominees. See each movie in a different theater. (This point is critical, as it elevates the day from casual outing to *Amazing Race*—we often have to sprint to make the next showing, popcorn still digesting as we race across Union Square.)

Lastly, our core objective: Aim to be as broken as possible by end of day. In accordance with our general masochism, we structure the lineup to get harder as we go.

When Joey tells me about LA, "What will happen to Oscarpalooza?" is the first question I ask. I barely make it through the words, thanks to the lump in my throat—it feels eerily like I'm getting dumped.

"I'll fly back for it," he insists. "I swear."

I nod but don't believe him. He's clearly set on his West

---

* My favorite of which was *Dietland*—Joy Nash hive, rise up!
† Our record was *The Shape of Water* at 8:03 a.m., and we weren't the only ones in the theater.

Coast life with his super attractive, super serious boyfriend—why would he return to the city of hot garbage and untimely deaths?

Despite the fact that no one is perfect, Joey's boyfriend, Adam, happens to be. Adam is Israeli, a silver fox who cooks Palestinian food for Shabbat as his own small act of dissent. He worships Jamie Lee Curtis and goes to a ceramics studio "for fun." I knew it was real when I heard Joey call Adam by his first name (unlike his ex-hookups, whom he referred to only as phrases: "Small Guy with Huge Apartment Who Gave Me a Rim Job While I Ate Popeyes" or "Greenpoint Dad I Bottomed for Before I Knew How to Douche"). This means Adam is special, and as much as I hate to admit it, their love is special too.

I'm not losing Joey to some sudden tragedy, the way we've always pictured—he won't be hit by debris or eaten alive by a Grindr hookup (at least not until he and Adam open things up). The loss has been years in the making, starting with neighborhood date nights and progressing into weeklong European vacations.

And now: LA. Not just for a week—for good. I'm bitter, but at the same time, I know Joey deserves his new life. He deserves California's perfect weather and all-consuming wellness culture. He deserves home-cooked meals with a political bent and a cabinet packed with hand-thrown plates. He deserves to raise a beautiful queer family in a beautiful hillside house. He deserves to escape our nihilistic world of imaginary accidents, Priuses, and one-night stands.

But losing him guts me. To add insult to injury, I can hardly communicate my pain—there are no terms like "breakup" or "divorce" for friendship. How do you say you're missing someone when you weren't married, weren't "in love," and were never intimate (unless you count the time you made out at that Avicii concert)?* A falling-out would've been easier—at least then we'd have a clean break and someone to blame.

After Joey leaves, we still text daily. From the second he takes off he sends updates on the move, including commentary on the storage company's branding ("Guess they ran out of budget for a logo designer") and a play-by-play of what he's watching on the plane (*Gloria Bell*, *Red Sparrow* for the second time). He forwards me the desperate, GIF-heavy emails he gets from apartment brokers. He sends photos of his new place along with articles about accidents on the 405. Nothing changes, yet everything does. Because now I realize that I'm alone.

I get a Craigslist roommate who is a twenty-one-year-old NYU student, which is great because she doesn't think it's weird when I binge-watch '90s rom-coms and finish several pints of Talenti per night. One day I'm bored enough to scroll to the bottom of my Instagram feed. It's underwhelming ("You're all caught up!") but it makes me realize how much energy my platonic love consumed. I wouldn't have traded our commitment for anything, but it overshadowed my drive to look for a romantic partner in someone else. Whether I knew it or not, I was emotionally unavailable. Spoken for. And the next day I wake up with even more clarity: I want to meet someone. I want to fall in love.

Joey does, in fact, fly back to New York for the fifth year of Oscarpalooza. We end our showcase with *Bombshell*, which he jokes will be the film that breaks us—by that point in the day, our moral compasses might be too weak to hold empathy for the women of Fox News.

---

* RIP.

But we begin the day masochistically: with a nine a.m. showing of *Uncut Gems*. We eat breakfast at the theater, watching the shaky cinematography and struggling to hold down our eggs. The movie is torturous, chaotic, and upsetting—just the way we like it.

"What's your review?" I ask as we run toward the escalator.

"That the whole thing was a reenactment of yesterday when I didn't complete your twenty-dollar Venmo charge," he replies. We sprint out of the theater, dodging pedestrians en route to film number two. The Manhattan air rushes around us; it's a shockingly warm day for January—perfect for a run. I start getting winded but remind myself that Joey won't leave me behind. He'll lead us safely to our next feature film—all I have to do is keep up.

PART IV

I WANT TOO MUCH
AND THEN SOME

A QUEER LOVE STORY

IT'S NOT VERY 2021/yes bitch!/you do you to end this book with a love story. For starters, love is often happy, and happiness, as they say, does not stain the page.* Yes, it's important (radical even!) to see people of all identities experiencing joy, but unless you're talking about that blissed-out roller skater on Instagram,† watching someone else share their contentment kind of blows. Audiences are looking for drama! Conflict! Pain! The hero should be tormented by a longing, a want—that way, the audience can root for them to achieve it (spoiler for every piece of media ever: They *will* achieve it, but not in

---

* The French writer Henry de Montherlant said: "Happiness is white ink on a white page," meaning we can't describe it and also we don't care. I opted not to quote this author directly because (1) his quote seems kinda racist, and (2) turns out he was a pedophile. (Tell me you're from the nineteenth century without telling me you're from the nineteenth century.)
† Thank god for @oumi_janta.

the way they expected!). While heroes often do seek out love itself, the juiciest parts of those stories will always be the chase. Resolutions masquerade as critical plot points but they're usually preordained throwaways, driveways that we already know we're going to pull into. It's why so many rom-coms put the much-anticipated kiss right before the credits: No one wants to see the protagonists cook a healthy dinner and go to bed by nine.

To craft an exciting love story, the goal must remain just out of reach at all times. Maybe that's why many adults wander the earth like kids who still believe in Santa, searching for True Love, not realizing that the idea is faker than Hilaria Baldwin's accent. I didn't find this out until I was twenty, and only because I was enrolled in an elective called the Philosophy of Love. Every week, the professor showed us how the romantic sausage got made, taking us through marriage's economic origins, Aristophanes's "two halves," and the poetic bigotry of Don Draper.* We read *Tristan and Iseult*, Plato, and Kierkegaard, charting the centuries-long dawn of a concept that still rules our day-to-day.

Naturally, the only reason I paid attention in this class was to make one of my friends fall in love with me: a creative writing major with extremely flat feet who always had his nose in a book. One day he said my syllabus looked "neat" (he wasn't being sarcastic—that was just how he talked), and before I knew it, I'd finished every reading. At the end of the class, I asked the TA if he'd write me a letter of recommendation to apply for a philosophy PhD. (He said no

---

* "What you call love was invented by guys like me to sell nylons."

and I was fine with that—I never picked up a philosophy book again.)

After I understood basic feminism (which I credit entirely to a rousing listen of P!nk's *M!ssundaztood*),* I realized how deeply the idea of True Love had manipulated me. For women, the indoctrination starts early and never lets up—one minute we're watching *Sleeping Beauty*, the next we've finished nineteen seasons of *Say Yes to the Dress*. The True Love industrial complex feeds us grandiose dreams to occupy our dainty brains, hopeful that wedding planning will distract from thoughts of uprising and masturbation.

One of True Love's cruelest jokes is that the entire concept hinges on scarcity. According to season one of *Emily in Paris*, a Netflix show that I definitely did not watch, the defining characteristic of "the one" is someone who exists in close quarters but remains perpetually out of reach. According to more scholarly sources like *Sex and the City*,† "the one" can only be in every fifth episode (you'll know him when he does show up because he'll stare at you like he forgot your name). A helpful way to cut through the bullshit is to ask yourself who the characters would be in real life and my favorite method to do this consists of imagining who they would've voted for in the 2020 U.S. elections. In *SATC*'s case, it would've played out as follows:

- **Carrie:** Campaigned for Mayor Pete in the primary, then bubbled in Biden but forgot to mail in her absentee ballot

---

* I know what you're thinking—two P!nk references in one book? Go OFF.
† Before the reboot. #TeamKimCattrall

- **Charlotte:** Voted Trump in 2016 but 2020's BLM protests persuaded her to go blue (also probably shared several infographics to her Instagram story with the caption "now more than ever")
- **Samantha:** Biden, but only because she had terrible sex with Melania Trump in college
- **Miranda:** Bernie in the primary, then Biden on New York's Working Families Party line
- **Steve:** Same as Miranda but also volunteered as a poll worker
- **Big:** Trump

As Big himself embodies, True Love is nothing without capitalist markers of success. Cognitively, the connection begins with gifts—we've been programmed to think that an $18.99 drugstore bouquet of roses on Valentine's Day means something, while the absence of those roses warrants spiraling out and second-guessing every emoji we've ever sent. Romance and capitalism are so enmeshed that our aspirations of love often include aspirations of money. Focus Features even marketed *Fifty Shades of Grey* with a digital tour of Christian's penthouse apartment, proving that the fantasy was as much about being rich as it was about BDSM.

As icing on the proverbial wedding cake of horrors, the concept of True Love has always been heteronormative. That said, it's important to note this flawed ideology isn't just reserved for straight people—it's equal opportunity bullshit, happy to ruin your life no matter how you identify. Anyone of any gender can blame True Love if they care more about being in "a relationship" than they care about the person they're in said relationship with.

While the myth of True Love hurts everyone, it's patriarchal in nature, meaning it comes for women and femmes especially hard. On top of all the other nonsense we're supposed to live up to, we're also supposed to become "the perfect wife."

I've said "I love you" to four men throughout my life,* but every time I uttered those words, I wondered if I was lying. In each relationship I had the nagging sense that I'd compromised myself, and that I'd done so because I was desperate for a storybook romance. At the time I sincerely believed that staying silent about my needs and regularly shaving my legs were necessary investments in "us."

But in each case, I could never maintain this illusion for long. I usually blew my cover with something hygiene-related (e.g., disposable contacts I'd left on their floor), but by the time those slipups happened I'd already been stifling myself for months. For example: My love language is Words of Affirmation, and I feel most cared for when my partner showers me with compliments.† But instead of voicing that to my boyfriends (which would've set both of us up for success), I simply contorted my personality into something I thought they *might* compliment: an amalgamation of their interests, passions, and visions of "the perfect girl." I listened to Bill Simmons's podcast. I took a Skillshare course on cryptocurrency. I left my own calendar for dead in an effort to center their volatile schedules, once bailing on a friend's birthday because Ian was in town and wanted to watch *Westworld*. (He fell asleep halfway through.)

---

* Ian, Ben, the flat-footed creative writing major, and a high school boyfriend whose chapter didn't make the cut.

† If you're reading this, please go to my Instagram and comment something nice about this book. ☺

Why was I so willing to discard myself? You guessed it: because I wanted True Love, and I didn't care if that love was fake as fuck. It's hard to admit but I clung to the hope that one of these dudes would give me jewelry, chocolate, or—best case—a proposal. I didn't have a Pinterest board (not a public one, anyway) but that didn't stop me from fantasizing. (The ceremony begins at sunset in a Neukölln courtyard—I step out in a red jumpsuit wearing a graphic *Euphoria* eye, and the crowd goes wild.)

In hindsight, all my love stories with men had only been performances—one-woman shows furthering the True Love agenda, perpetuating the harmful idea that a woman's sole purpose is to provide sex and free therapy to her husband until one of them dies. Sure, a feminist can still "fall in love," but she should do it only if it's what *she* wants. But where's the line? There's things we want, and then there's things the world *tells us* to want. But how can we determine where one ends and the other begins?

If I'd "fallen in love" with a cis man, I'd probably still be out there squashing myself. This book's ending would consist of sugarcoated essays that spoke to his strengths, concluding with a chapter called "Actually, Not All Men! Who Knew?" A close reading would indicate severe gaslighting on both the guy's part and the patriarchy's, but since I'd failed to "hold myself accountable" and call this out, Empowerment Instagram would deplatform me immediately (rightfully so).

This isn't to say that healthy relationships with cis men cannot exist—just that it seems like they cannot exist for me. Thanks to heaps of internalized misogyny, I tend to make myself smaller—I abide by traditional gender roles until a hip queer person on the internet tells me it's time to stop. Fortunately the hip queers are usually right—and since systemic sexism has impacted far more lives than just mine, I bet I'm not alone.

But luckily for me (and for you, dear reader, since you are somehow still here), my love story isn't about True Love. It's about Queer Love. And that one, I didn't study in school.

Queer Love, it turns out, is everything True Love wishes it could be, and the same goes for Queer Love stories—they're the best kind of love stories because they're forced to self-determine, which means they do their own world-building (*Lord of the Rings*, but make it gay . . . er than it already is). David Halperin writes, "Love has seemed too intimately bound up with institutions and discourses of the 'normal,' too deeply embedded in standard narratives of romance, to be available for 'queering.'" Queer Love then requires us to create something entirely new—it must be different than the heteronormative, patriarchal tropes from whence we came.

Before I go any further with this and wake the "BuT WhAt AbOuT sTrAiGhT pRiDe" crowd, I should clarify: You don't have to be an LGBTQ+ person to experience Queer Love. The only thing queer love requires is authenticity, and you can have that no matter who your partner(s) is/are. You can also lack it—being queer doesn't inherently make you down-to-earth (*see*: Jeffree Star, Rachel Dolezal, or Ursula in *The Little Mermaid*).* I'm no authenticity role model either: I've been bisexual my whole life, thus all of my relationships with men

---

* Any queer-coded Disney villain, really.

were *technically* queer relationships. But was I honest? Did I show up with my full self? The tattoo I got to impress a high school crush says no. (Actually it says "this too shall pass" and I'm in the process of getting it removed.)

People tend to focus on the practical appeal of queer relationships—plenty of think pieces have celebrated these bonds for the way they transcend gender roles. When sexism doesn't tell you who should cook, who cooks? The better cook. Beautiful.

But as I said, a Queer Love story isn't just a straight love story featuring queer people—it's about a love that is rooted in radical, asymmetrical truth. Queer Love is inherently political—an action that bell hooks defined as "the practice of freedom."* Queer Love takes up space—it is earth-shattering and expansive, yet somehow remains vulnerable even in its strongest form.

When I say Queer Love, I don't mean love in a legal sense. I don't mean domestic partnerships, divorces, or whatever it's called when two white gays start a joint TikTok account.

When I say Queer Love, I mean love that makes its own rules. Love that exists without borders and thrives without clean lines. Love that creates more space than it takes up.†

So yes—this book ends with a Queer Love story, and that story happens to involve two queer people. Sometimes I wonder if my partner and I were drawn to each other because we both struggle with binaries, each of us viewing the world as

---

* Interesting that we didn't read bell hooks or *checks notes* any Black queer authors in my Philosophy of Love course.

† This last sentiment was inspired by the hilarious and ever thoughtful writer Mamoudou N'Diaye—it's his personal and professional ethos, and it stuck with me.

overlapping Venn diagrams where everything happens to be something else too. Maybe we shared an intuitive understanding about the power in shades of gray.

Or maybe, like a ditzy girl in a rom-com, I just happened to get lost in their eyes.

BRINLEY JAMES FORD

YOU FIRST HEAR their name in September 2019, when even the leaves are in transition. You are finally starting to understand that autumn isn't just a pathway to winter but a permanent state; that flux itself can be a final form.

The person who says their name is your friend Julia—she and her girlfriend want to set you up. At first Julia describes your mysterious suitor only using pronouns, enunciating "they" and "them" like a study abroad student pronouncing "Barth-el-ona." She isn't showing off as much as wanting to make sure you notice—that way you won't mess up when you meet.

"They think you're hot," Julia says. "And just a heads-up—they're intense. Chances are they're going to pursue you. Hard."

"What's their name?" you ask, searching for anything that will help you Instagram-stalk later. You try to stay calm but

feel your face light up, enamored with the thought that someone has already chosen you.

"It's . . . Brinley," Julia answers, and from her hesitation,
you realize this name must be relatively new, something Julia
herself has likely just learned. You take the word into your
head, learning its curves, tossing it over like a tongue unwrap-
ping a Starburst. In that moment you must see the future,
because somehow you know that this word—their name—
will be important. A lump forms in your throat, but in a good
way—like you're at the top of a roller coaster ready to drop.

✳

The first time they look at you happens one week later—
despite being thirty, you feel like a preteen with a crush. The
South Williamsburg coffee shop-slash-gallery turns out to
be more elegant than you'd expected: velvet chartreuse furniture, a chandelier, and mezcal cocktails on tap. It's an art
show, and they're the artist—Julia has invited you but has also
made it clear that you aren't supposed to know the deets; the
artist wishes to remain anonymous. You think of a tweet by
@ayoedebiri: "no pronouns // do not refer to me ever," and
wonder about Brinley's sense of humor—if they'd balk at this,
or laugh.

You're checking out a photo of a bearded Barbie wearing a strap-on when you feel their gaze, white-hot, searing
into your skin. You look up to meet their eyes and they strut
toward you, wearing a leopard button-up with matching leopard socks. You feel your spine straighten, as if someone just
tossed an ice cube down your back.

Once they're close to you, you introduce yourself, spitting out "hellomynameisjen" just to fill the silence.

"I know who you are." They smirk. Though you've been warned, their forwardness still strikes like a gust of wind, so strong you almost have to steady yourself. By now you know who they are too—you've already spent hours studying their social media, hovering your thumb above the phone so you didn't accidentally double-tap. But you would never admit your interest in them *to* them (at least not until your fifth date).

Up close they look just like their pictures—though you've only seen the recent ones. You'd stopped yourself from scrolling more than a few months back, having seen a meme along the lines of TRANS PEOPLE DO NOT OWE YOU ANY INFORMATION ABOUT THEIR LIVES PRE-TRANSITION. The earliest post you saw featured a professional portrait, date-stamped in June. They stood against a gray studio backdrop with their crisp white shirt unbuttoned, revealing the topography of their chest: two long gold necklaces, scars from top surgery, and three prominent tattoos (with the hint of more). They looked like a suave Irish boy—dark hair styled into a dull peak, face slightly flushed, hinting at the type of heat that shows up after a good cry. The photo felt familiar, as if you'd already been carrying it in your wallet for years. You sensed it was meaningful before you even read the caption:

> Happy pride month! I've decided to officially come out as a queer, trans/nonbinary person who takes a low dose of testosterone. I am done hiding myself to prioritize anyone else's comfort. ♥

I use they/them pronouns. Using these pronouns makes me feel seen. If you're unclear, "they" replaces she/he and "them" replaces her/him when speaking to me or about me, whether or not I'm in the room. NO—it's not plural. It's singular. Hear it, believe it, take it seriously.

The trans/nonbinary identity suits me because I am not a man or woman. I am neither and also both. Put another way, sometimes I feel more masculine than feminine, and vice versa. Nonbinary people do not need to look a certain way.

Here's a quote from Banksy that stuck with me: "Parents will do anything for their kids, except let them be themselves." I've been fortunate to have friends/family who've supported me. I recognize many people have not.

But here's a fun fact: Did you know that less than 50% of teens identify as straight in 2019?

Thanks for reading and supporting me. Learning to use they/them pronouns can be tricky—I mess up too! But keep trying, and don't feel bad when you're called out—as long as you're putting in effort, you're on the right side of history.

When you read the Banksy quote, you smile—at least you'll have one thing to talk about.

Until this point, your interactions with people who iden-tify as nonbinary have happened entirely through the internet. But while comment sections have their perils, reality magni-fies the horrors, bringing the threat of physical violence, con-stant social anxiety, and "accidental" microaggressions (which are microaggressions nonetheless). Later, with Brinley, you'll witness all this IRL—how often people stare, or think they're being polite by saying "ma'am."

Since you're constantly comparing your queerness to other people's, it's hard not to do it here. Yet putting yourself under the same LGBTQ+ umbrella as Brinley seems absurd—you've spent your whole life performing femininity, taking gender's easiest road, and here they are, marching off-path to live their truth. You already admire their confidence and courage, but you also understand that this is gross on multiple levels: By projecting your own insecurities you become a problematic cliché, yet another cis person lauding trans people for being "brave." Besides, there are already so many real compliments you could give—acknowledge their fashion sense, their pho-tos, their stunning ice-blue eyes.

You must have zoned out because suddenly they're look-ing at you like you fainted.

"Sooooo . . . ?" Their impatience snaps you back to reality.

"So what?"

"So can I get you a drink?"

*

You schedule your first date for the following Sunday after-noon, which affords you one week of texting after the gallery, and your digital chemistry exceeds expectations:

im either going as harry styles
or Elton john for Halloween

> hell ya. im going as jennifer
> melfi from the sopranos

yes yes im into this therapist
cosplay

> what makes you feel
> that way?

are u asking or is that cosplay?

wow

can i come lie on your couch
later?

> def

ok great
date the smart girl they said

> oh shit, are you dating
> someone else? :(

very funny

When the day rolls around you meet at the Hoxton, a hotel that screams Brooklyn chic (high ceilings, millennial-pink wallpaper, and staff who look like they want to go home). You spot Brinley at the bar downstairs, face bright red, frantically begging two women to move. The women do, and when you take a seat Brinley explains those are their friends who happened to be here for brunch.

"I don't want anyone spying on us," they admit. You simper and hop onto a barstool—seeing them flustered boosts your confidence. You're ready. You feel good.

When the get-to-know-you portion begins, you focus on

your upbringing so you can make your best jokes about Indiana (e.g., "My dad is also my brother," "Heard of corn? That's us!"). Brinley goes next—they gloss over their childhood in upstate New York, then change the subject, telling you that they have particular tastes.

"Don't judge me, but I snuck in two sugar-free Red Bulls." Gesturing under the table, they flash you the contents of a plastic bag.

"How do you know they don't sell those here?"

Their tone grows brazen, self-assured. "Because I know every place in the city that carries these."

"Okay, NOW I'm judging." You laugh. "I thought being queer meant I didn't have to date frat guys anymore."

"Oh, I'm sorry—based on your obnoxiously huge sneakers, I just assumed 'frat guy' was your type."

"I will have you know that these are Balenciaga . . . knock-offs."

"My mistake." They lift their hand, mocking you, and start mixing their drink. "Also—if anything, I'm a *gay* frat guy."

You grin. "Now *that* is my type."

They order vodka on ice, then covertly mix in the Red Bull—with one sip their shoulders settle; they seem much more at ease. Comfortable now, they tell you about their coming-out. You realize that swapping these stories is indeed the "standard first-date thing" and will probably occur on every first date for the rest of your life (unless, by some twist of fate, this one happens to be your last). You lean forward, ready to pretend you haven't fawned over that photo with the gray backdrop and read the caption enough to have it memorized. But then they tell you things you don't already know. They say they've come out multiple times: When they were twenty-three as gay. Ten years later as nonbinary. On several occasions over the next three years—as someone getting top surgery, as a trans person, then as a trans person taking T.

"Which was the hardest?"

"They all sucked." Brinley shrugs.

You last an hour at the hotel before heading to a dive bar—a honky-tonk with horseshoe decals on the windows and Johnny Cash on repeat inside. You snag a booth and Brinley sifts through a pile of worn-out board games, pulling out Connect 4.

"Ask a personal question when you put in a chip—I'll start." They drop in a red piece. "When was the last time you had sex?"

"Uh . . . a few weeks ago," you estimate, remembering that speechwriter.

"Good for you, honey!" they respond in an accent, Jewish mother meets Spanish twink. "Who with?"

Gulp. The gender reveal. "Um, some dude."

"Oh yeah—you're bi, right?" Their voice softens; they seem unfazed. "I think I'm the same. It's funny, I've been sleeping with women for so long that sleeping with men actually sounds more risque."

"That's fascinating." You lean forward. "Bisexuality is interesting because everyone thinks it's, like, a synonym for 'slut.' But they don't know that if someone's calling me a slut, I'm taking that as a compliment."

"How else would you take it?" They slide out of the booth to go to the bathroom, leaving you swooning, missing them already. You decide to surprise them with more drinks when they emerge.

"Vodka Red Bulls and Connect 4?" the bartender asks.

"How'd you know? Do they do this with all the girls?" You giggle.

The bartender shrugs. "Third time this week."

This shocks you for a second, but thankfully it doesn't scare you off. On the contrary, it intrigues you—the threat of rejection registers as both repulsive and familiar, like the scent of a lover's BO. Suddenly your brain does its fantasy thing, imagining a luxury vacation to Marrakesh: you and Brinley weaving through labyrinthian markets, staying in your own private riad, feasting on bottomless Michelin-star tagine. But this fantasy feels different, more like a premonition. There's no turning back—you're hooked.

Despite owning the title of "slut," you don't want to seem easy, or worse—to reveal that you don't even know how to have queer sex. But when Brinley comes back from the bathroom and kisses you in the booth, you realize with certainty that you're going back to their place. The intimacy feels addicting and long overdue, decades of denial crumbling like segments of a blown-up bridge.

Their apartment feels industrial but also quirky—a silver table, vintage pillows, and too many plants to count, including the biggest bird-of-paradise you've ever seen. You're in awe of the greenery, but since you can't keep a succulent alive and don't know how to give a compliment without revealing that, you say nothing. A year later, during a fight, Brinley will tell you that they wish you'd been more forthcoming about being such a hot mess. (Maybe the murderous bisexual trope was about killing plants all along.)

They microwave a leftover panini and after devouring it, you somehow feel sexier than before. You're both too buzzed to notice each other's garlic breath and blissfully make out on the couch. At one point the taste changes, and you open your eyes to find that the tongue in your mouth belongs to their dog.

"EW!" You frantically down a glass of water nearby.

"I was wondering how long before you'd notice," they tease.

Eventually you move to Brinley's bedroom—there's a window open; it smells like Nag Champa and fresh air. They press you onto their bed, fingers slipping under your waistband, collectively agile, a tiny troop of soldiers undoing your jeans. Once the battalion succeeds Brinley charges, sliding their palm down your pants.

You tilt your head back and think, *Thank god this feeling was worth the hype.*

✳

The first time you cry in front of them, you're in an Italian restaurant on the Lower East Side. You ducked inside due to a sudden thunderstorm—the place has incredible lighting, but, you discover, half a star on Yelp. You order drinks and mozzarella sticks, the hardest things to mess up, but when the wine arrives, it somehow tastes stale. You chug it anyway and weep.

You should be proud of yourself. You just finished speaking on a panel of queer activists—an opportunity that thrilled you when it came your way. You'd hyped it up in your mind because it felt gratifying to be seen as LGBTQ+, but also because Brinley planned to attend and you wanted to show off. But onstage you made a fool of yourself—you became a broken record, trying to check your "bi privilege" by repeatedly insisting that you shouldn't take up space. You did this ad nauseum, trying to de-center yourself by talking about yourself, ultimately making the conversation all about you. The other panelists offered their consolation: "You deserve to be here, you know." But you disagreed, especially in hindsight, knowing that you'd aired your impostor syndrome for all to see. On top of that, your performance had been racist—you'd hogged the mic to talk about how white cis women needed to *pass* the mic. You embarassment. You hypocrite. You fake.

Hoping you haven't ruined your makeup yet, you wipe your eyes, but your finger comes away covered in soot. Brinley overlooks this, then points to themself and says, "Hey, at least one trans person thinks you did great." Tears stream harder as you dismiss their kind words: "You're white. Your opinion doesn't matter right now."

They shrug. "Fair."

"Besides," you continue, "I'm not crying about the panel."

Confused, they touch the back of their neck. "Okay, then—why?"

It's a reasonable question and even though you provoked it, you're not sure you know how to respond. You just know you're terrified, and if you dig into it, you might realize what you're scared of is falling in love with them. Your relationship feels too good to be true—because Brinley uplifts and supports you, but also because being with someone both masculine and feminine affirms the fact that you're bi. You've found a partner whose identity alone could communicate your sexuality to the world, yet you know even thinking about that upside isn't fair—to the relationship or to Brinley. Your love doesn't deserve this burden, the task of erasing your sense of lack. You now understand that your fluidity makes you high-maintenance—it requires constant validation, a steady stream of "yes, you exist." Brinley gives that to you—through their gender, but also by not treating your history with men like a past life you need to shed. They validate you when the two of you talk about the future, and agree that you could fuck with polyamory someday. They validate you when they tease you about the time you dated Ben. They validate you when they refer to you in the third person—"if the bisexual wants takeout, guess we're getting takeout!" (Sure, that's just how they flirt, but if there's one thing that's bi culture, it's feeling affirmed by a joke.)

By now you know that "bi privilege" is not a thing—your sexuality has not done you many favors thus far. But you realize why you continually dismissed your queerness—why, when the notification popped up, you chose "remind me tomorrow" every damn time.

You did it because owning your sexuality is hard. Period. And though you've been queer all along, loving Brinley means living that queerness. Your life will change. You'll have to explain pronouns to coworkers. Based on several homophobic news stories, you can't take that trip to Morocco. If you want to have kids, it'll be expensive—you'll need to inseminate or adopt. And no matter how hard it is, you'll still be a cis person—whatever inconveniences you face will be nothing compared to the ones Brinley does.

Those challenges aside, it's also wholly terrifying to actually be yourself. Authenticity comes with an existential ultimatum—if you're unhappy after coming out, maybe the problem is simply . . . you.

Your appetizer arrives looking rubbery and Brinley stabs the fried cheese with a fork. "Are you crying because these look gross or because we're obviously still gonna finish them?"

"Yes," you say. They feed you a bite.

✳

The first time they say "I love you" it's two months later, when you're both still in bed at noon. The dog, once your lover, now feels like your child—he* sleeps between you, curled up like a preschooler recovering from a bad dream. The afternoon sun pours in and you realize you're hungover. Your stomach growls from the Oreo Blizzard you had at two a.m.

"I'm telling you: I love you. You don't believe me," they say, and they're right. You don't believe they love you. Not yet. Sure, you know they *care* for you—you've been dating a total of three months and they manage to prove their compassion daily. They bought a table for your side of the bed. They stocked their fridge with tuna salad, your favorite midday snack. They share their fears with you—their fear that you will leave them (you have no plans to), their fear that you will think of them as a lesbian (you wouldn't—and since lesbians don't seem to like you, you're relieved they're not one), their fear that they don't look nonbinary enough (even though, according to their own Instagram caption, nonbinary people don't have to look a certain way). They often ask you to marry them, and you always give the same response: "Ask me again in thirty minutes." Until right now, you thought the whole thing was a joke.

Coming on too strong is usually a red flag (if a cis man proposed to you within the first six years of dating, you'd turn around and run). But Brinley is not a cis man, so with them it hits different. In spite of that bartender's observation, they've turned out to be the most committed, honest, and transparent

---

* Their dog uses all pronouns, so he/him will do.

person you've ever met. They have no filter, which means no barrier between who they are and who they show the world. (When you got them a bread machine for their birthday, they said, "Thanks, baby! Can we return it?") They're always lucid, able to articulate their feelings: "I'm anxious," "I'm over-whelmed," "I'm stressed," "I'm pleased." You envy them for this, especially since years of dating men trained you to do the opposite: under-communicate until the relationship implodes. It may be a queer stereotype to fall in love fast, but maybe that's not such a bad thing. Maybe it means you're more in touch with yourself and your feelings. Maybe we'd all fall in love fast if we thought we were allowed.

"You're right, baby," you say. "I don't believe you, but I do appreciate it." A knowing smirk crosses their face. They get out of bed, walk to their kitchen, and return with a note.

In blue ink the paper says, "I love you Jen Winston!" Below that, in black: "I wrote that last week to make sure I believed myself before I told you. And I do believe myself. I love you, it's true! I have faith that you'll meet me here."

You clutch the note to your chest and notice Brinley glow-ing, swaying on their feet. You kiss them, but before you can come up with something sweet to say, something terrible hap-pens: you fart.

This fart isn't femme. It isn't delicate. It's raucous, like an out-of-tune trumpet being stomped on. Your blood runs cold—no one has ever heard your body make a sound like this.* Congruent with your tendency to squish your emotions,

---

* Aside from Joey and twelve people in a restaurant at Helsinki Airport. (It's worth bring-ing up that incident to give you, dear reader, full context, but it should be noted that a com-parison would be flawed, as the Helsinki fart was in a league of its own. The Helsinki fart

you're not one to talk about piss and shit with your partner. No—you would rather conceal your biology forever, upholding the sexist tyranny of "Girls don't poop."

"I'm—I'm sorry." You sprint to the bathroom, where you sit on the toilet with your head in your hands. Your worst nightmare just got worse because the bathroom isn't soundproof— through the shut door, you hear Brinley's muffled laugh.

One month later, you finally say it back. It's a leisurely Saturday morning, the two of you toting iced matcha lattes around Williamsburg, waltzing into cooking stores, gardening shops, and sample sales whose markdowns you still couldn't afford. At one point, you walk past the pharmacy and they agree to come inside while you pick up a prescription. When you reach the register, Brinley realizes they need something too.

"Hi, I'm looking for syringes," they say.

"For what?" The pharmacist sounds pained that anyone might ask her to do anything.

Brinley takes a deep breath. "For testosterone."

You squeeze their hand and they frown as if to say, *I don't need your help*.

"What's your name?" The pharmacist has decided to put forth effort now, but you watch the color drain from Brinley's face. For most people this question means nothing, but

---

rivaled the decibel levels of commercial flights taking off. After the Helsinki fart happened, each of the twelve people turned their heads as if you'd just said their name. You and Joey cried real tears as you cracked up for thirty minutes straight and came dangerously close to missing your flight.)

for them it's almost a threat—three words guaranteed to ruin their day.

Ever since you've known them they've been trying to legally change their name. They've already chosen a great one, which impresses you—the selection process seems like the hardest part. You would've buried yourself in research, cycling through pop culture references, ultimately vetoing everything due to associations with problematic men. But you are not a trans person. They are. And so it makes sense that their decision took more practical matters into account.

For most of their life, Brinley was their last name, assigned at birth along with a binary gender marker and a feminine first name that never felt right. When they started going by that name instead, people understood—everyone gets the concept of nicknames, nbd. Now, regardless of whether that name was actually the one they wanted, they'd decided to keep it rather than force another change. They knew that they weren't supposed to make decisions to accommodate other people's comfort (and their Instagram caption had claimed to be done with that, anyway), but how could they ignore other people when other people had the power to make them feel whole? Andrea Long Chu writes, "If there is any lesson of gender transition—from the simplest request regarding pronouns to the most invasive surgeries—it's that gender is something other people have to *give* you. Gender exists, if it is to exist at all, only in the structural generosity of strangers."

Intellectually Brinley knew that their nonbinary identity was intrinsic to them, something no misgendering family member could ever take away. But one could do only so many mirror affirmations, and so they chose their last name as their new first, hoping this would help their loved ones get it right.

For the middle and surname they added "James" and "Ford," giving themselves a few splashes of masculinity. And boom—they had a name.

Well, almost. Because now that they've finished the appellative portion, the paperwork begins. As women who've taken their husband's surnames know well, legal name changes are a complex and bureaucratic process—they involve digging through the DMV website, emailing customer service reps, and attending multiple webinars to demystify the fine print. Changing your first name makes things even harder, so Brinley's reward for answering profound questions of selfhood will be a nightmarish onslaught of tasks: In the coming months, they will pay to print their name in a newspaper ad. They will track down a virtual notary during a pandemic. They will mail out their passport while USPS reports to be facing bankruptcy. (And then they'll mail it out two more times since it will accidentally get returned to sender twice.)

That Saturday, Brinley is relieved to not be thinking about this administrative labyrinth. But again the fate of the day lies with strangers, and the tight-lipped pharmacist has no idea.

"My name is Brinley," Brinley eventually says. You chew your lip, nervous about how this will go. *They mentioned testosterone earlier*, you remind yourself. *Maybe the pharmacist caught the hint.*

"Aaaaand first name?" She clacks her nails against the keyboard and before Brinley can respond says "Oh! Is it . . ." and reads their deadname aloud.

This moment could never hurt you the way it hurts Brinley, but even secondhand it still hurts like hell. You want to hold Brinley—to heal them, to somehow steal their pain and take it as your own. But that's impossible (and probably cis-saviory anyway). Instead you just stand there holding their hand until the pharmacist retrieves the syringes and you leave.

One block away from Duane Reade you blurt it out: "I love you." You're practically shouting even though they're right by your side.

They stop mid-step and face you. "What did you say?"

"I love you."

"Really?"

"Really." You smile. "I am in love with you, Brinley James Ford."

Though you can't heal them, you hope this truth—and it is your truth—provides a much-deserved respite. For a few seconds it does: Brinley beams, and seeing them happy renders the pharmacy powerless—a distant memory. But then their demeanor shifts—they furrow their brow, narrow their eyes. They press their tongue between their lips and make a fart sound.

"You fucker!" You slap them on the shoulder. "Can I take it back?"

They kiss you hard, then shake their head.

✴

Your first consultation with a couples therapist happens a year later and unfortunately it does more harm than good. Though her website claims she's LGBTQ+ friendly, her bedside manner says differently.

"Just a heads-up, I'm awful with pronouns!" the therapist chirps. You promptly hang up the phone.

The next one seems decent enough—she specializes in queer relationships and tells you she wrote her thesis on "trans people and trauma." That's vague but she's covered by insurance, so vague will have to do. Together you and Brinley fill out an eight-page questionnaire about why you're here: "We're here preemptively—not because our relationship is in trouble, but because we want to build a life together! We hope to establish a strong foundation for the way we communicate."

This sounds like a great reason to start couples therapy, and it would be, except it's a lie. By now you've been through a lot—good dates, bad dates, screaming fights, make-up sex, kink parties, dry spells, weekend trips, meeting their mom—and you're stuck in a phase where you fight constantly, never sure whether you should blame quarantine or just break up. You don't live together (yet) but you do live within walking distance, and since there's nothing else to do, you often wind up staying at Brinley's for weeks on end. The close quarters always seem lovely until one of you explodes and you, the guest, are forced to storm back home. During the pandemic, you learn that Brinley's OCD and your ADHD are each worse than either of you thought. Yes, opposites attract, but sometimes they also crash into each other too hard.

You fight about:

- The dishes (Brinley needs you to wash them NOW)
- Your iPhone alarm (Brinley begs you to stop hitting snooze)
- What to watch (Brinley suggests another shitty action movie)
- What not to watch (Brinley says if you choose another art film they'll scream)
- Zoom meetings (Brinley thinks you talk too loud)
- Back massages (Brinley asks if you're intentionally doing a bad job)

- Ordering food (Brinley thinks you do it too much—true)
- Showering (Brinley thinks you don't do it enough—also true)

By now (thanks but no thanks to COVID), you've both realized that "healthy relationship" doesn't mean "relationship that's conflict-free." As frustrating as it is, "healthy" means communication and that means therapy, which today you're each taking from your respective home. You only do this when you're already mad at each other and it usually leads to a shouting match via video chat. Today tears stream down both your faces as the queer-affirming therapist remains on mute.

After forty-five minutes of screaming, an exasperated Brinley gets the guts to ask: "Do you think our fights are quarantine-related, or are we just . . . not compatible? Are we a bad match?"

Despite this being the therapist's one chance to offer any substance to your session, her eyes dart to the clock. "Actually, we have to wrap up for today."

You gasp and notice Brinley's mouth fall open too. Right after the session ends, they FaceTime you.

"Literally what the fuck," they scoff. "She's the worst."

"The AUDACITY," you reply. "She can't spare five minutes?"

"Like, bitch, we KNOW you don't have any other patients to get to right now, because you suck."

"So much." You laugh.

"I mean, come on," Brinley continues, "when I get mad about you leaving out the dishes overnight, it's clearly rooted in a lack of control that stems from gender trauma. But maybe her trans thesis didn't cover that?!"

"I miss you," you say, and it's true—even though you were just at their apartment yesterday. Brinley smiles and tells you to "get your ass back." When you walk in you scoop up the dog and the three of you huddle on the couch, a family, a bundle of warmth and fur. You don't need a mental health professional to tell you that quarantine's been hard—sure, you've become codependent, but you'll do whatever it takes to get through it, no matter how many self-help books you have to read. Though you've discussed that stricter boundaries and more alone time would probably curb most of your fights, neither of you have the strength right now—it's a pandemic and just in case the world actually ends, you don't ever want to be apart again. Your therapist might be ready to quit on you (maybe she turns into a pumpkin at 6:46 p.m.?), but you and Brinley aren't ready to quit on yourselves.

"We can find a new doctor next week." Brinley softly kisses your neck. "But right now I wanna watch this Liam Neeson movie."

"Oooh, supposed to be good?"

"Got thirty-three percent on Rotten Tomatoes."

You roll your eyes while curling up in their arms. "Baby, that sounds perfect."

GENDER IS A DRAG: A TIMELINE

3500 BCE: Ancient Mesopotamians worship Inanna, the multi-hyphenate goddess of love, sex, and justice. Inanna becomes known for the ability to transform people's genders, leading a group of priests called the Gala who are neither "men" nor "women" (and who might be described as gender-fluid today).

✳

Fifteenth century: The Bugis people of Indonesia recognize five genders, including one encompassing gender-fluid or intersex identity, and those people call themselves bissu. The bissu often take on powerful roles in their culture, serving as "kingmakers" at coronations and mediators between people and gods. (Despite increasing persecution, bissu people persist for centuries, with a small population still alive in 2021.)

＊

Nineteenth century: The sex binary emerges, a product of co-lonial medicine. The word "women" refers exclusively to white women, since the racist scientists making decisions don't be-lieve Black people, Indigenous people, and people of color are "civilized" enough to distinguish between women and men.

＊

1978, a decade before my birth: My dad graduates from Yale with a PhD in data science and immediately gets a teaching position at Indiana University. Almost just as immediately, he realizes he hates it—as a twenty-eight-year-old introvert who recently lost his virginity, the thought of public speaking fills him with dread. His voice quivers. His body shakes. He has flashbacks to childhood bullies that make him terrified to be himself in front of a crowd. He's smart, but smart isn't enough anymore. He assumes he'll never thrive on the teach-er's stage.

But then he learns about a special doctor—a "psychiatrist" who can, allegedly, help him stop being afraid. For the next six months, that "psychiatrist" beats the shit out of him—punching until his skin grows bruised and bloody; until he screams; until his inhibitions fade and he has nothing left to fear.

The worst part about the "treatment" is that it works—afterward my dad addresses his class with strong posture, finally anxiety-free. He starts approaching women (and gets rejected, but bounces back). Three years after that he gets tenure. Ten years later—when I'm born—he wins several faculty awards.

Thirty years after that he will tell me this story, and I'll stare at him in shock.

"Are you glad you did it?" I'll ask.

"No question," he'll reply. "Changed my life. It's the only reason I had the guts to talk to your mom."

✷

1997, grade school: My mother always cooks and never asks for help. I assume it's because I can barely boil water, but maybe it's because she enjoys her alone time—though she began cooking out of obligation, the kitchen has become her sacred space. Whether she wants my help or not, I always feel guilty that I have no interest in joining her. I'm a girl, after all—I should be in there feeding my family, assisting with pot roasts and stews.

Years later I will be grateful that she didn't pressure me, though I will still feel guilty that I forced her to shoulder the burden alone. She'll tell me it's fine—she loves Food Network and "now that your father put a TV in the kitchen, I never want to leave!"

For my mom, being a woman isn't about manicures, eyebrow waxes, or a stocked makeup bag. She grew up too poor for that—raised in Evansville, Indiana, as the daughter of a coal miner, she was always tasked with making ends meet. Femininity was a luxury afforded only to women in magazines, and even now that she can pay for jewelry, perfume, and skin care products, she obsesses over them less than I do. (The exception being her La Mer cream, which I am not allowed to touch.)

Maybe that's why my mother's womanhood now feels so

enmeshed with kindness. Being nice has always been a free way to accomplish the very thing women are supposed to do: delight. My mom gives out thank-yous with abandon, waves cars ahead at stop signs. In buildings, she holds the door for everyone no matter how long she has to wait.

✳

2002, middle school: The first time I question my gender it's not by choice—it's because Sloane asks Laney, Becca, Erin, and me to do an experiment. Her brother, a high schooler who has recently done a flawed reading of *Middlesex*, told her he knows how to find out if we're really boys or girls—we each have to look at our nails.

I flip my palm up and curl my fingers down. *That was easy.* Then I notice everyone else has kept their palms facing the floor. Their hands are outstretched, fingers long.

"You guys do it weird!" I shout.

"Oh my god, Jen—YOU do it weird!" Sloane gasps. "You must be a BOY!"

They all laugh. I laugh too, joining in to mask my embarrassment. But more than embarrassed, I'm confused. I *thought* I was a girl, but maybe I'm not a good one. What should I do: Show more cleavage? Start using tampons? Have a baby ASAP? All of that feels out of reach. I spend the next few weeks training myself to look at my nails from the top.

✳

2013, two years after college: My friend Ari hosts a costume party with the theme of "Daddy's Gay." Years later Ari will tell me they've started using they/them pronouns, and we'll celebrate with joints and orange wine. But in 2013, I primarily know them as my friend with the two-story penthouse in downtown LA—a queer Jay Gatsby known for outrageous soirees.

Ari's parties involve extreme levels of commitment to taboo themes—the most provocative one was "Sexy Kids," where Ari managed to transform one bedroom into a ball pit. (The costumes that night were in especially poor taste—three women showed up dressed as JonBenét.)

The invitations usually arrive as an email that helps build out the story. In the case of "Daddy's Gay," it was written as a note from Daddy himself:

> Hey buddy, it's Daddy! How's summer camp? They still have archery this year?
> So listen champ. Daddy needs to talk to you about something: DADDY'S GAY. After you get back from camp, maybe you could come get a glimpse into my life? Just do Daddy a favor and don't tell your mom. 😉

I show up wearing fishnet stockings with lingerie and say I'm "a housewife grasping at straws." I think I might take home Best Dressed until one of Ari's other female friends arrives, tits out, wearing four-inch heels, showing off a drawn-on beard.

"I'm Daddy and Mommy at once!" she explains. "And I don't know whether my character should laugh or cry."

I fawn over her but stew underneath: *Why didn't I think of that?*

*

2016, five years after college: After the coworker I punched in the face ghosts me, I find solace in feminine angsty dreampop—specifically Empress Of. Her albums feel like love letters to herself. In my favorite song she croons over and over, "I'm only a woman if woman is a word." The lyrics repeat in my head on a loop but I can't figure out what they mean.

✳

2016, the day Trump is elected: I put on a red-white-and-blue top, then strut to the polls. After I'm done, exhilarated, I take a photo with my "I Voted" sticker and flash a toothy grin. I caption it: "I don't always take smiling selfies, but when I do, it's after voting for the first woman president!" I include several emojis of the U.S. flag.

✳

2016, the night Trump is elected: I sit on my couch watching CNN and sob. Scrolling through my camera roll lets me replay the devastation in real time—my screenshots gradually shift from hopeful tweets to that damn needle from the *New York Times*. I stay up until four a.m. taking more screenshots, though these are of memes, quotes, and protest signs featuring phrases like MIKE PENCE LIKES NICKELBACK and TREAT WOMEN AS PEOPLE, NOT AS WIVES. I grip my phone like it's a weapon, capturing posts that teach me something, make me laugh, or both.

Writing sponsored lists was an embarrassing job, but at

least it taught me how to make content—and how to make that content spread.* I decide I will use my marketing skills for good—I will start a platform and share these edifying jpegs with the world.

Instagram asks me to create a handle so I type in the most obvious phrase I can think of—"girlpower"—and pause for a moment before adding "supply." The handle is available (not a hot commodity apparently) so I claim it and write my bio: "Your anti-Trump energy source—keeping you pissed off through 2020 and beyond." After this I post nine protest signs and marvel at my empowering new grid. Maybe the revolution can, in fact, be memed. It might not fix everything, but it's a start.

✳

2017, three months into Trump's presidency: I purchase a shirt that says the words "Hysterical Female" in a Metallica-esque font. I love this shirt so much that I sleep in it every night and still manage to wear it out of the house once a week. I purchase many similar shirts and eventually collaborate with a designer to make some of our own—we sell graphic tees with phrases like "2 FEMINIST, 2 FURIOUS," "GIRLS RULE, TRUMP DROOLS," and most regretfully, the Migos-inspired "BAD AND BOOBY" (which also comes in a tote!).

I don't yet understand that capitalist feminism is an oxymoron—don't yet see why I can't use the revolution to

---

* The cardinal rule being that there are no rules—the only way to grow your audience is to experiment and find what sticks.

get rich. At protests for #MeToo I rock my own shirts with pride, styling them with statement earrings and striped pants. I chant "Hey-hey! Ho-ho! Sexism has got to go!" and while I believe what I'm saying, I am oblivious to the extent of my privilege while shouting it: the history of racism, transphobia, and discrimination within the feminist movement; the complexities of gender itself. What I do know is that embracing my womanhood makes me feel like a rock star—a left-of-center rebel whose existence is radical enough.

✳

2017, six months into Trump's presidency: I watch the documentary *The Mask You Live In* and it upturns my entire life. I'd thought patriarchy only held back women but I learn that the system actually harms men too. (I won't learn that nonbinary people exist for at least another few months.) In the film, Dr. Caroline Heldman explains, "Masculinity is not organic. It's reactive. It's not something that just happens. It's a rejection of everything that is feminine." I can hardly wrap my mind around the implications of this: If society teaches men that the worst thing to be is a woman, Heldman probes, is it really a surprise when men treat women like shit?

The film points out that in Western countries, being "a man" usually means three things: (1) be athletic, (2) have sex with women, and (3) make lots of money. But what if you're a poor man, or a fat man, or a nervous wreck like my dad? Are you still a man? Who gets to decide?

✳

2017, ten months into Trump's presidency: At twenty-nine years old I finally realize I don't need to enjoy cooking in order to "count" as a woman. Eden gives me this permission even though she herself loves it—she often bursts into the office, gushing about a dish she made last night. When we aren't talking about politics, Eden spends the day deciding what to make that night, drafting up a shopping list she'll use on her commute home. She locates specialty stores that sell shichimi togarashi. She calls ten boutique grocers to ask how much their oysters are, looking disgusted every time she hangs up. "THREE DOLLARS? An outrage."

Each time Eden mentions a recipe, I interpret it as a threat—*she's rubbing it in my face that I can't do what she does.* One day it breaks me and I confess: I hate cooking. It's monotonous. It's overwhelming—especially as someone with ADHD. (Ableist much?)

"I really fucking hate it!" I yell.

Eden shrugs. "That's cool."

"No—you don't understand—I never want to cook again. I'd rather spend every cent of my salary on takeout." I expect her to be outraged and try to convince me otherwise. That's what everyone else has always done.

"You don't have to like it," she replies. "I *like* it, but I don't love it."

"But you do it every day?" I'm confused.

"Yeah, because it's cheaper, and because my fiancé who works late hours always wants to come home to a HoMe-CoOkEd MeAL." She rolls her eyes, then turns back to the Katsu sandwich recipe on her screen. "Eh, I dunno. Sometimes it's pretty great."

A few months later she breaks off her engagement and finds the joy in cooking for one.

✳

2018, one year into Trump's presidency: Joey and I become obsessed with *RuPaul's Drag Race*, fully aware that we're late to the game. Naturally we make up for our delay with fervor, binging all ten seasons in less than a month.

A cis white girl who vehemently stans *Drag Race* is very "tell me you have a gay best friend without telling me you have a gay best friend." But the shame doesn't faze me—I love the show too much. Each season transports us to a fantasy gender playground where fake blood is fashion and latex grows on trees.

Once we finish the episodes, Joey and I legitimize our obsession with drag—we go to local shows so we can support Brooklyn queens. Around the same time, RuPaul makes headlines for transphobic remarks—specifically for suggesting that any trans woman on his show is breaking the rules. His tweets frame drag as a competitive sport and frame gender-affirming surgeries as a form of cheating: "You can take performance-enhancing drugs and still be an athlete, just not in the Olympics."

I can tell this tweet is offensive but I don't fully understand why. As far as I know drag is about trying to be a woman. Through that lens, RuPaul's logic makes sense.

Eager to understand, I google it and stumble upon an article by Amrou Al-Kadhi. I keep the tab open for weeks and read until the concept clicks: "Femininity is a social construct that doesn't belong to women *or* men, and can be explored by anybody," Al-Kadhi writes. "If femininity is something arti-ficial, then biological sex shouldn't have anything to do with performing it."

This sentence breaks new ground for me, peeling apart "femininity" and "womanhood"—concepts I once thought were one and the same. Just months ago, womanhood gave me a purpose, an outline, but the concept now seems heavy—especially when compared to femininity. Femininity floats, suspended in the air above us. Intrinsically it belongs to no one, but we can use it as we please.

2018, one year and eight months into Trump's presidency: The second time I question my gender, Eden and I attend a workshop called "Beyond the Binary" at, ironically, a swanky women's club. We grab millennial-pink cocktails and sit on a velvet love seat near the front.

The workshop is hosted by the sex and racial justice edu-cator Ericka Hart (@ihartericka). Ericka asks all one hundred people in the audience to do an exercise. We are to reflect on our gender identity: How do we identify? When did we first realize we identified that way?

I fly through the first prompt, but the second one stumps me. I don't recall ever "realizing" my womanhood—aside from the nail incident, the matter has never been up for debate. I've always known I'm a woman. But how have I known? Because people have told me. And how have they told me? By not tell-ing me that I could be otherwise.

When it comes time to share our responses, a woman in the audience shoots her hand up. Floral perfume wafts out as her arm stretches toward the sky; the fabric of her tufted dress spills out around her chair.

"I didn't understand the second question." She sounds on edge, like she's about to ask for the manager. "I've always known I'm a woman. I never *realized* anything." I relate to the sentiment but see other audience members fidget in their chairs, which tells me this perspective must be flawed. Ashamed, I look at the floor, trying to distance myself while also paying attention.

"That's valid," Ericka says patiently. "And what do we call that?"

"I don't know." The woman shifts in her chair, her dress rustling.

"It starts with a 'p.'"

"No idea."

"Anyone else?"

Silence.

"P . . . rivilege," Ericka eventually tells us. "It's called 'cisgender privilege' if you've never had to 'realize' your gender. You have cisgender privilege if you identify with the gender that you were assigned at birth."

I start to say "ohhh!" out loud but catch myself—I don't want to let on that I didn't already know.

✳

2019, two years into Trump's presidency: I finally leave the PR agency for a different job in tech, maintaining my friendship with Eden as well as @girlpowersupply on the side. I use the account as a vessel for my frustration—a place to react to whatever headline infuriates me that day. I also document my own unlearning and share when I get things wrong. (I've gotten good at this, since I mess up a lot.)

One day during work hours Trump does god knows what, and his actions inspire a political discussion with two clients. It's not the fighting kind of discussion that gets you fired but the beautiful kind where everyone builds on each other's ideas. We spend the whole afternoon swapping anti-capitalist talking points, ignoring that our paychecks depend on conversions and clicks.

When I mention my meme Instagram, one client seems impressed. I love the attention until she asks hard questions: "Curious—are you at all concerned about the word 'girl' infantilizing women?"

"I've thought about it," I lie. "But the whole name is ironic. Gender is a construct, after all!"

When I leave our meeting there's a lump in my throat— the question of "girl" remains stuck, an identity crisis I can't escape. I agree with the client (for once, amirite?!)—the infantilization is a problem, but so is the reliance on gender at all. Every day, I learn more about people who live outside the binary. Every day, I gain understanding of the harm that gender can cause for all of us—trans and cis alike—when we don't live up to its roles.

@girlpowersupply feels like a dress I've outgrown—I'd better change fast lest I burst through a seam. Eventually I do, swapping the username for my personal. I'm finally myself again—@jenerous. The handle is a pun on my name, no problematic terms in sight. (Sure—the pun ties back to my mom's concept of womanhood, but even I barely recognize that yet.)

✳

2019, two years and eight months into Trump's presidency:
On my third date with Brinley, I drag them to another gallery show I'm supposed to attend. It's a promotion event for a documentary on immigration. Attractive art snobs mill about the room, ambling in their designer clothes.

Brinley and I post up at a tall table directly in catering's line of fire, stuffing our faces with tiny puff pastries as catering staff walk past. I shovel hors d'oeuvres into my mouth as Brinley excuses themself to go pee, but when they return the color has drained from their face. They get closer and I notice their eyes ignited like flames on a gas stove, each one searing with pain and rage.

"Someone just screamed at me in the women's bathroom," they mutter. "So I went to the men's. Then got yelled at there too."

"WHAT?!" I spit out a mini hot dog. "Let's fucking leave."

"No." Brinley lifts their hand. "Not yet. That's not what I want." They're quiet and calm, and I realize I'm the one making a scene.

"Okay, okay—sorry." I take circular breaths, curbing my performative outburst—I'm this worked up and it didn't even happen to me. "What do you want?"

They think for a moment, then smirk. "I want YOU to go pee in the men's."

I don't ask Brinley why they want this. I assume it's to help me feel their pain—or because this is the closest thing to retribution against the gender binary that they can get. Later I find out they just thought it seemed like a cute way to handle such a serious subject on a third date. (It also made me disappear, giving them space to process their feelings in peace.)

I give a sharp nod like an agent accepting a mission, honored to do anything that might lessen their pain. Inside the men's stall I scrunch my face at the smell—out there it's Diptyque candles; in here it's a zoo.

"How was it?" Brinley asks when I come back.

"Horrible," I say, pulling them into a hug. "Let's go."

✳

2020, three years into Trump's presidency: I notice several people on Instagram using she/her and they/them pronouns, often abbreviated as "she/they." I learn (again from Ericka Hart) that pronouns don't necessarily correspond with gender identity, though many nonbinary people do choose to use they/them. A graphic novel, Maia Kobabe's *Gender Queer*, helps me understand that infinite pronouns exist—many nonbinary people use e/eir, ze/zim, and beyond. Much like other words about gender, queerness, and identity, pronouns don't have inherent meaning, so ascribing that significance is entirely up to us.

"I'm considering using she/they pronouns," I tell Brinley one day.

"That's rad, baby! Are you nonbinary? Not that you have to be."

"No, no—of course not." The nonbinary label feels like a stretch, far from something I deserve. For Brinley and so many others, they/them pronouns are a necessity—changing mine would feel like a choice. She/they pronouns sound affirming in a way I can't exactly articulate, but at the same time, I wonder if using them would feel like straddling a line—clinging to the binary with one foot, stepping outside with another.

At this, a voice inside irks me: *Hey, Jen—why is straddling a line so bad? Isn't that what you've done most of your life? Your bisexuality has always been more than a "choice"—maybe this is the same way and you just don't know that yet.*

I clear my throat. "Actually, wait. What *is* nonbinary?"

Brinley shrugs. "Your guess is as good as mine."

✳

2020, three years and two months into Trump's presidency: The third time I question my gender, I've been quarantining for about three weeks. I'm still processing the new work-from-home reality and I handle my shock by staring into my phone. My reality becomes one endless blue light, until one day I see a pickle-green Instagram post from @matisse.dupont sitting in my explore page. The post—"Some Gender Questions You Could Ask Yourself"—features four prompts, but I get caught on the first one: "Why are you performing gendered habits while staying home and social distancing?"

I take stock of my habits. I still wear makeup: eyeliner, CC cream, and sometimes lipstick (to distract from the dark circles under my eyes). I baby-talk to Brinley's dog, which is arguably maternal. And then there's my raging PMS tantrums—unintentional, but as stereotypes go, about as womanly as I can get.

Beyond that, most of my feminine traits have already fallen by the wayside. I don't dress up anymore, not even for the internet. I have no reason to wear heels. I hardly even enjoy the femme concept of "self-care" these days—doing a face mask by candlelight feels impossible when I can barely remember to brush my teeth.

What is a "woman"? Does wearing makeup, baby-talking,

or sobbing into a Shake Shack bag make me a good one? I don't know. But I know the word itself doesn't ring as empowering as it once did.

Gender feels restrictive. It feels like quarantine.

Maybe it's time to go outside.

＊

2020, three years and three months into Trump's presidency: I tell Brinley I'm doing it: I'm changing my pronouns to she/they.

"Exciting, baby!" they exclaim, kissing me on the cheek. Then they walk to their dresser and toss me a balled-up T-shirt. "You should sleep in this tonight."

I unfold it and realize it's their favorite: the soft one that says "they/them" on the chest that they never used to let me wear. I put it on, then nuzzle myself in Brinley's arms. The casual affirmation feels better than I'd expected. I can't tell why exactly, but I'm holding back tears.

＊

2021, three years and eleven months into Trump's presidency: I drive through the night toward a house in Vermont, the Hobbit-esque Airbnb where I hope to finish this book—to somehow tie together threads of femininity, queer theory, and my sex life into a sturdy double-knotted bow. I think the final chapter will be about gender, and I also think that if I hear one more second of news about the white nationalists raiding the Capitol, I might crash into a tree. Instead of NPR, I spend the drive listening to an audiobook of *Beyond the Gender Binary* by the poet Alok Vaid-Menon.

Vaid-Menon says that our reliance on existing gender roles is "like being handed over a Scantron sheet and demanded to paint a self-portrait on it. Is it really a choice when you don't get to select the options you are given to begin with?"

The car blows hot air on my face and I feel a sense of peace. I'm overcome with understanding, though understanding of what, I'm not sure. If I got goose bumps while listening to this book, does it mean I'm nonbinary? I have no idea. But the world is not a Scantron, so maybe not knowing is okay.

What I do know is that my attachment to being a woman—my faith in the idea—has waned. Womanhood once brought me strength but now feels worn and tattered, and what good is a down jacket covered in holes? This warmth-based metaphor reminds me of another by the writer and organizer Prishita Maheshwari-Aplin: "Womanhood, for me, feels like a weighted blanket that's kept me comfortable and warm . . . but now I feel trapped underneath."

Sliding my hands over the smooth leather of the steering wheel, I recall an improv teacher who went on frequent spiritual tirades—"Let go of that which no longer serves you," he once said. Though I'm talking about gender (and he was talking about the litigious priest character I'd played in the last scene), his epithet still applies.

Regardless of nightclubs, jean cuffs, or self-doubt brought on by bad cologne, my sexuality has always been fluid—expansive, consuming, and impossible to contain. Bisexuality brought me here—it taught me that I can find stability in a state of flux. And I had to understand that—this part of myself—in all its vastness before I could unpack the rest.

Now I'm surrounded by trees, headed toward a writing

retreat during a moment of national unrest. Right before I left I saw a tweet: "Men will literally storm the Capitol instead of going to therapy." I think of masculinity. I think of my dad. I think of the Empress Of song that still gets stuck in my head.

The question of gender remains daunting, unanswerable—especially since it took me thirty-two years to realize it was even a question at all. But maybe there's an accomplishment in there somewhere—maybe there's power in just understanding the need to ask. I wonder—what would happen if I didn't seek concrete answers? If I let question marks dangle on my own accord—for their own sake—rather than because a lover didn't respond?

I've switched gears, blasting *Fetch the Bolt Cutters* at full volume when I finally reach the house. My rental sedan creeps up the snowy driveway, and near the top starts gliding on the ice. I've never been great in a crisis (must be nice for Fiona Apple that Sebastian thinks she's "a good man in a storm"), but somehow I wrangle the steering wheel easily, without panicking even a bit. I manage to park, then sit in the passenger's seat, proud of myself for my aplomb, even though no one else saw. I consider that this makes for an on-the-nose metaphor—if there's one thing that makes me comfortable these days, it's uncertainty. I look up at the house, and even with an unfinished manuscript hanging over my head, I feel calm. I guess I know what to do from here: Make like a bisexual and stay confused for good.

ACKNOWLEDGMENTS

It's impossible to thank everyone who brought this book to life, but apparently it's customary for authors to try.

First and foremost: Thank you to every queer person who has ever shared their experiences, and every bi person who has ever named their identity—you gave me the confidence to know myself. Shiri Eisner, Robyn Ochs, Meg-John Barker—thank you for helping me make sense of the world and my place in it.

Melanie. Thank you for being an incredible reader, editor, and human who champions these stories, and for tolerating me. You made this work better, more inclusive, and more self-aware at every turn.

Wendy. Thank you for believing in me and answering every panicked text.

Richelle. Thank you for helping me with the hardest part: the bones.

Diana. For building me into the writer I was, am, and will be. For teaching me about passive voice even after it was too late.

Rodrigo. For translating my confusion into something beautiful.

Kelli, Jimmy, Megan, Isabel, Raaga, Lexy, Elisa, Beth, Sarah, D. Ann, Sossity, Gabriella, and Sara. Thank you for your brilliance, patience, and understanding at every turn.

Emily. I owe any and all aesthetic to you.

Marla. For helping me live my biggest value: this.

Joey. Every good joke in this book is because of you, whether you ghostwrote it or just trained me to be funnier. Also, the only reason this book exists in the world is to serve as a placeholder until you write yours (the Popeyes guy deserves more time to shine). I love you like you love that "Oy Mista! You me Dad?" meme, which is to say: endlessly.

Ben. For being a teacher, a rock, and a best friend. You've given me the priceless, frustrating gift of an obsession with personal growth. Thank you for being so consistently self-serving that it doesn't matter when I'm self-serving back. You're the best.

JAC. Every thought, feeling, or idea in here began with you. Thank you.

Jamie. My first college friend, my ever-present moral compass. Forever grateful to know you and grow alongside you.

Eden. A constant inspiration and an impossibly cool friend. Thank you for challenging me and supporting me at the same time, and from halfway across the world.

Danielle, Lily, Natasha, Naz, Rachel. Thank you for showing me all sides of womanhood, from intelligence to audacity.

Thank you for holding me accountable, even indirectly, and for cleaning my pee off too many bar floors.

Ari. My bold bisexual friend. I love that we can always pick up wherever we left off.

Josh. Thank you for being so talented, and so generous with that talent. Your jokes make me look good.

David. I promise the next book will be called *Maybe Dick*.

Darin and Joe. My adulting role models, my grumpy but grateful inspo. Blair, I already love you.

Everyone who helped with brainstorms, sent me readings, consulted on covers, forwarded me old emails, looked at old proposals, or critiqued these pieces in writing workshops long ago: Buster. Landon. Thomas. Emily O. Sara. Edwin. Nereya. Larissa. Ida. Ryan. Toy. Katie. Ji. Francesca. Tony. Candy. David. Courtney. Mike. Charles. Jeremy.

Simi. For reading, writing, and thinking the way you do.

Lina. For your powerful work about power.

Mary and Lachrista. For your honesty and resilience.

Maggie, for being the best mentor a girl (slash gender-confused femme person) could ask for.

Jim, Finola, Jeff, Mafé, and everyone else who picked up my slack while I faded away to write this, as well as everyone who supported me when I hit a mental health wall a few weeks later. Thank you.

Michael Bauer. For showing me that two truths can exist at once.

Zoe and Joanna. For therapy.

Mom. For everything, but especially for showing me how to be kind. You're one of the most powerful creative minds I know, even though you would never believe that. Everything good in my brain, I learned from you.

Dad. For being a character too singular for my words to ever capture, and for teaching me that all types of wealth are supposed to be shared. You are an incredible role model, father, and friend.

Greg. For being hilarious, strong, and the only one who understands.

Grandma. For a wisdom even beyond your hundred years.

Navy and Astro. I finally understand why people write boring books about dog friendships: because how else can you comprehend such pure, overwhelming love? I adore you both. Thank you for cuddling with me during the hard parts. I hope you don't chew this up.

Brinley. My LOMO, my baby. Thank you for being no-bullshit, and for loving me in a way I never thought possible. Thank you for singing to the babies, for making me coffee even though you only drink chai, and for forcing me to shower (at least a few times) while writing this. I am unbearable and I am beyond lucky. You've shown me what queerness means and have taught me that it can be breezy—something far more personal and meaningful than the heady spirals I tend to tumble down. Words fail, so I'll go with the standard ones: I love you. So much. Thank you. A toast to us.

Thank you to every person who follows me on social media. Thank you for your support, your ability to see nuance, and your constant reminders that bisexual stories deserve to be told.

And you. Yes, you. Thank you for reading. It means the world. You mean the world.

Really. Thank you.

REFERENCES

WHAT I TALK ABOUT WHEN I TALK ABOUT BISEXUALITY

xxiv *"skeptical"*: Josh Milton, "Scientist Who Denied Bisexual Men Exist Finally Comes to His Senses and Discovers, Yes, Bi Guys Are Telling the Truth," PinkNews, 07/21/20.

xxv *Nearly half of bi women*: Katherine Schreiber, MFA LMSW, "Why So Many Bisexuals Are Victimized," *Psychology Today*, 05/22/14.

xxv *men earn*: Trenton Mize, "Sexual Orientation in the Labor Market," *American Sociological Review* 81, no. 6 (2016): 1132–1160.

xxvi *monogamous relationships*: Samantha Joel, PhD, "3 Myths About Bisexuality Debunked by Science," *Psychology Today*, 05/22/14.

xxvii *"no, we're not greedy"*: Shiri Eisner, interview by Emily Zak, "More People Are Identifying As Bisexual, and That's Great!" Bitch Media, 09/22/15.

CUFFED JEANS AND FEELING SEEN

4 *bisexuals will be*: @thecherryghoul on Twitter, 06/18/20 at 2:13 p.m. EST, accessed on 04/17/21 via https://twitter.com/thecherryghoul/status/1262446212290142208.

4 *"pray for all bisexuals' exposed ankles"*: @sianvconway on Twitter, 01/17/19 at 7:35 p.m. EST, accessed 02/26/21 via https://twitter.com/sianvconway/status/1086059425109102592.

5   *"memetic"*: Richard Dawkins, *The Selfish Gene* (Oxford: Oxford University Press, 1976).

5   *"2 Girls 1 Cup"*: Jen Winston, "The Memeing of Life: Repetition Keeps Memes Afloat," Daily Trojan, 09/15/09. (And can I just say that citing yourself in your own book is big semicolon energy?)

7   *"then there are bisexuals"*: *Friends*, Season 2, Episode 12, "The One After the Superbowl: Part 1," directed by Michael Lembeck, aired 01/28/1996.

10n   *28 percent of bisexual people*: Emily Alpert, "Why Bisexuals Stay in the Closet," *Los Angeles Times*, 07/04/13.

11   *Reading* Gay Bar: Jeremy Atherton Lin, *Gay Bar* (Hachette Book Group: New York, 2021).

11   *"spatially scattered"*: Manuel Castells, *The City and the Grassroots* (London: Edward Arnold, 1983), 181.

11–12 *encounter biphobic comments*: Shiri Eisner, *Bi: Notes for a Bisexual Revolution* (Berkeley, CA: Seal Press, 2013), 78–87.

12   *only 8 percent*: Eliel Cruz, "REPORT: Bisexuals Face Biphobia at Doctor's Office, LGBT Groups," *The Advocate*, 05/27/15.

12   *"tend to get lost"*: Rory Gory, "Want to Celebrate Bisexual Visibility? Build a Better World for Bi People," them., 09/23/20.

HOT AND COOL

20   *Black people were*: ACLU, Marijuana Arrests by the Numbers, 2021, accessed 04/26/21 via https://www.aclu.org/gallery/marijuana-arrests-numbers.

TRUE LIFE: I MASTURBATE WRONG

45   *"don't owe prettiness"*: Erin McKean, "You Don't Have to Be Pretty," *A Dress a Day*, 10/20/06.

46n   *sexual assault, revenge porn*: Emily Ratajkowski, "Buying Myself Back," *The Cut*, 09/15/20.

47   *"move toward the ugly"*: Mia Mingus, "Moving Toward the Ugly: A Politic Beyond Desirability" (Speech, Femmes of Color Symposium, Oakland, CA, 08/21/11), transcript accessed 02/17/21 via https://leavingevidence.wordpress.com/2011/08/22/moving-toward-the-ugly-a-politic-beyond-desirability.

48   *vision of "perfection"*: Ibid.

49   *"Ugly Law"*: Susan M. Schweik, *The Ugly Laws: Disability in Public* (New York: NYU Press, 2009), 291.

49   *over 50 percent of doctors*: Gary D. Foster, Thomas A. Wadden, Angela P. Makris, et al., "Primary Care Physicians' Attitudes About Obesity and Its Treatment," *Obesity Research* 11, no. 10 (October 2003): 1168–1177.

49   *spend less time*: Michael Hobbes, "Everything You Know About Obesity Is Wrong," Huffington Post Highline, 09/19/18.

49   *"being called fat"*: Aubrey Gordon (@yrfatfriend), "Please, Just Call Me Fat," Human Parts, 08/28/18.

50   *"Exercise brings me the most anxiety"*: Imani Barbarin, "We Need to Talk About Ableism-Related Anxiety," CrutchesAndSpice.com, 11/09/19, accessed 02/17/21 via https://crutchesandspice.com/2019/11/09/we -need-to-talk-about-ableism-related-anxiety.

50   *"power to glorify"*: Jacob Tobia, "Sissy Diaries: How Beauty Brands Can Help Shape Queer and Trans Acceptance," *them.*, 04/03/18.

A GIRL CALLED RHONDA

82   *overlook that fact*: Michelle Garcia, "Whitewashing the Orlando Shooting Victims Only Makes LGBTQ People of Color More Vulnerable to Violence," Vox, 06/16/16.

THE POWER DYNAMIC

111   *"fellatio"*: Andrea Long Chu, *Females* (Brooklyn, NY: Verso Books, 2019), 45.

116   *substance abuse*: Nicole Johnson and MaryBeth Grove, "Why Us? Toward an Understanding of Bisexual Women's Vulnerability for and Negative Consequences of Sexual Violence," *Journal of Bisexuality* 17, no. 4 (2017): 1–16.

118n   *"rhetoric of consent"*: Katherine Angel, *Tomorrow Sex Will Be Good Again* (Brooklyn, NY: Verso Books, 2021), 38.

THE NEON SWEATER

124   *"anti-racist"*: Lauren Michele Jackson, "What Is an Anti-Racism Reading List For?", Vulture, 06/04/20.

125n   *"not a self-improvement exercise"*: Rachel Cargle (@rachel.cargle) on Instagram, 07/07/20, accessed 02/17/21 via https://www.instagram.com/p /CC_gVzvJRl6/.

128   *"remain unchanged"*: Hyejin Shim, "Consenting to Normal," 01/17/18, accessed on 04/11/21 via https://medium.com/@persimmontree/con senting-to-normal-d3c5ec2c5b99.

133n   *"Euphemisms are death"*: Carmen Maria Machado, "How Promising Young Woman Refigures the R*pe-Revenge Movie," *The New Yorker*, 01/29/21.

135   *waiting at a Starbucks*: Emily Stewart, "Two Black Men Were Arrested in a Philadelphia Starbucks for Doing Absolutely Nothing," Vox, 04/05/18.

135   *golfing too slowly*: Christina Caron, "5 Black Women Were Told to Golf Faster. Then the Club Called the Police," *New York Times*, 04/25/18.

135   *refusing to pay*: German Lopez, "Police Throw Black Woman to Floor, Say They Will 'Break' Her Arm During Arrest at Waffle House," Vox, 04/25/18.

135   *three times more likely*: Harvard School of Public Health, News, "Black People More Than Three Times as Likely as White People to Be Killed During a Police Encounter," 06/24/20, accessed 02/17/21 via https:// www.hsph.harvard.edu/news/hsph-in-the-news/blacks-whites-police -deaths-disparity/.

135   *prison system was rigged*: *13th*, written by Ava DuVernay and Spencer Averick, released October 2016, on Netflix.

135   *"Instead of Calling the Police"*: Aaron Rose, "What to Do Instead of Calling the Police: A Guide, a Syllabus, a Conversation, a Process," accessed 02/17/21 via https://uaptsd.org/take-action/what-to-do-instead -of-calling-the-police.

137   *out of every 1,000*: RAINN, "The Vast Majority of Perpetrators Will Not Go to Jail or Prison," Criminal Justice System: Statistics, accessed 02/17/21 via https://www.rainn.org/statistics/criminal -justice-system.

KNOTS

145   *to fear the "yes"*: Audre Lorde, "Uses of the Erotic: The Erotic as Power" in *The Lesbian and Gay Studies Reader,* ed. Henry Abelove et al. (New York and London: Routledge, 1993), 341.

155n   *"You can't give away"*: Lina Dune, "A Beginner's Guide to Submission," *Dipsea* (blog), 02/27/20, accessed on 04/11/21 via https://www.dipsea stories.com/blog/a-beginners-guide-to-submission/.

156n   *views came from women*: Denise Noe, "Why Women Watch Gay Porn," The Gay & Lesbian Review, March–April 2020.

156n   *less sexually and romantically attractive*: Neil Gleason, Jennifer A. Vencill, and Eric Sprankle, "Swipe Left on the Bi Guys: Examining Attitudes Toward Dating and Being Sexual with Bisexual Individuals," *Journal of Bisexuality* 18, no. 4 (2018): 516–534.

OUT OF THE WOODS

162   *"The beginning is the end"*: Chuck Klosterman, *Killing Yourself to Live* (New York: Scribner), 160.

162   *"Queers who ride"*: Billy-Ray Belcourt, *A History of My Brief Body* (Canada: Penguin Random House Canada, 2020), 68.

162n   *"For more on this"*: Rachel Cargle, "When Feminism Is Just White Feminism In Heels," *Harper's Bazaar*, 08/16/18; Kimberly Seals Allers, "Rethinking Work-Life Balance for Women of Color," *Slate*, 03/05/18.

162n   *risk of criminalization*: Daiana Griffith, "LGBTQ Youth Are at Greater Risk of Homelessness and Incarceration," 01/22/19, accessed 02/17/21 via https://www.prisonpolicy.org/blog/2019/01/22/lgbtq_youth.

162n   *unemployment rate*: National LGBTQ Task Force, "New Analysis Shows Startling Levels of Discrimination Against Black Transgender People," 2020, accessed 02/17/21 via https://www.thetaskforce.org/new-analysis -shows-startling-levels-of-discrimination-against-black-transgender -people.

162n   *experienced homelessness in their lives*: Gabriella Velasco and Melanie Langness, "COVID-19 Action That Centers Black LGBTQ People Can Address Housing Inequities," Urban.org, 06/23/20, accessed 02/17/21 via https://www.urban.org/urban-wire/covid-19-action-centers-black-lgbtq -people-can-address-housing-inequities.

165   *"cook dinner forever"*: Lisa Duggan, "The New Homonormativity: The Sexual Politics of Neoliberalism" in *Materializing Democracy: Toward a Revitalized Cultural Politics*, ed. Russ Castronovo et al. (Durham: Duke University Press, 2002), 189.

165n   *seventy-two countries*: Josh Lederman, "Trump Administration Launches Global Effort to End Criminalization of Homosexuality," NBC News, 02/19/19.

165n   *"born to shop"*: Sherrie Inness as quoted by Ann M. Ciasullo, "Making Her (In)Visible: Cultural Representations of Lesbianism and the Lesbian Body in the 1990s," *Feminist Studies* 27, no. 3 (2001), 577–608.

168n   *nonetheless maligned*: Kerry Manders, "The Renegades," *New York Times*, 04/13/20.

171   *"possibility for another world"*: José Esteban Muñoz, *Cruising Utopia: The Then and There of Queer Futurity* (New York: New York University Press, 2009), 1.

171   *impacts Black trans women*: Anushka Patil, "How a March for Black Trans Lives Became a Huge Event," *New York Times*, 06/15/20, updated 06/27 /20.

172   *largest trans-based protest*: Fran Tirado (@fransquishco) on Twitter, 06/24/20 at 10:04 p.m. EST, accessed 02/17/21 via https://twitter.com/fransquishco /status/1272349301163859968.

173   *"built on cooperation"*: Mariame Kaba, "Yes, We Literally Mean Abolish the Police," *New York Times*, 06/12/20.

173n   *An example case study*: Lucas Manfield, "Dallas Has Been Dispatching Social Workers to Some 911 Calls. It's Working," *Dallas Observer*, 12/10/19.

173   *"queer people everywhere"*: Adam Eli, *The New Queer Conscience* (New York: Penguin Workshop, 2020), 60.

174   *none of us is free*: Audre Lorde, "The Uses of Anger: Women Responding to Racism" (Speech, National Women's Studies Association Conference, Storrs, CT, 06/1981), transcript accessed 02/17/21 via https://www.blackpast.org/african-american-history/1981-audre-lorde-uses-anger-women-responding-racism.

A QUEER LOVE STORY

240   *Christian's penthouse*: David Rudin, "The Virtual Tour of Christian Grey's Penthouse Is the Best Version of *Fifty Shades of Grey*," Kill Screen, 02/18/15.

243   *"too intimately bound"*: David M. Halperin, "Queer Love," *Critical Inquiry* 45, no. 2 (Winter 2019): 396–419.

244   *"practice of freedom"*: bell hooks, "Love as the Practice of Freedom," *Outlaw Culture: Resisting Representations* (New York and London: Routledge Classics, 2006), 250.

BRINLEY JAMES FORD

248   *"no pronouns"*: Ayo Edebiri (@ayodebiri) on Twitter, 02/28/19 at 11:47 p.m. EST, accessed 03/01/21 via https://twitter.com/ayoedebiri/status/1101162074749788160.

249   *"Happy pride month!"*: Brinley Ford (@brinley4u) on Instagram, 06/10/19, accessed 03/01/21 via https://www.instagram.com/p/ByikxofB0Rk/.

262   *"structural generosity"*: Long Chu, *Females*, accessed via e-reader 03/01/21, location 354.

GENDER IS A DRAG: A TIMELINE

269   *transform people's genders*: Jessica Cale, "Trans and Nonbinary Identities from Mesopotamia to Ancient Rome: Inanna, Cybele, and the Gallai," Dirty, Sexy History, 03/09/20.

269   *bissu people persist*: Farid M. Ibrahim, "Homophobia and Rising Islamic Intolerance Push Indonesia's Intersex Bissu Priests to the Brink," ABCnews.ne.aut, 02/26/19, accessed 02/17/21 via https://www.abc.net.au/news/2019-02-27/indonesia-fifth-gender-might-soon-disappear/10846570.

270   *sex binary emerges*: Kyla Schuller, *The Biopolitics of Feeling: Race, Sex, and Science in the Nineteenth Century* (Durham: Duke University Press, 2017).

276   *"rejection of everything"*: Jennifer Siebel Newsom et al., *The Mask You Live In*, Representation Project (2015).

278 *"if femininity is something artificial"*: Amrou Al-Kadhi, "What RuPaul's Problematic Comments Mean for the Future of Drag," i-D, 03/09/18.

284 *"Some Gender Questions"*: Matisse DuPont (@matisse.dupont) on Instagram, 04/09/20, accessed 03/01/21 via https://www.instagram.com/p/B-w9i5sAxha/.

285 *"handed over a Scantron"*: Alok Vaid-Menon, *Beyond the Gender Binary* (New York: Penguin Workshop, 2020), 9–10.

286 *"a weighted blanket"*: Prishita Maheshwari-Aplin (@prishita_eloise) on Instagram, 07/23/20, accessed 03/01/21 via https://www.instagram.com/p/CC_gVzvJRl6/.

287 *"Men will literally"*: @gokuw33dlord on Twitter, 01/06/21 at 3:24 p.m. EST, accessed 03/01/21 via https://twitter.com/gokuw33dlord/status/1346915460097433606.

ABOUT THE AUTHOR

JEN WINSTON (she/they) is a writer, creator, and—you guessed it—bisexual. Their writing has appeared in *Marie Claire*, McSweeney's Internet Tendency, BuzzFeed, and more, while their digital advocacy has been featured by CNN, the *Wall Street Journal*, and the *Washington Post*, among others.

Jen lives in Brooklyn with their partner, dogs, and iPhone. This is their first book.

Follow Jen on Twitter, TikTok, and Instagram: @jenerous.